Earthed

Christian perspectives on nature connection

Edited by
Bruce Stanley and **Steve Hollinghurst**

First Published in the UK in August 2014 by

Mystic Christ Press
Troed Yr Esgair Barn
Llangurig
Powys, SY18 6RS

10 9 8 7 6 5 4 3 2 1

Typeset and design by www.embody.co.uk/design

British Library Cataloguing in Publication Data. A catalogue record for this book is available from the British Library.

ISBN: 978-0-9575383-2-0

Printed in the UK on Forest Stewardship Council certified paper.

Table of Contents

Foreword

This book is a resource for people practically exploring the relationship between spirituality and nature connection. You may be developing your own individual practice or joining with others through groups like Forest Church. You may be a passionate environmental campaigner, a bird watcher, a walker or gardener or painter or angler or someone that simply notices natural things on the way to work but I think we all have something in common. Amongst the writing emerging from different seemingly unconnected sources around the world one word keeps appearing – **participation.** If you're new to the subject of nature connection, that is one of the distinct ideas defining it. The connection is just the start, the aim is to participate.

There is plenty written about ecology, environmentalism and creation from a Christian perspective but that writing might not tell you much practically about nature connection as a spiritual practice. Contemporary thinking and writing on nature connection from Christian perspectives is only just exploring the foothills of a forgotten, uncharted wilderness and if you're drawn to the adventure it can help to connect with others on the journey – that is how this book came about. Our intention is to pull together a collection of thoughts, theological perspectives and practical suggestions that both encourage those interested in the subject and also portray some of the various ways further into the territory.

These authors come from a variety of backgrounds and are drawn to different aspects of nature connection and that is reflected in this book. It is not a work of academic theology and thus is not referenced that way, though there are some chapters from people with backgrounds in academic theology. Many are by people exploring their own spiritual journeys and some explore various traditions that inform the subject. There is in all of these much that is profoundly theological.

It is not a book that argues a particular position or comes from a particular theological basis; chapters come from a range of people with different approaches and experiences and you will find differences of opinion between them. What all have in common is they believe Christianity's relationship with nature matters and it is something that needs to be on the agenda not just of the church but others too for whom nature and spirituality are in dialogue.

So, we stand together at the head of the trails map – **You Are Here** – and 16 routes lead off before you, some following distinctly unique paths, others cross each other in places. If you read these chapters sequentially you'll go from overview to detail or from introduction through scripture and tradition to experience but there is a little of each in most so head off whichever way you fancy.

Bruce Stanley
Steve Hollinghurst

Editors

Chapter 1 – Cate Williams

Contemporary Spirituality, Theology and Nature Connection.

What I intend to do in this chapter is to explore, within a Trinitarian framework, some of the theological issues associated with nature connection. I will be opening out some significant issues, looking at the rationale for believing that connection with nature can support and enable our connection with God, and that nature connection is an expression of legitimate Christian spirituality. There are other things that could be said about creation, redemption and the place of non-human creation within these things, the majority of which I am leaving for others to say. My focus here will be to examine human connection with nature in the context of the Trinity, the God we know as Father, Son and Holy Spirit; Creator, Redeemer and Sustainer.

It is essential we give thought to these matters because some within the Christian tradition are suspicious of a material and earthed spirituality, suspecting that it is a kind of idolatry. Some say that only something which is purely spiritual is real prayer and connection with God. That we always need to move beyond the physical towards a purer form of prayer, even if we have begun with something physical. They say that any kind of prayer in which a connection with the physical is an integral part is dangerously close to worshipping the physical, to putting something else in God's rightful place.

And yet in our contemporary culture, many of the people around us are more drawn to an earthed than a transcendent spirituality which is assumed to be otherworldly. They are drawn to a spirituality that engages with the physical world and find the concept of unearthed spirituality dissatisfying.

Christians need to explore how our own tradition relates to this contemporary instinct. If Christians resist this impulse then it puts obstacles in the way of our conversations about the spiritual life. Yet at the same time, if it is truly incompatible with Christianity then we need to be honest and say so.

This move towards an earthed spirituality and a focus on the immanent is part of the background to the culture in which Forest Church has emerged. The question we are exploring here is whether Forest Church and other forms of earthed spirituality have been led astray by contemporary culture, or whether nature connection as a spiritual discipline is in fact a move of the Spirit within society. If the latter, then it is an opportunity for Christians to rediscover an element which is authentically Christian but which has been side-lined in recent expressions of faith.

We need to examine these things within Christian theology and understand what we believe and why in order to discover whether the contemporary move towards an earthed spirituality is something we can celebrate with integrity within our own tradition. Those of us who are a part of the Forest Church movement give a resounding 'yes' and very much celebrate God within creation. What I write here is some comment about what allows us to do so.

Biblical background

I would like to make reference by way of introduction, to two key passages in the New Testament that refer to the natural world and which are in the background of this kind of thinking. The first, Colossians 1.15-20, reminds us of the participation of all of creation in God.

> *He is the image of the invisible God, the firstborn of all creation; for in him all things in heaven and on earth were created, things visible and invisible, whether thrones or dominions or rulers or powers—all things have been created through him and for him. He himself is before all things, and in him all things hold together. He is the head of the body, the church; he is the beginning, the firstborn from the dead, so that he might come to have first place in everything. For in him all the fullness of God was pleased to dwell, and through him God was pleased to reconcile to himself all things, whether on earth or in heaven, by making peace through the blood of his cross.*[1]

Key points to note here are all of nature being created in and through him. There is a sense of the interweaving of the divine and the material as God participates in all of nature, and it is in fact held together in God. Alongside this is the inclusion of the whole of creation in the work of the cross. All things, whether on heaven and earth reconciled by the cross, not just individual human beings. It seems that perhaps redemption is bigger and more inclusive than we sometimes seem to express in our churches. The theme continues in another key passage, Romans 8.19-25

> *For the creation waits with eager longing for the revealing of the children of God; for the creation was subjected to futility, not of its own will but by the will of the one who*

1 Biblical references here and following from NRSV (Oxford: OUP 1995)

subjected it, in hope that the creation itself will be set free from its bondage to decay and will obtain the freedom of the glory of the children of God. We know that the whole creation has been groaning in labour pains until now; and not only the creation, but we ourselves, who have the first fruits of the Spirit, groan inwardly while we wait for adoption, the redemption of our bodies. For in hope we were saved. Now hope that is seen is not hope. For who hopes for what is seen? But if we hope for what we do not see, we wait for it with patience.[2]

Here again is a reminder that it is the whole of creation longing for fulfilment in Christ, not just humanity. If we narrow down our sense of God at work in creation primarily to the human world, then we are missing many aspects of God's work that evidently were important enough to Paul to be included in this passage that is often considered key to his understanding.

Contemporary spirituality

In the introduction I made reference to contemporary spirituality outside the church. In this section we will examine this some more as it forms a significant backdrop to the exploration of earthed spirituality within Christianity, of which Forest Church is a part. Others have written at length on this subject so there is no attempt here to write a definitive study, more to point out some trends.

The primary thing to note here is the fact that the spirituality of those outside the church is drawn more to an earthed spirituality, suspicious of the otherworldliness of recent Christianity. David Hay and Kate Hunt undertook an extensive study into unchurched spirituality based on research conversations, or informal interviews, with participants in the study. They were exploring various questions about the spiritual experience

2 Romans 8.19-25 NRSV (Oxford: OUP 1995)

and understanding of contemporary British people outside the church.[3] One of the recurring themes they express in this way:

> As we have seen, one doctrinal difficulty that crops up regularly with a number of people is the unacceptability of God seen as transcendent. God's immanence is much more acceptable.[4]

Other studies have come to similar conclusions. One from Australia for example, referring to the spiritual attitudes of Generation Y, notes how although dogma is mistrusted, the real Jesus of the Gospels connects with people's experience of being human:

> One of the heartening findings of the ACU study, however, is that while Gen Y has little or no time for the institutional Church its youth do relate very positively to the no-nonsense, down to earth and challenging figure of Jesus.[5]

Cole Moreton reflecting on contemporary British spirituality writes:

> It is not quantifiable, in a census or a survey, because our new way of believing does not want to sign up or be pinned down, it is elusive and private, but it is also obvious and all around us. We want a spirituality that relates to the earth.[6]

Down-to-earth, connection with real lives and environmental concerns are all recurring themes as people reflect on the spirituality within wider society. Other-worldliness however, the traditional realm of much Christianity, is not something that people warm to. Practical, down to earth and connected with all of nature is how people around us seek spirituality. This

3 D. Hay & K. Hunt *The Spiritual Life of People who don't go to Church* (Nottingham: University of Nottingham 2000) p6
4 Hay and Hunt *Spiritual Life* p. 35.
5 David Tims *Spirituality that appeals to Gen Y* http://www.cath-news.com/article.aspx?aeid=22934 accessed 24 January 2013
6 Cole Moreton *Is God still an Englishman?* (London: Little Brown 2010) p. 340.

is frequently expressed in references to 'The Universe' which many of us will have heard from family and friends.

All of this means that there is a growing gap between contemporary spirituality outside the church and Christianity in its most prevalent form. Reflection on this gap can take us in one of two directions: either we emphasise our difference and continue to focus on the transcendent and the uniqueness of the Christian message, or we find ourselves wondering whether traditional Christianity has something to learn, or rather to rediscover about earthed and connected faith.

Paganism

Many who are disaffected by the church but still seeking a spiritual path find a home in Neo-Paganism.[7] A fascinating discussion took place over a series of articles in the Pagan journal 'Pomegranate' discussing idolatry within Paganism, icons within Christianity and the relationship of spirituality to the material world. Michael York, in the article that initiated the discussion, writes:

From a Pagan perspective, matter matters, and it matters much. The tangible is accepted as sacred in and of itself. If the holy "bleeds" into a transcendental, it does not begin with it. Instead, the sacrosanct is understood first and foremost in material being.[8]

Gareth Redford's article summarising the debate contrasts the Pagan affirmation of the material world with the Christian insistence that an icon must always be a vehicle into the transcendent rather than God being met in the material world itself. In Paganism, he writes:

....
7 Moreton *Englishman* p. 334.
8 Michael York *Idolatry, Ecology,and the Sacred as Tangible* The Pomegranate 12.1 (2010) 74-93 p. 76.

As religious foci the idol becomes primus inter pares (meaning first among equals) in a belief system in which all can be recognised as sacred or divine. In a sense the idol is like an inverted icon. Whereas the concern of the Christian is in that the icon is not equated with God and it that is God emanating through the object, not its physical form that makes it holy.[9]

Holiness within Paganism is found within the material world not beyond it, whereas in Christianity, at least in the form that has been handed down filtered through Platonic thought, the transcendent as otherworldly is the focus. In this Platonic approach though Christians may start with the physical, the expectation is to move beyond, with an experience of the transcending the physical as the goal.

And yet Christianity is an incarnational religion, one founded on the fact that God became flesh and blood, God inhabited the material world and lived among us. Incarnational faith is about as earthed and rooted as it is possible to be. It seems strange given this is at the heart of Christianity that there should be any ambivalence concerning the physical as a legitimate part of spirituality.

This critique of an otherworldly Christianity from a Pagan perspective, when put alongside the incarnational heart of our faith, leaves us questioning how much of such an understanding of the experience of God in the material world is truly Christian. How much is true to Christ, and how much borrowed from Platonic ideas and leading us away from our incarnational and earthed faith?[10]

9 Gareth Redford *A different perspective on idolatry* https://docs.google.com/file/d/0B-2oGQwIYvXFcF9WaldUdDRsMlU/edit?pli=1 p. 9. accessed 23 Oct 2012
10 For a discussion on the interaction between Platonic thought and Christianity see Trevor Hart *Hearing, Seeing and touching Truth* Jeremy Begbie (ed) in *Beholding the Glory* (London: DLT 2000)

Christian responses to contemporary spirituality

Christians are divided in their reactions to the contemporary impulse towards earthed spirituality. Many within the Christian tradition resist it, for example Savage, Collins-Mayo, Mayo and Cray in their book *'Generation Y'*, here paraphrasing and quoting Colin Gunton:

> *The Holy Spirit is not an impersonal immanent force, as in Star Wars, but the presence of the transcendent God. 'Talk of the Spirit is not a way of speaking of God's immanence, but of his transcendence. The Spirit may be active within the world, but he does not become a part of the world.'* [11]

Here Gunton appears to insist on a radical separation between God and nature. He is certainly understood this way by the authors who are quoting him. In this understanding, God may be at work by the Holy Spirit, but is never actually a part of the created order.

When viewed from this perspective, the hunger for spirituality is missed. Seeing as they do a lack of desire for the transcendent, they miss the desire for spirituality expressed in a more earthed form than we have been used to in recent centuries. They write:

> *I am now convinced that there is, in the Church, a tendency to exaggerate the extent of interest in spirituality in Western culture.* [12]

It is true that if you are looking for openness to a spirituality that transcends this world you may well conclude that there is a lack of interest. Yet this is by no means the end of the story, and misses much of the picture.

....

11 Sara Savage, Sylvia Collins-Mayo, Bob Mayo, & Graham Cray
Making sense of Generation Y (London: CHP 2006) p. 168.
12 Savage et al *Generation Y* p. 136.

There is however a contrasting response from Christians that is more positive about the contemporary trend. In this, the rediscovery of the spiritual imperative of the material realm is to embraced and celebrated.

One such are those approaches to Christianity that have profound influence from liberation theologies. Here a contrast is made between two priorities within the life of faith, given the terms orthopraxis and orthodoxy. Orthopraxis means right practice, the day to day living out of faith in the material world, whereas orthodoxy (when not using the term to refer to a denomination) means right belief. Within liberation theology, orthopraxis is valued more highly than orthodoxy.[13] To value orthopraxis over orthodoxy is to be more concerned about whether faith is being lived out in everyday life than whether an individual can express their faith in the terms deemed correct. It is earthed in the sense that the primary concern is about how faith is lived out in this life. Tomlinson writes:

> *The important issue raised by the question of who Christ really is for us today is not primarily about which boxes of 'orthodoxy' we will tick, but rather, how will we live out the liberating, life-affirming, peace-making, people-redeeming good news of Christ in the world today.*[14]

In expressions of Church like Forest Church there is a different, but overlapping theme. Faith lived out comes to play as we consider how we care for the natural world, and how we engage with the global issues raised by the Green movement. However the question we are asking here is not just about ethics, but even more about spirituality. So we take our focus

13 See for example Jon Sobrino *Spirituality and the Following of Jesus* Sobrino and Ellacuria (eds) in Systematic Theology (London: SCM 1996)
14 Dave Tomlinson *Re-enchanting Christianity* (London: SCM Canterbury Press 2008) pp. 50-51.

now to that core question as we explore whether nature connection is a legitimate route for connection with God within the Christian tradition.

God and the physical realm

So what then do Christians believe about the relationship between God and non-human creation? Is God purely Spirit who can only be experienced apart from the material, or is God present in some way in all that is his, in the whole of the created order, human or otherwise?

This next section is going to make reference to some major debates and theological concepts. If we are going to answer the question about the appropriateness of nature connection within Christianity, we need to dive into the middle of the arguments!

All of this is a question that has created controversy for the majority of Christian history, most notably during the periods of church history known as iconoclasm when Christians were divided over whether or not icons were appropriate in Christian worship.[15] The heart of this debate was about whether or not it was appropriate for a Christian to use an image of Christ as a focus for worship. Of this debate, Ware writes:

> *The struggle was not merely a conflict between two conceptions of Christian art. Deeper issues were involved, the character of Christ's human nature, the Christian attitude towards matter, the true meaning of Christian redemption.*[16]

As Christianity has developed through the centuries, two broad streams of understanding have developed with core

---

15 See for example Timothy Ware *The Orthodox Church* 2nd edn (London: Penguin 1997) pp. 30ff
16 Ware *Orthodox Church* p. 30.

ideas that go back to those of this debate. The Western strand includes Roman Catholic and reformed churches, and the East is largely the Orthodox churches.

Western theology has traditionally made a clear distinction between creation and creator.[17] If this is true then God is clearly apart from the material world. In the Eastern understanding, where icons have continued to have a core role within worship through the centuries, it is seen differently; we will come to that in a moment.

In the Western framework of understanding as we have seen, creation and creator can be seen as separate: God as apart from creation though with the exception of the incarnation whereby God lived among us in Jesus. So, apart from those few years, God is usually viewed as wholly other.

Pentecost of course followed as Jesus returned to his Father's side, and with this in mind, many make an exception of the church: God is only fully present within creation in those people who have accepted the reconciling power of the cross. For example, Miroslav Volf in seeking a Protestant rediscovery of the Trinity, sees the immanence of the Holy Spirit primarily within professing Christians.

> *Human beings can be in the triune God only insofar as the Son is in them ... It is not the mutual perichoresis of human beings, but rather the indwelling of the Spirit in common to everyone that makes the church into a communion corresponding to the Trinity.*[18]

In this extract from his work he uses the technical term perichoresis, much used within Trinitarian theology. Its meaning doesn't have an exact equivalent in English, but carries

....

17 J. Moltmann *God in Creation* transl. Margaret Kohl (London: SCM 1985) p. 1.
18 Miroslav Volf *After our likeness: the church as the image of the Trinity* (Grand Rapids MI: Eerdmans 1998) pp. 212-3.

nuances of relationship, intimacy, indwelling, and there is a sense of joyful dance in the indwelling and mutual reaching out. It is used primarily to describe the relationship between Father, Son and Holy Spirit. John 17.21 is a good biblical reference:

As you, Father, are in me and I am in you, may they also be in us, so that the world may believe that you have sent me.

So returning to Volf, he sees the intimacy and indwelling between the persons of the Trinity extended towards those people who have accepted Christ and are therefore invited to be a part of this relationship. This however is seen as the sole way in which God is present in the material world, through redeemed humanity.

Colin Gunton seems on an initial reading to join him in resisting a theology of the immanence of the Holy Spirit in all creation. He is certainly understood in this way by the authors of Generation Y, quoted above. He writes:

In particular, arguments like those of Lampe for varieties of a single immanence of God will not do, particularly in view of John Zizioulas' observation that talk of the Spirit is not a way of speaking of God's immanence, but of his transcendence.[19]

This however is a misunderstanding of the point he is making. Zizioulas, who he quotes, is working within the Orthodox framework of understanding. Within this, the Trinity is understood in two ways: God as Trinity who is separate from creation (known as immanent, or essence) and God who is at work within creation (known as economic, or energies). Thus the Orthodox can say that God is fully transcendent as Father, Son and Holy Spirit (immanent Trinity), but is also fully

19 Colin Gunton *The Spirit in the Trinity* Alasdair Heron (ed) in The Forgotten Trinity (London: CCBI 1991) p. 123.

present and working within all that has been made (economic Trinity). Timothy Ware writes that God is absolutely transcendent and God is 'everywhere present filling all things'.[20]

Orthodoxy therefore distinguishes between God's essence and His energies, thus safeguarding both divine transcendence and divine immanence.[21]

Within this framework then Zizioulas can understand within the immanent Trinity the Holy Spirit to be wholly apart from creation and therefore considered as transcendent. This is to be balanced however with the counterpoint of the economic Trinity – the Holy Spirit is also actively present within creation.

Gunton follows this framework and therefore his comments on the transcendence of the Holy Spirit picked up by the authors of 'Generation Y' need to be balanced against the counterpoint of the economic Trinity. Overall he appears to be arguing against a total identification of the Spirit with creation, against a kind of practical pantheism. He affirms the Spirit's presence and work within nature though remaining reluctant to use the word immanent.

The one who 'everywhere diffused, sustains all things' is the agent of redemption as well as the creation of all things.[22]

He specifically argues that the work of the Spirit is not confined to the church but within the whole of creation.

Although the present action of the Spirit is identified ecclesiologically, it should not be so limited.[23]

---

20 Ware *Orthodox Church* pp. 208-9.
21 Ware *Orthodox Church* p. 209.
22 Gunton, C. *The Spirit in the Trinity* Alasdair Heron (ed) in The Forgotten Trinity (London: CCBI 1991) p. 129.
23 Gunton *The Spirit in the Trinity* p. 129.

So here we are beginning to find theologians affirming the presence of God within the whole created order, affirming the instinct of communities like Forest Church that seek to engage and connect with nature is a legitimate means to seek God, who is present within all of nature. We find this way of thinking more fully worked out within the Eastern and Orthodox stream of Christian thought, though with an awareness that Western theology in our own time is looking more and more to the East for insight and understanding.

Ian Mobsby writes on the logical conclusion of the Eastern way of thinking:

> *The Eastern churches have a more* **panentheistic** *theology, where God is understood to be omnipotent, eternal and other, and yet present in all creation, enabling it to exist. Put another way, God's energy maintains all things and all beings, even if those things have explicitly rejected God... So rather than creation being just dirt, there is a mystical relationship between all matter and the Divine.*[24]

Within Western theology, many shy away from the division between economic and immanent Trinity, understanding instead that what God does comes from the heart of God's being. Within the contemporary rediscovery of the Trinity many would argue that immanence (now using the word differently to mean presence within the material world) is led in our own era by the Holy Spirit, having been lived out in the person of Jesus. Transcendence, separateness from the material world, is led by the Father, though through perichoretical relationship, where one person of the Trinity is present, so are they all.

---

24 Ian Mobsby *God unknown* (Norwich: Canterbury 2008) p. 61.

Alistair McGrath follows this approach. Having written about how if God was just the Father then God would only be apart from Creation, he then reflects on the Holy Spirit:

> *If God was just the Holy Spirit, we would have to think of him as just part of the world of nature, caught up in the natural process, or in terms similar to nineteenth-century idealist philosophies. But once more, Christians know that God just isn't like this.*[25]

Within this framework there is a growing movement that sees God as more fundamentally present within creation than has previously been understood, at least in the west.

Moltmann is a leading theologian in this field. The following is an extract from his book 'God in Creation':

> *Through the powers and potentialities of the Spirit, the Creator indwells the creatures he has made, animates them, holds them in life, and leads them into the future of his kingdom.*[26]

This is often known as panentheism: not that all is God, as in the pantheism of Paganism, but that all is in God and God is in all, an understanding which when held within Trinitarian framework is within the bounds of Christian orthodoxy. Essentially it is this way of understanding God's relationship with creation that allows us to understand our interaction with nature as a participation in God and a legitimate Christian spirituality. If God is in all, if God is sustaining all, animating, holding in life, leading forwards, then to relate to nature is to relate to God as God is present within nature.

....
25 Alister McGrath *Understanding the Trinity* in McGrath *Studies in Doctrine* (Grand Rapids MI: Zondervan 1997) p. 214.
26 Moltmann *God in Creation* p. 14.

Panentheism, Forest Church and Christian mission

This brings us to the heart of our question, which is whether we can legitimately understand our connection with nature to aid and strengthen our connection with God. And thankfully the answer is yes. If God is present in all of nature then it is just as legitimate to seek the face of God in the natural world as it is to look for God in the people around us or in the pages of scripture.

God is both greater than the created order and intimately a part of it. This remains, whether we understand it within the Eastern framework of immanent and economic Trinity, or within the Western framework whereby the different persons of the Trinity are, though united by perichoresis, assigned different roles. Either way, it is no bigger leap to seek God within nature than to seek God within one another. This means that Forest Church and other nature connection initiatives are on a firm footing within Christian orthodoxy. It is good news for Christians who find the natural world an inspiration for faith.

This is also a positive discovery in missiological terms as it leaves us in a good position to connect with those around us who, suspicious of Christianity's traditional focus on the transcendent are more open to engagement with a spirituality that is earthed, that can be seen, touched and felt. It means that, while remaining rooted with integrity within our own tradition, we can have conversations with others who find inspiration in the direction that spirituality has been taking in the past decades.

The most important conclusion however, is simply that nature connection is legitimately Christian. We have forgotten it through the centuries and become rather otherworldly in our focus. But when we start exploring, we discover that Christianity itself is deeply earthed and with much that is positive to say about the physical world that God has made. We are not abandoning our roots when we find ourselves drawn to aspects of contemporary spirituality, rather rediscovering a forgotten strand that goes deep within the Christian tradition.

Incarnation is at the heart of our faith, as is a celebration of God's enduring presence within all of creation. It is absolutely right therefore that authentically Christian spirituality reaches out to seek God in the fullness of all that God has made including the variety of nature around us.

*Cate **Williams** is an ordained Anglican priest. She is currently the Mission and Evangelism Officer for Gloucester Diocese having previously worked in parish ministry for 14 years in Middlesbrough and Milton Keynes, the latter in an ecumenical team.*

Chapter 2 – Annie Heppenstall

Do I Not Fill Heaven And Earth?

[handwritten margin note: this should be a footnote]

This article uses familiar terms in Christian vocabulary such as 'God' and 'creation' with caution. By 'God' I hope it becomes clear that I do *not* mean a temperamental old man with a white beard, 'up there', and in using the word 'creation' I am *not* asserting or encouraging a literal understanding of the creation account in Genesis (or the Bible in general). Masculine gender will only be used of deity when quoting directly from the Bible; all quotations are from the NRSV translation.

I've always felt love of and affinity with the natural world to be an essential element of Christianity, which is the faith important to my parents, in which I was brought up. As a child, I enjoyed a large garden to play in and a park at the back of the house, with huge and beautiful trees. Childhood holidays invariably involved camping in places of natural and ancient historical interest, in the British Isles and France. There were three of us girls, Mum and Dad, in a relatively small home and smaller tent. Sometimes, from an early age, I wanted peace, solitude, *space*. The garden, the trees, or if we were away, whatever standing stone, hill or seashore we were nearest to, became temporary sanctuary. Stones, the moon, a tree, a river, these seemed to be watchful guardian companions and I tended to feel very safe alone outdoors with them. The more I sat and watched and listened and let my environment touch me, the more I came to experience awe and beauty, great, yearning love, a sense of 'other'. That, I would say, was the emergence of my sense of spiritual experience.

My parents read a lot to us, and many of the stories we heard from the earliest days were Bible stories. I regularly went to church with Dad, it was a lovely 'together' time. One of my earliest identifiable memories, at about 2 ½, is of being in an old Methodist church, with daffodils, a drawing book and crayons, on the occasion of Mothering Sunday. As a young teenager, I gravitated towards the local parish church which had an excellent youth club, and was drawn into participation in the liturgy as a 'server' or altar-girl. This was a socially active, very caring and inclusive church, one might perhaps call it 'liberal catholic', and through my teenage years it became as family to me, communicating a great deal of warmth, acceptance, support and inspiration. Without this influence I would not have chosen to study Theology and Religious Studies as my degree, and probably would not have chosen teaching as a profession. Here, my social conscience was nurtured, a sense of community and also an appreciation for the depth and mysticism of the Christian tradition. I also have an abiding love of candles, incense, white robes and the elements of a Eucharist done 'properly'!

My sense of the sacred, of Divine Presence, of awe and fascination, was - and is - often strongest outdoors. When I first realised that not all Christians seek and find God this way, indeed, mistrust too deep an engagement with the natural world, I felt incomprehension and a great sadness. Much of my writing comes from a desire to open the door for Jesus-lovers, to give a little confidence that it is safe, worthwhile and spiritually enriching to engage with creation. One of my favourite passages in the Bible is the call of the lover to the beloved in the Song of Songs, to come outdoors into a beautiful garden. Christian mystics have suggested that the lover can be seen as Christ and the beloved, the church or the human soul – although of course the Rabbis have different interpretations:

My beloved speaks and says to me:
'Arise, my love, my fair one,
and come away;
for now the winter is past,
the rain is over and gone.
The flowers appear on the earth;
the time of singing has come,
and the voice of the turtle-dove
is heard in our land.
The fig tree puts forth its figs,
and the vines are in blossom;
they give forth fragrance.
Arise, my love, my fair one,
and come away.
Song of Songs 2:10-13

It's time for the beloved to step outdoors! Christianity *needs* intimacy with the natural world and is lost without it; following a human being who walked the earth, used the environment constantly to illustrate his wisdom and chose bread and wine as the focus for his continued presence, how can Christianity *not* look constantly to creation to gain insight into the divine? The issue, to me, is not so much about justifying nature-love to Christians, but asking how any spiritual path can possibly be healthy *without* a love of and communion with nature. Personally, I don't understand how anyone could choose to follow a faith path that does not have this desire for intimacy with creation.

Let's think about Jesus. In Jesus we find someone who turned to the natural world for peace and quiet, for inspiration – wisdom – for God. He prayed alone at night on mountainsides.

He submitted to a fasting ordeal in a desert. Following a busy day of healing people, he withdrew outside the village to the grassy hills. He talked often about the natural world and used it to illustrate his teachings, in particular the grain cycle. He (or the Gospel writers) said he was like a grain of wheat which had to die to bear fruit. He said he was like the dying and rising grain. He didn't just commune with God in nature, he was, it seems to me, telling his listeners, 'I *am* nature...' In the Gospel message, I hear, *'I am the bread and wine, I am the living water, I am giving myself sacrificially for the good of all. I am the earth.'*

Jesus of course was also a people-lover. He didn't stay out in the wilderness, he came to people where they lived, including sharing worship in synagogues and the temple. He participated in the Jewish prayer, reflection and community life of his people. He offered interpretation of scripture and provoked heated debate; he spoke prophetically, forcefully, sometimes controversially. The synagogues were meeting places, places of debate and learning, places of togetherness, conflict and resolution of conflict: they were at the heart of community dynamics. Church follows this model -which is as it should be - and tends to concern itself with the bustle of the community, where the people are. But despite Jesus's homeless wandering and attraction to the wilderness, 'the Church' seems a bit bewildered on the whole by the outdoors. Why is this? When Jesus said 'follow me', did he mean 'follow me to church and community but when I go up the mountain or out on the lake you can stay home.'? I don't think so.

Jesus's own faith, as a Jew, was rooted in the Hebrew scriptures, which often have a deep earthiness. (At the time of the earliest church of course, what Christians now call the 'Old Testament', the mainly Hebraic texts of Judaism, were the only scriptures. Many in the 1st Century region of the Mediterranean, including Jews of the Diaspora, relied on versions of these which had been translated into Greek. The writings which came to form the 'New Testament' were dependent on these translations and were also written in Greek.) In these properly Hebrew texts, there is often a sense of heaven (the skies and beyond) meeting earth, Divine presence here in creation: God with us. God is often described as God of 'heaven and earth', not just 'in heaven' as we find in the prayer attributed to Jesus. The title of this article comes from a couple of verses in the writings attributed to the prophet Jeremiah, who, like other prophets, often articulated what he felt to be the mood or the will of God:

> *Am I a God near by, says the LORD* [27] *and not a God far off? Who can hide in secret places so that I cannot see them? says the LORD. Do I not fill heaven and earth? says the LORD.*
>
> *Jeremiah 23:23-24*

'Do I not fill heaven and earth?' It's a rhetorical question. 'Yes,' the reader responds, in their heart, 'Yes, you fill heaven and earth. Nowhere and nothing is outside of or beyond your presence.' *'Panentheism'* is a term meaning all-in-God: God is present in all that is, and all creation exists within God. There are many books on the concept of panentheism, which are well worth exploring further, but as a passage for simple, faithful meditation, Jeremiah 23:23-24 is a nugget of gold.

The context of the passage is a powerful chapter in which 'false' prophets and dreamers are condemned for misleading the people with messages contrary to the message of God. The prophetic message of God is repeatedly – especially in Jeremiah - an insistence on compassion for the poor and oppressed, and

....
27 LORD is used in English translations to show that the sacred name of God appears in the text but has been respectfully replaced to avoid pronunciation. It is unfortunately a gendered title, whereas the Name of God is a non-gendered statement of pure existence, something like 'I AM': Exodus 3:14.

on the practice of social justice by those with power: a message of radical concern for the most vulnerable in society. The 'laws' of the Hebrew Scriptures (see above), in the context of the time in which they arose, outlined to society how this was – and is – achievable. Doing God's will was – and is – very much about merciful living day by day, in harmony with the natural cycles of the earth. Many of the guidelines of ancient scripture concern living off the land and care of creatures.

Insistence on loyalty to God₁in the time of Jeremiah, meant loyalty to a particular ethical code which placed value on human, animal and plant life in a world which, according to the Bible at least, practised bodily mutilation, child sacrifice, the exploitation of minors in cultic prostitution and homage to deities who were not interested in human well-being but which had frightening, amoral 'lives' to which humans were subject. Loyalty to God in the pages of the 'Old Testament,' is through responsible living in a particular way, as part of creation, in the here-and-now. Christians are often brought up to be disparaging of 'the Law', believing ourselves to be acceptable to God through faith and by grace, but if we are excused from the minutiae, it is because the spirit of the Law is supposed to be written on our hearts. We are supposed to intuit God's desire, through our connection with Jesus.

It has often been said that a verse in the Book of Micah sums up the Hebrew Scriptures:

> *He has told you, O mortal, what is good;*
> *and what does the LORD require of you*
> *but to do justice, and to love kindness,*
> *and to walk humbly with your God?*
>
> *Micah 6:8*

Walking with God is reminiscent of the time-before-time of the Garden of Eden, when it is said that God walked in the garden with the first people:

They heard the sound of the LORD God walking in the garden at the time of the evening breeze, and the man and his wife hid themselves from the presence of the LORD God among the trees of the garden.

Genesis 3:8

'False' prophecy and teaching is often expressed by the prophets as ignoring the plight of the oppressed, leading to lack of respect for life and encouraging worship of things that are 'made' rather than the 'maker'. There is a consistent attitude in the Bible, that God is creator, Source of All and is omnipresent, Being itself, within, around and beyond all, and that selecting any one aspect of creation for worship, from creature to hand-made object, narrows the enormity of God down to meaninglessness. We might find something of this expressed in Paul's encounter with the many deities of the Athenians, according to Acts 17, and his quotation of one of their own poets, to describe God:

For as I went through the city and looked carefully at the objects of your worship, I found among them an altar with the inscription, "To an unknown god." What therefore you worship as unknown, this I proclaim to you. The God who made the world and everything in it, he who is Lord of heaven and earth, does not live in shrines made by human hands, nor is he served by human hands, as though he needed anything, since he himself gives to all mortals life and breath and all things. From one ancestor he made all nations to inhabit the whole earth, and he allotted the times of their existence and the boundaries of the places where they would live, so that they would search for God and perhaps grope for him and find him—though indeed he is not far from each one of us. For "In him we live and move and have our being"; as even some of your own poets have said,

"For we too are his offspring." Acts 17:23-28

In God we live and move and have our being. If Jeremiah 23:24 is one golden nugget for meditation, then Paul's words here in Acts 17:28 are another. We live in God, like a fish in water or an embryo in the womb. We can think of God as our environment, our atmosphere, which sustains us like the air we breathe. We are in God – and God is in us. Thinking of God as intelligent, loving environment, ups the value of environment somewhat.

Respect for life, incidentally, is not limited to regard for humans. Take the Sabbath rule of rest. All are given one day a week of complete rest, and this rest extends to the labouring classes and to domestic animals. Oxen threshing grain should not be muzzled to stop them eating. A mother bird should not be killed at the same time as her eggs being taken, nor a lamb stewed in its mothers' milk. In times of war, fruit trees are not to be destroyed -

> *If you besiege a town for a long time, making war against it in order to take it, you must not destroy its trees by wielding an axe against them. Although you may take food from them, you must not cut them down. Are trees in the field human beings that they should come under siege from you?*
>
> *Deuteronomy 20:19*

In killing an animal, the blood must return to the earth:

> *And anyone of the people of Israel, or of the aliens who reside among them, who hunts down an animal or bird that may be eaten shall pour out its blood and cover it with earth. For the life of every creature—its blood is its life; therefore I have said to the people of Israel: You shall not eat the blood of any creature, for the life of every creature is its blood...*
>
> *Leviticus 17:13-14*

The life-blood is to be poured on the earth because the creature is of God. In some mysterious way, pouring the life-blood on the earth returns the life to the Divine source, like a river flowing back to the sea:

> *I will not accept a bull from your house,*
> *or goats from your folds.*
> *For every wild animal of the forest is mine,*
> *the cattle on a thousand hills.*
> *I know all the birds of the air,*
> *and all that moves in the field is mine.*
>
> *Psalm 50:9-11*

Respect for the life-blood remained a requirement of the gentile dimension of faith as advised by the apostles according to Acts 15:28-29:

> *For it has seemed good to the Holy Spirit and to us to impose on you no further burden than these essentials: that you abstain from what has been sacrificed to idols and from blood and from what is strangled and from fornication. If you keep yourselves from these, you will do well. Farewell.'*

Respect for life runs deep in the Hebrew Scriptures, not least in the psalms, used for centuries in the liturgical worship of both Jews and Christians. Take Psalm 104:

> *The trees of the LORD are watered abundantly,*
> *the cedars of Lebanon that he planted.*
> *In them the birds build their nests;*
> *the stork has its home in the fir trees.*
> *The high mountains are for the wild goats;*
> *the rocks are a refuge for the coneys.*
> *You have made the moon to mark the seasons;*
> *the sun knows its time for setting.*
> *O LORD, how manifold are your works!*
> *In wisdom you have made them all;*
> *the earth is full of your creatures.*

Yonder is the sea, great and wide,
creeping things innumerable are there,
living things both small and great.
There go the ships,
and Leviathan that you formed to sport in it.
These all look to you
to give them their food in due season;
when you give to them, they gather it up;
when you open your hand, they are filled with good things.
When you hide your face, they are dismayed;
when you take away their breath, they die
and return to their dust.
When you send forth your spirit, they are created;
and you renew the face of the ground.

Psalm 104:16-19, 24-30 (read the whole psalm!)

The concept of God as 'Creator of Heaven and Earth', is one which we encounter immediately in the opening chapters of Genesis. There is a repeated phrase which appears like a refrain in a storyteller's performance: *'and God saw that is was good.'* The natural world, as dreamed, wished, sung, commanded, willed, imagined, whispered, fashioned into being by the Supreme Being, is *good*. Humanity, according to the account in Genesis, is the notable exception to this inherent goodness: we can *choose* to be good. Or at least, we can choose to *try* to be good, whatever 'good' means to us. For Christians, Jesus is the model of how to be good, how to live life as God intended – so to be truly human is to touch the divine. Becoming like Jesus, taking on the mind of Christ, means allowing God to free us from the 'sins' or obstacles that stop us living in complete harmony with God's desire. Paradoxically, discovering how to be fully human, is the mystical Christ-path to divinity.

One of the traits of the natural world is, according to many passages of scripture, an innate capacity for praise of the creator. Again, we find such passages especially in the psalms:

Praise him* [God], sun and moon;
praise him, all you shining stars!
Praise him, you highest heavens,
and you waters above the heavens
Let them praise the name of the LORD,
for he commanded and they were created.
He established them for ever and ever;
he fixed their bounds, which cannot be passed.
Praise the LORD from the earth,
you sea monsters and all deeps,
fire and hail, snow and frost,
stormy wind fulfilling his command!

Psalm 148:3-8

The last verse of the last psalm exhorts, *'Let everything that breathes praise the LORD! Praise the LORD!'* (Psalm 150:6) Humanity is not alone in praising God, but is called to join nature in praise. Praise, the psalms imply, should be as natural to us as it is to mountains and forests, birds and whales. The chorus of true worship, lamentably, is often without the human note. By what strange twist then, do we presume to separate ourselves from the natural world and assume that it is only *we* who offer true praise? If we recall the question from God in the title of this article, 'do I not fill heaven and earth?' We are faced with an interesting notion of natural praise as the unstoppable joyousness of God's sacred breath, the breath by which all utter their praises, the 'all' which is or are filled by the Divine.

It is often imagined that the Judeo-Christian deity is 'out there' and 'up there', an imageless and mysterious transcendent heavenly being, for Christians (and according to some Christians for anybody else too) only accessible through Jesus – or worse, some Father Christmas-like rather unpredictable old man. It is interesting that for Christians, it is important that the Divine comes to earth, incarnate as a human being who is born and dies before he is raised and assumes the cosmic status of the Christ. It does matter to the Christian story, that God is present on earth and it is a heresy to claim that Jesus was not a human but purely a heavenly being. But the notion of God's presence on earth is not unique to Christianity. Once again, we can turn to the psalms. Take Psalm 139:

> O LORD, you have searched me and known me.
> You know when I sit down and when I rise up;
> you discern my thoughts from far away.
> You search out my path and my lying down,
> and are acquainted with all my ways.
> Even before a word is on my tongue,
> O Lord, you know it completely.
> You hem me in, behind and before,
> and lay your hand upon me.
> Such knowledge is too wonderful for me;
> it is so high that I cannot attain it.
> Where can I go from your spirit?
> Or where can I flee from your presence?
> If I ascend to heaven, you are there;
> if I make my bed in Sheol, you are there.
> If I take the wings of the morning
> and settle at the farthest limits of the sea,
> even there your hand shall lead me,
> and your right hand shall hold me fast.
> If I say, 'Surely the darkness shall cover me,
> and the light around me become night',
> even the darkness is not dark to you;
> the night is as bright as the day,
> for darkness is as light to you.
> For it was you who formed my inward parts;
> you knit me together in my mother's womb.
> I praise you, for I am fearfully and wonderfully made.
> Wonderful are your works;

that I know very well.
My frame was not hidden from you,
when I was being made in secret,
intricately woven in the depths of the earth.
Your eyes beheld my unformed substance.
In your book were written
all the days that were formed for me,
when none of them as yet existed.
How weighty to me are your thoughts, O God!
How vast is the sum of them!
I try to count them—they are more than the sand;
I come to the end—I am still with you.
Search me, O God, and know my heart;
test me and know my thoughts.
See if there is any wicked way in me,
and lead me in the way everlasting.

Psalm 139:1-18, 23-24

To me, Psalm 139 implies that God is immediate. God is in our environment. We might even say, as above, that God *is* our environment. (Acts 17:28) The natural world is not just made and left to carry on, watched over by a distant deity who creams off the obedient from a select species for a heavenly idyll; the natural world is inseparably infused with God, inextricably bound in relationship with God, helplessly in love with God, dependant on God, filled with God. When we are told to recognise our nature as temples of God's Spirit (1 Corinthians), we are, to my mind, reminded that there is nowhere outside of God's presence, *except* perhaps the closed human heart which chooses to shut God out. 'Creation' is God's temple. We, like the natural world, can let God in.

So where is Christ in this? The writer of John's Gospel describes Jesus talking about the interiority of God's presence, in a long and mystical discourse prior to Jesus's arrest:

In a little while the world will no longer see me, but you
will see me; because I live, you also will live. On that day
you will know that I am in my Father, and you in me, and
I in you.

John 14:19-20

God, as expressed in the Hebrew Scriptures, God as worshipped in Judaism, as praised by 'everything that breathes',
God who fills all heaven and earth, dwells in Jesus who lives
a life in harmony with God. For those who follow Jesus, he
will dwell in us, and thus in him, we will have God within
us. When I read John 14:19-20, I think of Russian dolls. But
it doesn't do to let mystical expressions get too cerebral. The
point, to me, is that the in-dwelling presence of God is for us
to realise and welcome, and this makes us rejoice – along with
the natural world which knows this intuitively. Our praise is
empty until it comes from a heart which is in awe of and in
love with the omni-present Divine.

In the Hebrew Scriptures and also in inter-testamental writings which influenced early Christianity (and perhaps Jesus
too), God's presence was sometimes expressed though the
personification of Wisdom, a feminine character present on
earth. Wisdom is an attribute, a quality of God, even perhaps
simply God, but can be gained to some degree by humans.
Solomon was famed as particularly wise, and his wisdom
included understanding of the ways of people and of nature.
In an extensive description of Solomon's majesty and might,
we read,

He would speak of trees, from the cedar that is in the
Lebanon to the hyssop that grows in the wall; he would
speak of animals, and birds, and reptiles, and fish. People
came from all the nations to hear the wisdom of Solomon;
they came from all the kings of the earth who had heard of
his wisdom. 1 Kings 4:33-34

In contrast, when Job expresses righteous indignation and challenges God about his suffering, he is made aware of his crushing ignorance of creation:

Then the LORD answered Job out of the whirlwind:
'Who is this that darkens counsel by words without
knowledge?
Gird up your loins like a man,
I will question you, and you shall declare to me.
'Where were you when I laid the foundation of the earth?
Tell me, if you have understanding.
Who determined its measurements—surely you know!
Or who stretched the line upon it?
On what were its bases sunk,
or who laid its cornerstone
when the morning stars sang together
and all the heavenly beings shouted for joy?

Job 38:1-7 (but continue reading the following chapters...)

Even for us for whom scientific discovery has revealed so much, awe and humility before God continue to be appropriate and it is often the natural world that draws that humility out of us. Scientific discovery enhances that humility and wonder. The prevalent attitude, that the earth simply exists as a resource for humanity to exploit, lacks the awe, reverence and the humility characteristic of a Biblically-rooted person of faith. It also lacks wisdom, in the same way that undermining the foundations of ones' house lacks wisdom. Worryingly, it is often also associated with a mind-set interested in pursuing economic prosperity for the chosen few, as we have seen for example in American politics and oil interests over the last few decades, and more recent developments closer to home such as fracking.

The notion that the earth, our home, and the earth's living things, our brothers and sisters, don't matter, and that our supposed destination (if we believe and do the right things), 'heaven', is more important, that earthly concerns are lesser than 'spiritual' ones, that natural and spiritual can be divorced like this at all, is not from the Hebrew Scriptures of Jesus's faith, but has a discernible root in Ancient Greek thought influential around the inception of Christianity. There was a belief in Greek society (and I simplify), that male was greatly superior to female, that male was associated with the rational, with light, clarity, logic, mind, strength, action, the divine, and goodness. The female was associated with earth, the carnal, instinct, darkness, weakness, passivity and evil. It's a kind of clumsy, inflexible parody of the yin yang symbol, which expresses oneness beyond division and the truth of flowing, ever-changing states of being. It goes without saying that women and the earth, nature, do not do well out of the outlook, and that the notion spawned misogynistic consequences right up to this day.

In the writings of the New Testament, we have a range of outlooks from a range of authors representing a range of diverse communities, some Jewish, some not Jewish – and therefore by default, old-style pagan of a Mediterranean kind. At this time too, to complicate things, Judaism was also exposed to and in some ways influenced by the surrounding culture of empire, whether Macedonian, Greek or Roman – 'Hellenist', although it held onto its particularism with amazing resilience.

Gradually, texts emerged out of the early Christian communities, and some of these texts, probably to the consternation of the authors had they still been alive at that point, eventually came to be thought of as scripture too. Among them, there are varying degrees of influence by a Hellenist binary outlook, where earth, carnality, women and darkness are associated with inferior status and absence of the divine. Sadly, in the climate of antagonism between early Christian communities and Jewish communities, and at a time when it paid to be respectful towards the Roman world, and as the faith spread predominantly among non-Jewish people, Christianity found itself heavily influenced by Ancient Greek philosophy and inclined to brush the Jewish roots under the carpet. This is the legacy we live with today. It is one of the reasons, I would suggest, that much of contemporary Christianity struggles so much to connect with the earth: it has lost touch with its true roots.

Not all expressions of Christianity shun the earth. In European tradition for example, we have St Francis, gentle lover of nature, who lived in utter poverty, preached to birds and tamed wolves. And we have the 'Celtic' Christians who lived lives of austerity and wove their love of the natural world into their prayer and everyday life. The Celtic church in particular was inspired by the austerity of the Desert Fathers and Mothers of the Mediterranean, who left the cities to seek God in the wilderness. The psalms, with their rich natural imagery, were an essential component of devotional life for all these people.

The invitation implicit in such 'desert' approaches is to live very simply in one's environment, and to uncover the Christ in all – a Christian way of searching for and finding the God who 'fills heaven and earth'. The following passage in Colossians can perhaps be read as a gateway back through to connection with creation, for Christians:

> *He is the image of the invisible God, the firstborn of all creation; for in him all things in heaven and on earth were created, things visible and invisible, whether thrones or dominions or rulers or powers—all things have been created through him and for him. He himself is before all things, and in him all things hold together. He is the head of the body, the church; he is the beginning, the firstborn from the dead, so that he might come to have first place in everything. For in him all the fullness of God was pleased to dwell, and through him God was pleased to reconcile*

to himself all things, whether on earth or in heaven, by
making peace through the blood of his cross.

Colossians 1:15-20

This hymn to Christ uses language that echoes Jewish praise of Wisdom, which we find in the book of Proverbs among other sources:

The LORD created me at the beginning of his work,
the first of his acts of long ago.
Ages ago I was set up,
at the first, before the beginning of the earth.
When there were no depths I was brought forth,
when there were no springs abounding with water.
Before the mountains had been shaped,
before the hills, I was brought forth—
when he had not yet made earth and fields,
or the world's first bits of soil.
When he established the heavens, I was there,
when he drew a circle on the face of the deep,
when he made firm the skies above,
when he established the fountains of the deep,
when he assigned to the sea its limit,
so that the waters might not transgress his command,
when he marked out the foundations of the earth,
then I was beside him, like a master worker;
and I was daily his delight,
rejoicing before him always,
rejoicing in his inhabited world
and delighting in the human race.

Proverbs 8:22-31

Writers of material in the New Testament often try to introduce the idea of Christ to both Pagan and Jewish listeners, by referring to the well-known concept of Divine Wisdom. She is equated strongly with the Christian understanding of

Christ. Some might say she *is* Christ or that Jesus as Christ *is* a manifestation of her.

Finding God present amongst us in the awe and wonder of the natural world is not a new idea but a very ancient one, inherent to the faith Christians claim as their root. To me, following Jesus is about appreciating his roots, which were fully embedded in the Jewish tradition and Hebrew Scriptures. This tradition - which still lives of course - is earth-loving as well as rich in transcendent and mystical visions of deity, and this supports the experience of God's presence on earth in the natural world, which is good, awesome and full of praise for God the source of all.

Departing from the Hebrew scriptures and the Jewishness of Jesus seems to me to risk the slippery slope of believing the earth to be disposable, of no real consequence, and the simplistic and erroneous division between earth / carnal / instinctive / female / dark / evil and heaven / spiritual / rational / male / light / good. I can think of a lot of Christians who would argue with me, and say that the 'God of the Old Testament' is different to the 'God of the New Testament', and that they find too much violence and wrath in the 'Old'. I would suggest, that we are conditioned to see this way and not helped to interpret or understand the 'Old Testament' by those who could be our guides. The people to really listen to if we want to understand the Hebrew scriptures and the God they reveal, are practising Jews, but sadly we have such a history of prejudice that it takes a great deal to admit our need for their wisdom. First perhaps comes the work of reconciliation preceded by our corporate willingness to be humble.

Humility, being humble, as has so often been said, is a word that derives from the earth. It means one who is low down on the earth, not in an elevated position. Down here, we see things differently, the little things, ants and blades of grass. Lying on the earth, we may be looking up to the heavens with

hope of a resurrection, whatever that means, but we also antic-
ipate our death, the decay of our bodies back to the soil, to
nurture new life, to *become* new life. The cycle that holds us,
we mortals, is the cycle that holds all life, and according to the
Biblical tradition it is made by God, is good, and is filled by
God, both heaven and earth; there is nowhere we can go from
the divine presence, there is no cell, no atom in our bodies that
is not filled with God. And that, is a great mystery.

***Annie Heppenstall** has a number of books, prayers
and reflections published on Christianity's potential for
earth-spirituality, drawing on her Theology degree and
love of nature. She is particularly drawn to the mystical
and earth-centred aspects of spiritual paths of the world,
the need for self-awareness and inner peace, as well as
ecological mindfulness, if we are to engage constructively
in the world today. Annie is a qualified teacher, especially
enjoys art and music, and is married, with one son.*

Chapter 3 – Matt Freer

The Power of Nature Connection To Change The World

Facing an uncertain future

It is increasingly clear that the earth and humanity are facing an uncertain and challenging future. The challenges facing all living things from the impacts of climate change and global warming are becoming clearer, especially if you live in the global South and are economically poor.[28]

Many of us want, if only reluctantly, to face up to the situation, to create new ways of living that minimise the challenges and navigate them in as a sustaining and life giving way as possible. But not everyone sees it that way, and those that do can find the response needed daunting and a challenge to identify, and a struggle to sustain.

All too often the problems facing the earth and her people are presented in a negative and fear inducing way, leaving us

....

28 This will be clear to some and contentious for others, there is lots of research and reading - the summary findings of the IPCC report of 2013 is a good starting place, whereas Bill McKibben (2010) *Eaarth - Making a life on a tough new planet* is more 'easy-reading' and covers the topic in some detail.

feeling guilty, burdened and immobile. The topic incites passion and confusion - igniting our flight or fight brain response, and making us want to be ostriches with our heads in the sand. In the global North we can remain well protected from the day to day realities of a changing climate – and so we can push them to one side for another day.

Time outdoors does not necessarily feel connected with these big challenges, such as climate change. Connecting with nature is not where we lobby our MPs or decide how to live or manage our carbon emissions. Going for a walk isn't going to the change the world, right?

Those people involved in raising awareness of the impacts of climate change can easily dismiss what the outdoors has to offer 'their world', whilst those engaged in nature connection activities might miss what that connection offers the 'big picture' issues. So in this chapter I want to examine how nature connection could change the world; summarising the growing research in this area; and explore how being outdoors can hugely help how we present and respond to these big social and environmental issues, and how nature connection activities could be crucial to how we engage other people with these.

Why connect with the outdoors...

> "Studies in disciplines of ecology, biology, psychology
> and psychiatry have attempted to empirically examine
> the human relationship with the natural world, some
> concluding that as well as being totally dependent on nature
> for material needs (food, water, shelter, etc.) humans also
> need nature for psychological, emotional and spiritual
> needs." [29]

29 Cecily Maller, et al (2005) Healthy nature healthy people: 'contact with nature' as an upstream health promotion intervention for populations, in

The key message from research into the possible benefits of nature connection is that time spent outdoors seems to make us happier and healthier - prisoners who can look out of their cells at nature get sick less often, patients in hospitals recover more quickly when their view is of greenery rather than concrete.[30] Being outdoors often brings about positive emotions and makes us feel good - and importantly it seems the benefits are not restricted to just the time we are outside either, they seem to be durable,[31] and may influence subsequent interests and behaviours.[32]

In addition to our minds and bodies, time outside enjoying nature is also good for our souls. The natural world doesn't come with an instruction manual, or a set range of possible outcomes; instead it holds infinite possibilities, and can often introduce transcendent moments, when we feel deeply connected to something bigger than ourselves. This wonder and awe is important for our spiritual growth.[33]

Yet at the moment we generally are not well connected to nature. There are plenty of depressing statistics about how little time children (and adults) spend outside. For example in the UK less than a quarter of children now regularly use their local patch of nature compared to over a half of all adults when they were children. In 1971, 80% of 7-8 yr olds walked to school, often alone or with their friends, whereas two decades later fewer than 10% did so, almost all accompanied by

....

Health Promotion International, Vol 21 No 1 (Oxford University Press) - see http://heapro.oxfordjournals.org/content/21/1/45.full
30 Ibid
31 http://www.theguardian.com/news/oliver-burkeman-s-blog/2014/jan/21/spending-time-nature-mental-health
32 C L E Rohde and A D Kendle (1994) *Human well-being, natural landscapes and wildlife in urban areas - A review*, English Nature - see http://publications.naturalengland.org.uk/publication/2320898
33 See Chapter 21 of Richard Louv, *Last Child in the Woods* (2005) and Edward Hoffman, *Visions of innocence – Spiritual and Inspirational Experiences of Childhood* (1992)

their parents.[34] In a single generation since the 1970s children's 'radius of activity' or 'home habitat', the area in which children are able to travel on their own, shrank to one-ninth of its former size.[35] Certain health and behavioural issues are starting to be attributed, at least in part, to this growing absence of time in nature.[36] Researchers have attributed, at least in part, increasing rates of obesity to a decrease in the time children spend outdoors, as well as an increase in Vitamin D deficiency. Childhood behavioural 'disorders' have also been linked to an absence of time in nature. Other less tangible consequences include declining emotional resilience and a declining ability to assess risk, both vital life skills. Interest in the benefits of time in nature is growing - and it has been the topic of bestselling books and even a film.[37]

One study of the research concluded:

> *"In the last few hundred years, there has been an extraordinary disengagement of humans from the natural environment. This is mostly due to the enormous shift of people away from rural areas into cities. In evolutionary terms, 'the urban environment is a spontaneous, changeable and historically unfamiliar habitat'. Never in history have humans spent so little time in physical contact with animals and plants, and the consequences are unknown. Already, some research has shown that too much artificial stimulation and an existence spent in purely human environments may cause exhaustion and produce a loss of vitality and health. Modern society, by its very essence,*

---

34 Stephen Moss/National Trust, *Natural Childhood report* 2012
35 Mayer Hillman, John Adams and John Whitelegg, *One False Move* 1990
36 See Richard Louv (2005) *Last Child in the Woods* and (2011) The Nature Principle: Human restoration and the end of nature-deficit disorder. *Health Benefits to Children From Contact with the Outdoors & Nature* (see http://www.childrenand-nature.org/research/) provides a synthesis of research and studies on health benefits, and in 2012 the National Trust gave a UK angle with the *Natural Childhood report.*
37 Project Wild Thing - see http://projectwildthing.com/film

insulates people from outdoor environmental stimuli and regular contact with nature. Some believe humans may not be fully adapted to an urban existence. With parks and public nature reserves often their only means of accessing nature, the majority of urban-dwelling individuals may have all but forgotten their connections with the natural world." [38]

Loving nature and protecting it...

This disconnection with nature brings with it a problem for responding to big environmental issues, such as climate change and biodiversity loss. People cannot emotionally engage with something they cannot see or connect with. They can feel no sense of loss or anger at it, if they cannot identify it. Surely our relationship with nature must affect how we respond to it and how we treat it?

Sara Maitland recently berated the way,

"Schools have abandoned the nature table – the "look-closely-and-see-what-you-can-see" approach – in favour of huge (and usually frightening) global perspectives in which the natural world is perceived as fragile, delicate and endangered by human beings. And it is all very far away." She concluded if, "Nature is over there, somewhere else – and ultimately if "nature" becomes Chinese pandas and Brazilian trees it becomes nothing to do with us: not our fault, not our problem and, saddest of all, not our joy or indeed our heritage." [39]

....

38 Cecily Maller, et al 2005.
39 Sara Maitland in *Do you know the names of the trees in your neighbourhood?* on The Guardian website (Tuesday 26 November 2013 - http://www.theguardian.com/commentisfree/2013/nov/26/trees-names-knowledge-of-nature-rainforests?CMP=twt_fd)

Others have argued that our disconnection with nature leads us into policies that 'sell' nature to the highest bidder:

> *"Spending less time in nature impacts on the way we feel about it and leads us to treat the natural world as simply another resource for us to exploit rather than something of inherent value. It is this type of relationship with nature that has resulted in proposals like biodiversity offsetting. Essentially moral issues about the value and importance of ancient woodland are reduced to one factor in a cost benefit analysis, which stands to lose against anything that can be calculated to have greater short-term economic gain."* [40]

If we spend more time exploring and enjoying the outdoors the way we view the natural world as a society will change.

However, when considering how we respond to these big issues there is much more to the benefit of nature connection than this. As important as being connected and knowing about the natural world is in helping us value it and wanting to protect it, being outdoors can help us process the bigger issues too, and open up our ability to respond. Studies into the way we respond to issues like climate change have identified that we need to engage positive emotions - and as we already know nature connection is ideal for bringing those emotions about.

Reframing the challenge...

Often our approach to raising awareness of injustice and climate change has been to give people facts and figures in the assumption that people will see the problems and be moved to respond. Research into empathy suggests that this approach is not as efficient as sharing the situation as a story, ideally concerning one particular person. Like it or not we seem to

....

40 Ralph Underhill in *The nature moral* on 27 January 2014
at http://projectwildthing.com/posts/view/233

favour emotional language over rational analysis.[41] Providing information and raising awareness is not enough, especially if it induces negative emotions.

Niki Harré has researched what we can learn from the world of psychology for engaging with environmental issues, what she calls the *psychology of sustainability*. Her book, *Psychology for a better world*,[42] is a helpful analysis of what happens psychologically when we are confronted by big environmental issues, and presents a strategy for how to work with that and encourage behaviour change. The core findings suggest that if we want to help ourselves and others in responding to the challenges humanity and the earth face, we need to recognise that people are happiness seekers, and social imitators. Why?

Firstly, we seem to be wired for seeking happiness. Research shows happiness and positive emotions bring out creativity, co-operation and an openness to change. So for people to change, and stick to those changes, it is argued we need to offer activities that create positive emotions. If we work in an atmosphere of positivity we'll also bring out creativity, co-operation and openness to change, and by working in a positive way we'll create immediate wellbeing for ourselves and those around us.

Secondly, research reviewed by Harré suggests people are social imitators. We copy what we see, especially if we see it as normal behaviour. Therefore, we should make visible, and obvious, practices and behaviours we want others to follow. Sharing stories of joy that express the change we want to see, however imperfect those changes are, is important.

41 See pg 137 of Niki Harré (2012) *Psychology for a better world - Strategies to Inspire Sustainability*. This book can be downloaded at http://www.psych.auckland.ac.nz/en/about/our-staff/academic-staff/niki-harre/psychologyforabetterworld.html - there is also a good 15 minute film of the main ideas in the book at https://www.youtube.com/watch?v=2zExibEV_PY
42 Ibid.

Psychologists also suggest we have a tendency to be outraged by big acts of recklessness, and give more time and space to those than 'good' acts that, say, benefit the environment.[43] This creates a dilemma in how we present and frame injustice and the impacts of climate change. Often we are given the big picture stories in a way that focuses on the 'bad', but these can often be fear-inducing messages that create in us a feeling of guilt and make us want to stick our heads in the sand or dismiss the evidence. Fearful messages often create fear based responses.

If we want to help people respond to the big and complex issues of our day we need to move away from tactics that bring shock, anger, fear and anxiety. These negative emotions stop us from responding effectively. Clearly we can't hide from the reality of these big issues, and research has shown that fearful messages can be effective when first heard, but we quickly become adept at avoiding the fear, rather than working to remove the threat itself. Drawing more attention to the severity of the problem only seems to increase our sense of helplessness.[44]

The report *Common Cause for Nature – Values and Frames in Conservation,* which cautions against using extrinsic values, such as economic frames and appeals to competition, status or money when communicating nature's value, is also important here. The report concludes a more viable way of communicating nature's value is to use intrinsic values, showing how amazing nature is; sharing the experience of wildlife, talking about people, society and compassion as well as the natural world; and encouraging active participation through exploration, enjoyment, and creativity.

....

43 Ibid pg 133.
44 Ibid pg 21.

Positive emotions make us more open-minded and improve our ability to handle threatening information, so being inspiring, uplifting, engaging and fun is part of what we need to help us overcome fear.[45] Studies by Barbara Fredrickson, that incidentally used films of nature to generate positive emotions, suggest that one of the differences between positive and negative emotions is that positive emotions broaden our sense of what we can do, whereas negative emotions narrow this sense.[46] This makes us more open-minded and again improves our ability to handle threatening information. The great thing about these positive emotions is that the knowledge, relationships and physical resources accumulated during these good times are still there afterwards, even if we become miserable.[47]

So to summarise, using positive emotions and framing messages carefully, using intrinsic values as much as possible, are important to how we engage people in facing up to the challenges of climate change. You might be thinking that this is all pretty obvious - that of course how we frame and present things matters to how we respond to them? But if we look at the above findings and then look at how 'we' and those around us (as individuals, faith groups, churches and NGOs) often pitch messages around climate change and injustice, we will probably find a disconnection with those findings. It is often sensationalised, fear-based and creates negative emotions - and predominantly uses extrinsic values.[48] Discussions around climate change and calls to campaign are often devoid of contact with nature. Conferences talking about the issues often take place in conference centres inside. We are asked to

....

45 Ibid pg 18.
46 Ibid pg 15.
47 Ibid pg 15, 17, 18, 31.
48 Elena Blackmore, Ralph Underhill, Jamie McQuilkin & Rosie Leach
with Public Interest Research Centre (2013) *Common Cause for Nature - Values and frames in conservation.* See http://valuesandframes.org/downloads/

sign petitions and write letters to MPs usually whilst inside on our computers.

How can nature connection help…

When despair for the world grows in me
and I wake in the night at the least sound
in fear of what my life and children's lives may be,
I go and lie down where the wood drake
rests in his beauty on the water, and the great heron feeds.
I come into the peace of wild things…
I rest in the grace of the world, and am free.

Wendell Berry [49]

"Our failure to address environmental issues is not a failure of information but a failure of imagination." [50]

We've already noted that there is plenty of research affirming what perhaps many of us instinctively know - time outdoors encourages positive emotions. Given the importance of positive emotions to how we respond to big issues, nature connection and being outdoors provides a great stage for helping bring about those good feelings, and hence a valuable tool when approaching big issues and identifying our response.

When looking at how we respond to the big issues like climate change, we need to be inspired to think creatively, and happiness and positive emotions inspire creative acts. [51] Liberating our minds is an important part of our creative response. Back in 1958 a study found that in the act of contemplating nature, the brain is relieved of 'excess' circulation and nervous system

....

49 Excerpt from *'The Peace of Wild Things'* from Wendell Berry (1998) The Selected Poems of Wendell Berry
50 Professor John Robinson of the University of British Columbia quoted by Joseph Zammit-Lucia in Guardian Professional, Friday 24 May 2013 - see http://www.theguardian.com/sustainable-business/art-sustainability-imagination-create-change
51 Niki Harré (2012).

activity is reduced.[52] Later studies found that an experience of nature can help strengthen the activities of the right hemisphere of the brain, and restore harmony to the functions of the brain as a whole; a technical explanation of the process that occurs when we 'clear our head' by going for a walk in a natural setting.[53]

It goes beyond people though - we seem to be moved even by animals and nature. "Imagination, not spreadsheets will create change," says Joseph Zammit-Lucia, who in experiments has shown pictures of animal portraits to people and analysed the impact they had on the viewers. He explains that there were no words, no explicit messages, no attempts to "educate" the viewers, they were just exposed to the image. Around 90% of people changed their, "...cultural perceptions of animals and spontaneously made statements about the need for more sustainable lifestyles that can help conserve these animals. This happened without a single word being uttered or printed about conservation or sustainability. Viewers were subjected to an emotional experience, allowed to internalise it for themselves and see where that took them. It is an approach that's fundamentally different from the idea of educating by bombarding people with facts and telling them exactly what to think using rational arguments." [54]

Interestingly when examining the benefits of contact with nature for migrants researchers found the benefits included: increased sense of identity and ownership of the country they

....
52 Yogendra, 1958; cited in Cecily Maller et al (2005) *Healthy nature healthy people: 'contact with nature' as an upstream health promotion intervention for populations*, Oxford University Press. See http://heapro.oxfordjournals.org/content/21/1/45.full
53 Furnass, 1979; cited in Cecily Maller et al (2005) *Healthy nature healthy people: 'contact with nature' as an upstream health promotion intervention for populations*, Oxford University Press. See http://heapro.oxfordjournals.org/content/21/1/45.full
54 Joseph Zammit-Lucia in Guardian Professional, Friday 24 May 2013 - see http://www.theguardian.com/sustainable-business/art-sustainability-imagination-create-change. His work can be seen at http://www.jzlimages.com

live in; sense of integration rather than isolation; a reunion with nature; the reawakening of a sense of possibility; restoration and a relief from daily struggles; empowerment, skill development and the enabling of opportunity to participate in caring for the environment.[55]

In responding to big issues we need to get away from the idea that there is one right way forward that we should all follow. Rather we need to respond in a locally appropriate way, and individually we need to find our place of greatest fit, what Frederick Buechner has quite wonderfully described as where, "our deep gladness and the world's deep need meet."[56] That will require inspiration, creativity and being open, and it seems that spending time outdoors is likely to be a great place for that to happen. It grounds us and widens our sense of what we can do, opening us up to new possibilities, and helping us find our own response. By nurturing these experiences of interconnectedness we enhance our sense of belonging to the world, deepening our sense of who we are, and to quote Psychologist Marilyn Brewer, "When the definition of 'self' changes, the meaning of self-interest and self-serving motivations changes accordingly."[57]

The sustaining nature of the outdoors...

"Our objective for the future should be healthy people in a healthy environment, with healthy relations to that environment. Natural spaces and public-owned parks not only preserve and protect the environment; they also encourage and

....

55 Wong, 1997; cited in Cecily Maller et al (2005) *Healthy nature healthy people: 'contact with nature' as an upstream health promotion intervention for populations.*
56 Frederich Buechner (see http://www.pbs.org/wnet/religionandethics/?p=15314) cited on pg 218 in Joanna Macy & Chris Johnstone (2012) *Active Hope - How to face the mess we're in without going crazy*
57 Cited on pg 88 in Joanna Macy & Chris Johnstone (2012) *Active Hope - How to face the mess we're in without going crazy*

enable people to relate to the natural world, hence they have a key role to play in a socio-ecological approach to health."[58]

When we've faced up to the problems the world is facing and decided how we're going to respond we all face the challenge of how to keep going. The reality can be tough and depressing. Again nature connection offers help. We've already mentioned positive emotions and how being outdoors seems to nurture them, but research suggests that connecting with the natural environment is also powerfully restorative to our wellbeing. For example, when comparing a walk in a natural setting, a walk in an urban setting, and relaxing in a comfortable chair, a study found that mental fatigue was most successfully relieved by a walk in a park.[59] Flow, the mental state in which a person performing an activity is fully immersed in a feeling of energised focus and enjoyment, is key to our commitment and keeping going.[60] For many of us activities that create flow are conducive to being outdoors and connecting with nature.

Contact with nature seems to improve our cognitive functioning (for example through better attention or less fatigue) and cognitive contents may also arise (for example a high self-concept and sense of a symbiotic expansion of the self). The first of these acts directly on the person's thinking processes, whilst the second sets the occasion for the emergence of positive thoughts This can help us see the benefits which contact with nature may have on people's behaviour - on the one hand exposure to nature may exert a direct influence on the behaviour in which a person engages, and on the other it may

....

58 Pg 51 in Cecily Maller et al (2005) *Healthy nature healthy people: 'contact with nature' as an upstream health promotion intervention for populations*
59 Hartig et al., 1991; cited in Cecily Maller et al (2005) *Healthy nature healthy people: 'contact with nature' as an upstream health promotion intervention for populations.*
60 See Mihaly Csikszentmihalyi (2002) *Flow: The Psychology of Happiness* - the classic work on how to achieve happiness, and Niki Harré (2012).

provide a setting which encourages constructive behaviours which enhance the person's psychological well-being.[61]

It may seem obvious, but again how often do we integrate time outdoors with our responses to these issues? In developing a context that supports us in working for our world, we need to include contact with nature.

Research also suggests that being in natural environments can invoke a sense of 'oneness' with nature and the universe, and that being in nature can lead to transcendental experiences.[62] Nature has the power to bring the over there, in here. In nature you can often overcome that sense of separateness and know you are a part of the whole. Recognising that everything in nature, including us, is interconnected is important to restoring hope for a better future. More fundamental than the feel-good factor of pleasant views, being outdoors connects us with the biological reality that we are part of nature, that, "...We wouldn't have the food we eat if it weren't for the rich living matrix of soil, plants, pollinating insects, and other forms of life. When we carry within us a deep appreciation of how our life is sustained by other living beings, we strengthen our desire to give back."[63]

A shift in our understanding of nature and how we relate to it can bring us a greater purpose to what we are doing and a greater sense of support too. Following in the footsteps of St Francis we see the trees, the insects, and birds as our kith and kin, as our extended family, as parts of our larger, ecological self. We are thus surrounded by allies. This opens up the possibility that our, "...desire that life continue is larger than we

....

61 See pg 101, C L E Rohde and A D Kendle (1994) *Human well-being, natural landscapes and wildlife in urban areas - A review*
62 Rohde and Kendle 1994; cited in Cecily Maller et al (2005) *Healthy nature healthy people: 'contact with nature' as an upstream health promotion intervention for populations.*
63 Pg 211 in Joanna Macy & Chris Johnstone (2012).

are, and when our actions are guided by this desire, we can imagine all around us the cheering of all those sharing our aims."[64]

Bringing us together...

The benefit of contact with nature goes beyond the self though, it can, "...not only help one to increase or re-establish one's identity with one's own self, but also that with one's social and physical surroundings."[65] Again this seems crucial to a desire to bring about change and engaging with environmental issues.

Nurturing this sense of ecological identity is something that we can share through nature connection activities with others. You can walk along a river everyday of your life and not necessarily connect with it, but spending time with someone who understands the river and how it 'works', can quickly enable you to identify with that ecosystem in a way that will transform your daily commute.

This approach provides an opportunity to, "...move beyond egotistic motives for behavioural change, and away from trying to persuade people that they *should* make their choices with a series of ecocentric concerns in mind... [often favoured by faith-based groups]," and instead, "...work to uncover, and make explicit, the innate sense of connection to other living things... We might use this to develop peoples' sense of self, such that this is more inclusive, in the expectation that people will then want to make behavioural choices with a broader set of interests at heart."[66]

....

64 Ibid pg 211-212
65 Pg 136 in C L E Rohde and A D Kendle (1994) *Human well-being, natural landscapes and wildlife in urban areas - A review*
66 Tom Crompton (June 18, 2007) *Self-identity and Connection to Nature - discussing the work of psychologist Wesley Schultz.* See http://valuesandframes.org/self-identity-and-connection-to-nature/

Nature is a good leveller and a great space to explore solutions together. In their review of studies in this area Rhode and Kendle concluded that, "Nature perhaps has subversive potential - or to put it another way, the informality of the nature setting allows people with a common goal to discard societal 'straightjackets' and relate to each other in a spontaneous and immediate way. The results of this 'subversion' of social roles are usually constructive and may extend beyond the boundaries of the nature setting. Thus children felt more grown up and responsible because of their conservation work, and adults and youngsters alike felt it had motivated them to take a greater interest in the community at large. Thus it would appear that work with nature in whichever context may generate within and amongst the participants processes which encourage them to take on responsibilities not only for their own actions but also for the wellbeing of the community around them."[67]

Being outside in nature is not the only setting where these desirable and necessary social processes for change are set in motion, but they do offer a great stage for them that is often overlooked. The informality of these settings is not easily matched elsewhere, particularly for example in church settings.

Being together is also important for sustaining our responses, as people often require social affirmation to keep going. Zavesoski's research with deep ecologists (i.e., those practising a philosophy of environmentalism that explicitly calls for the expansion of the self-concept to include nature), found that maintaining an "ecological identity" is challenging. In our society we often communicate information about the self through consumer goods, and people trying to maintain an

....
67 Pg 148 in C L E Rohde and A D Kendle (1994) Human well-being, natural landscapes and wildlife in urban areas - A review.

ecological identity are often forced to communicate this part of themselves to others primarily through their actions, such as not owning a car. It seems we need affirmation that others understand who we are, but many of the actions one may take to communicate an ecological identity fail to elicit affirmative responses from others using this consumer approach.[68]

Hence a supportive community seems vital not just for helping create ideas but also for sustaining people. Perhaps with a greater understanding of what is going on here, we could also see new spaces developed by our faith communities for support and modelling? Forest Church groups would be a natural place to start - and are already helping provide such sustaining environments.

Just connect

Our response to climate change is not simply about global agreements on carbon emissions (important though they are), but also about how we respond as individuals and communities. As we do that we need to be aware that how we frame engagement with climate change and its impacts is important to how people will respond. Nature connection and engaging with people outdoors in nature is a valuable tool for raising awareness and developing responses. Those of us engaged in raising awareness of environmental issues like climate change need to be aware of the importance of examining our attitude to, and relationship with, our natural environment. Whilst those of us engaged in leading nature connection and creating opportunities for time outdoors need to be aware that we have such a valuable tool within our grasp. No doubt we need resources and ways to know how to do that - and hopefully with growing interest they will be developed - but even if it

68 Stephen Zavestoski in comments of Tom Crompton (July 27, 2007) Response from Wesley Schultz - see http://valuesandframes.org/response-from-wesley-schultz/

is 'just' a walk, it really could help you and others change the world.

Matt Freer lives on a small-holding on the edge of the Black Mountains, where his family are developing a new venture providing space for retreats, holidays and workshops that connect with nature (www. warmthandwonder.co.uk). He is a project manager for the Quiet Garden Trust and works freelance on other projects. In the past he was the Environment Advisor to the Diocese of Oxford and has worked for a range of NGOs on community development and environmental issues in the UK and Africa (www.mattfreer.info).

Chapter 4 – Simon Marshall

Nature is My Church

Books are a place where treasure is discovered. What I hope to set down here is something which I would have loved to discover a few years ago - something to reassure me that the path I found myself on was the right one, that it was okay for me to be there and (and here I am not exaggerating) that I was not losing my sanity. What I needed at that time was to hear another voice saying, 'This is what I have discovered, and I'm not totally sure about it, but I share it with you because others may be feeling like this, too.' I have heard that writers are often told by their publisher: 'Write the book that you would love to read.' Well, this article will be considerably shorter than any book, but that's what I aim to do: to write what I would like to have read when I began this part of my journey.

Before I go any further, I think it would be helpful to say something of who I am and where I am coming from. First of all, I am a Christian, or, at least, I walk a Christ-centred path. Secondly, I am an Anglican priest, and Vicar of a church in the West Midlands. Indeed, for the last thirty five years of my life, church has been something of a second home to me: my thinking and my behaviour have been shaped by the patterns and rhythms of the worshipping life of the Church of England. I sang in my church choir as a child; I led the church youth group with my wife in the early years of our marriage; I led the prayers, read the lesson and occasionally served the coffee after the service. The words and phrases of the Church of England are part of my tapestry: I have grown up being able to chant psalms, recite creeds, sing the Magnificat and the Nunc Dimittis from memory and find my way around the Book of Common Prayer.

And now, as an Anglican priest for the last 12 years, I plan and lead acts of worship so that others are enabled to engage with God. I spend much of my working life preparing sermons, choosing hymns and writing liturgies for the different seasons of the Church's year. I also chair meetings, plan strategies and struggle with church finances. In addition, I also prepare couples for marriage, officiate at funerals and baptisms and visit schools to lead assemblies. I listen to the concerns and burdens of people at every stage of life, something which I count a great privilege. I play a small part in the lives of my parishioners at the most joyful and sorrowful times of their lives.

Mine is a varied and challenging role, which comes with a certain amount of authority, and even more responsibility. There are about an equal number of successes and failures, though I find that I recognise the failures more easily. And in the midst of all of these duties, I try to remind myself that I, too, am travelling on a spiritual journey.

However, a couple of years ago, I began to feel that something was changing. Many of the things which I had believed passionately in my twenties and thirties no longer gave me the same feelings of enthusiasm and energy. I began to find that much of the work I was called to do as a Christian priest felt dry and over-intellectual. I felt that many of the words I was called upon to say in Sunday services and in meetings no longer sounded genuine: it was as though a former version of myself was speaking them. I was also growing tired of constantly having to come up with something new to say about church life or some new way of thinking about the Christian faith. And underneath all of this, I couldn't shake the feeling that the way I was practising my faith was leading to a separation of body, mind and spirit.

In other words, my role as a Church of England priest required a very intellectual mode of operation: reading, analysing, discussing, planning, reviewing, writing and debating. And ironically, although it was my role to facilitate the spiritual growth of others, it seemed that my spirit was shrivelling. And my contact with the material world and with God's creation, though very important to me, was left to struggle along in last place. I was intellectually, spiritually and bodily tired. And though I continued to love the Church which had been part of my life for so long I felt that, sooner or later, something would have to give.

Throughout this time of change, I had begun to develop an interest in gardening. This came as a surprise - I'd never shown the least interest in gardening before - and I initially took it as a slightly depressing sign that I was heading towards middle-age. Nevertheless, I encouraged myself to embrace this new interest and to see where it led. I began by simply growing a few herbs such as marjoram, thyme and coriander - things which would be easy and satisfying to grow and also useful in the kitchen. I soon learned to appreciate the fact that the simple act of filling pots and planting seeds took me away from the computer and the phone, and provided a welcome pause in the middle of the working day. Little by little, I noticed that the half hour I spent in the garden each day had a particular quality - it contained both a sense of detachment and a sense of engagement. Although my desk was only a matter of yards away from my spot in the garden, I forgot about work for those few minutes.

And at the same time, I was drawn into another world where things happened more slowly, but with more purpose and, I believe, more truth. Not only that, but when I was in the garden my breathing slowed, the chatter in my head quietened and I shook off the layer of anxiety which I wore during many working days. As I grew accustomed to the rhythm of sowing, thinning, tending and harvesting I slowly realised that I had found the place I most wanted to be in the entire world. The garden was the place where I stepped outside myself, where I experienced joy and wonder, where I felt that I didn't have to live up to expectations, where I could express something of my creativity and where I felt at home. Though it was painful to admit it to myself, I slowly realised that something life-changing was emerging: the garden had become my church.

What do I mean by Church?

But then, there's a word to conjure with: church. As the Church of England said in the promotions for its recent Back to Church Sunday initiative, Church means different things to different people. The word 'church' may trigger thoughts of buildings, people, hymns, Sunday School, friends, history, division, belonging, authority, sermons, power, place, safety, irrelevance or any combination of these and other concepts. And, of course, to many 'church' may not mean much - or, indeed, anything - at all. But for the purposes of this article, I would like to try to define what I mean by the word 'church', so that we know where we're starting from.

When I refer to church in this article, I am talking about Church as I have experienced it over the last 35 years within the Church of England. Firstly, as a gathering of individuals seeking to engage with God as Trinity: Father, Son and Holy Spirit. This gathering takes place indoors in more-or-less the same location and at more-or-less the same time on a more-or-less weekly basis. Within that gathering, there will be opportunities for offering worship to God in spoken words and song, for affirming belief in God, for hearing texts read from the Bible, for the delivery of an explanation of the meaning of those texts, for prayers which address God and seek God's help in areas of personal and corporate need.

There may also be a sharing of bread and wine, involving some or all of those present, as a remembrance of the death and resurrection of Jesus, the Son of God. It is common for the whole of the proceedings to be directed by one person, male or female, who is a recognised figure of authority in the gathering and who may have been ordained to the priesthood of that church.

In addition to this, certain groups of those individuals may also meet at other times in order to learn more about the Christian faith, or to carry out charitable works in the name of the Church, or for social reasons, or to make decisions which direct the ongoing financial, material and spiritual direction of the gathering.

I hope that you will forgive the rather formal tone of the last couple of paragraphs, but I feel that it is important to at least try to define our terms, and I don't want to assume that all readers will have a readily-accessible picture of the sort of gathering I have in mind. Of course, I realise that in presenting my definition of church, I have omitted a hundred things that others would deem essential. I fully acknowledge and accept that, but it can't be helped!

What is 'wrong' with Church?

Over the last three years or so, I have been called to challenge and question things about my Christian faith which I have held dear for decades. The questions I have been exploring include:

- Who and what is God, and how can God be experienced?
- Can God be found only within the teachings and practices of the Christian Church or is God elsewhere, too?

- Who is Jesus, and what do I really think about the things I have been told about him?
- What does the created world teach us about God?
- What language can I use to describe and to experience God?
- How can I engage with God through my emotions and senses, rather than just my mind?

At the same time, I have felt a growing dissatisfaction with the Church I serve. It has been hard to admit this sometimes, and it has been a painful, exhausting and sometimes scary experience. For what if this questioning leads me to abandon the faith which has not only nurtured me for so many years, but which also provides my identity, my income and my home? Would God really take me on such a journey?

My journey into the green of the garden raised issues relating to the worship, language, symbolism and practice of Church. I felt increasingly limited by the way traditional church talked about and engaged with God and, as I began to encounter God outdoors and in nature in general, I became increasingly frustrated by many elements of the worshipping life of the church and often found it wanting.

The regular liturgies of the Church of England often take very little account of the existence of the natural world, and of our place within it. At best, it seems, an occasional paragraph will refer to creation in the midst of a much longer prayer, but even this is very limited in its scope. For example, within the Eucharistic Prayer, which comes at the approach to the high point of the liturgy, we find these words:

Father, you made the world and love your creation. You gave your Son Jesus Christ to be our Saviour. His dying and rising have set us free from sin and death. (Common Worship, Prayer E).

However, two of these prayers do slightly better:

> *You are worthy of our thanks and praise, Lord God of*
> *truth, for by the breath of your mouth you have spoken your*
> *word, and all things have come into being. You fashioned us*
> *in your image and placed us in the garden of your delight.*
> *(Common Worship, Prayer F).*

And:

> *From the beginning you have created all things and your*
> *works echo the silent music of your praise. In the fullness of*
> *time you made us in your image, the crown of all creation.*
> *(Common Worship, Prayer G).*

It should be noted that, within the last decade, the Church of England has published good liturgies for use at times such as Harvest- and Lammas-tide which are included in a resource called Festivals of the Agricultural Year. I have found these to be well-written and thoughtful resources. However, they are for occasional use and I find that the effect of such an approach can lead us to compartmentalise our belonging to nature, rather than to acknowledge it as a basis of our daily existence.

At the same time, the language of traditional church worship has become something of a stumbling-block to me. Much of it is very hierarchical and sounds like the language designed for use in the royal court, or in a legal setting. Of course, any language which addresses the Divine should be appropriately dignified and thoughtfully written. But my experience has increasingly led me to feel that the words of the liturgy build an unnecessary and unhelpful barrier between humanity and God, and that there is little sense of partnership or participation between the created world and the Creator.

Also, as the liturgy is written to express fundamental concepts of the Christian faith - salvation, Trinity, redemption, incarnation - it has to express itself in abstract terms. For example:

We believe in one Lord, Jesus Christ, the only Son of God, eternally begotten of the Father, God from God, Light from Light, true God from true God, begotten, not made, of one Being with the Father... (The Nicene Creed, Common Worship Order One).

These ancient words express a beautiful and significant truth about the Christian understanding of God, but they are hard to grasp and, I have to say, the way they are written does not easily move me or fill me with joy.

As my exploration of the created world has developed I have been increasingly uncertain about the Christian view that the world is 'broken' or is inherently 'less than good'. For Christians, this is a fundamental element in the concept that the work of Christ is about the restoration and redemption not just of human relationships and lives, but also of creation. And I accept the Christian understanding of humanity: that each of us is fallible and bears scars which are the result of the failings of others. I believe also that within each human being is a need for divine healing and renewal.

However, my experience of the natural world, whether sowing seeds in my garden or standing entranced by the blackbird's early morning song, leads me to question the idea that the world is intrinsically 'bad'. I do not generally experience the created world as broken, but rather as beautiful, mysterious and generous. In other words, the accepted teaching of the church and my personal experience of the created world do not match. Indeed, there is a tension here which leads me to feel almost guilty that my experience of the natural world is such a wonderful gift!

So how to deal with this mismatch? After much thought and reflection I have dared to trust my intuition and to choose experience over an element of the church's teaching which does not match what I feel. For many who have grown up in the life of any church, this may feel very challenging, rebellious or even impossible. But if we accept that God speaks to human beings through creation, that God expresses him or herself within nature, then surely we must take the risk of believing that God may reveal to us a richer and more beautiful understanding of who God is?

In addition to the limitations of language, I have also discovered other ways in which I feel myself walking a new path which often diverges from that of traditional church. Quite often, when standing at the lectern or the altar - two places where I feel enormously privileged to be - I find myself wondering, 'What are we doing here, inside these walls, away from all that God has created for us?' And it is then that it feels to me that traditional church can only work indoors.

What I mean is, we can say the words of our liturgies and prayers when we gather inside buildings and away from the sights and sounds of the created world, but I find that once we take these words into nature, they do not work. I don't mean that God disappears when we leave the sanctuary of the church building, but I find that when we immerse ourselves in God's creation these forms of words are not enough, yet at the same time they are too much. Perhaps what I mean is that we need new words, and sometimes no words at all.

In her book Green Spirituality, Rosa Romani captures something of this sense of limitation which I have experienced when she says:

> *Religion... is not about resurgence or growth in a natural verdant sense but about continuity and steadiness. It has little of the spontaneity or unpredictability of a living spirituality; rather it is a rigid structure that shelters us from other more unrefined ways of being.*

In a similar way, I have increasingly found that the regular worship of the Church of England as I have experienced it is not readily designed to engage the senses. Much of its worship is confined to the use of two senses, hearing and speaking. But the very starting point of nature connection is the expectation that we will use all five senses in our engagement with God's creation. And, in that way, the process of worship is reversed: it is not humans who take the lead and set the agenda, limiting the experience as we go, but it is nature itself which presents itself to us, and we who are then invited to open ourselves to the experience.

I hope that I have given a sense of my growing frustration and disconnection with the traditional worshipping life of the Church as I experience it, and also of its limitations as a way of encountering the Divine. But at the same time, I don't want to simply criticize the ways of traditional church: it has much within it which is truthful, beautiful and creative. I feel that a more creative way forward is to acknowledge the tensions between experiencing God in church and in nature and then to look for connections and new ways of exploring a relationship between them.

Looking for Jesus in the wood

At the heart of my journey of faith is the figure of Jesus Christ. Whenever I have doubted the meaning of the Christian tradition, or felt embarrassed at its apparent irrelevance, it is the life, teaching and character of Jesus which has restored my trust and my sense of purpose. But in recent times, I have found myself questioning this central aspect of my faith in a desire to connect Jesus with the calling to experience the Divine in nature. In a sense, I have found myself searching for Jesus amongst the trees and calling out his name on the shoreline.

And I have been relieved to find that I am not the only seeker who has been doing this. In the introduction to Mark

Townsend's remarkable book Jesus Through Pagan Eyes, I was intrigued to read these words by the author Barbara Erskine:

I found it hard to relate to the... God of the Old Testament. I wanted a god who understood the world I knew and loved; a god not of sand and desert and olive groves, but a god of misty green isles and apple orchards and verdant forests.

Although I had not put my searching into such romantic words, I identified with the tension between living in Britain and following the path of a religion whose imagery and language - drawn from its Holy Scriptures - is largely of Eastern origin. Of course, to a large extent, the liturgical year of the Church of England is based upon the seasons of the year, particularly with reference to Spring/Easter, Harvest and Christmas. But I was beginning to find it increasingly difficult to make the connections between the two, given the limitations I experienced in the way the Church interpreted these seasons in its worshipping life.

I am well aware of the roots of the Christian faith: its story begun in the wilderness, the village and on the hillside; its growth nurtured by the Mediterranean journeys of St Paul and the apostles; its practice shaped by the early Church and the historic Councils. This is a rich and precious heritage, but I found that it became more and more difficult to allow this story to shape my own, to touch the parts of my life which were now opening to the sights, sounds and touch of nature as I was experiencing it.

A good priest-friend of mine refers to his spiritual journey into nature as 'journeying into the green' - a phrase which I have found very helpful. In a sense, I am looking for an understanding of Jesus which can be taken 'into the green' of the wood, the garden, the forest, the orchard and the meadow. One way in which it is possible to make the connection between the

Jesus of traditional church and the Jesus of the wood is to explore the nature-based teachings of Jesus. Many scholars agree that Jesus himself came from a nature-based tradition:

> *He grew up in Galilee, the green belt and farming area of Israel, and his closeness to nature and her animals and her seasons and lessons is everywhere manifest in his parable and his teachings (Matthew Fox in his introduction to Mark Townsend's Jesus Through Pagan Eyes).*

We constantly find Jesus using nature-language in order to help his hearers understand the life of faith. In the gospels we find pictures of seeds being sown, patterns in the weather, crops being harvested, the problem of weeds amongst the wheat, sparrows and flowers, floods and vineyards, sheep, birds and goats. Jesus, it seems, is a dweller in nature - he seems to understand how the changes, challenges, patterns and signs of the natural world shape who we are and how we think and feel.

In that way, I have begun to see a picture of the rootedness of Jesus. Of course, the Christian faith teaches that Jesus came as light for the whole world, and not just for one place or time, but, for me, to know that Jesus had a belonging to particular places - many of which are recorded by the gospel writers - helps me to meet him in the places which are important and significant to me.

This idea of the being rooted in one place should not be underestimated. For most of my life I was content to worship God whenever and wherever - I wasn't too worried about being linked to particular places and locations. But as I have grown older, this has changed. It is now extremely important to me to know a place well, to be familiar with its rhythms and character.

I have lived in my current home for nearly nine years, and over that time I have enjoyed getting to know the place where

I live. In particular, I have drawn strength from the rhythm of the seasons as I have seen them played out in the garden: I can now watch for the first growth of leaves on individuals trees; I can look ahead to the ripening of berries and the arrival of the migrant birds who come to feast on them; I can enjoy the changes in the fall of sunlight as the trees in our little wood regain their leaves through the Spring and Summer; I know where the robin and blackbird cross paths at dawn. And I can tell what time of day it is (and when it is time for lunch!) by the position of the sun across the study window.

This knowledge, gained over nearly a decade, is precious to me: it is an intimacy with this particular place, which, although outwardly unremarkable, is like no other on earth. And it is here that I sometimes find I can encounter the spirit of Jesus, amongst the quietness holly and hawthorn, as I reflect on the fact that he, too, regularly withdrew to be alone in contemplation.

One the most significant factors in my journey in the last two years has been my participation in a movement called Forest Church. My belonging to this network, a creative and pioneering initiative, has transformed the way in which I have begun to understand and encounter God in nature. There are many things I could write about what I have discovered over recent months through my involvement with Forest Church, but I would like to share one in particular - a reflection on my first experience of a Forest Church ritual held to celebrate the Celtic festival of Samhain in November 2012. After the ritual, I wrote the following reflection in my blog:

> *...as we celebrated Samhain, I was keenly aware of the way in which the ritual forged a connection to the earth. As the sacred space was woven we honoured the energy of the Life around us, in the place where we all stood:*

Here in this place we honour muntjac deer, robin and squirrel;

Magpie and owl, fox and badger, blue tit and chaffinch

...the mighty cedar in whose shade we meet...

Throughout the ritual I felt that what we were celebrating was rooted in that very place, in that garden, amongst those trees, with that group of people. As I reflect on the celebration I am aware of the intimacy of the ritual and of the way in which it drew on the experiences of those who were participating in it.

And although I had met the majority of the group only half an hour earlier, I felt a belonging and that what we were doing together mattered. This resulted in a connection and a rooted-ness which I find so often sadly absent from our weekly celebrations and services in church. Is this because our Anglican rites fail to take account of who is present, of the holy place in which we are meeting, of the connections we have to one another?

For me, this new experience of intentionally encountering the Divine was completely transforming. I was familiar with the practice of the Church of England: using an authorised, stand-ardised form of words which was intended for use in a huge variety of places from city-centre cathedrals to tiny churches on the edge of a hillside. I now realised what had I been miss-ing, and why the liturgies of the church I loved had come to seem so dry and empty: it was because they took so little account of the place in which they were being used.

Because they are the liturgies of the national Church, they have to be written in such a way that they can be used in all churches, everywhere. There is a clear sense of rootedness: the liturgies are rooted in the history of the Anglican Church, and in the wider story of God's action in the world. But, for me, their shortcoming is that they have very little sense of being rooted in the environment in which are were being used. However, a ritual which took account of the sights, sounds, presence and subtleties of a particular place allowed me to feel a sense of God's immanence. God was truly in that place, in each person, in the light, the darkness, the flame, the earth. Once again, nature was my church.

Why Nature? And where is God in all this?

As I said earlier in this chapter, I do not want suggest that, for the individual who seeks God in nature, traditional church is ineffective, or of no value. But my experience leads me to conclude that, once the journey into the green has begun, there is no easy turning back from that path. Also, I have found that my seeking (and sometimes finding!) God in nature has then led me to re-evaluate the practices and thinking of traditional Church and has often led to an 'opening out' of those practices which has been fruitful for myself and for those I am called to serve. For example, I have noticed that my preaching has become more 'rooted' in the place and the community of my church. I find it easier, and more important, to 'keep things local' in the hope that people will more easily be able to make their own connections between faith and life.

But, why nature? What do I find there which adds meaning and significance to the spiritual journey? Why not just stick with what I know, and keep going? After all, doesn't the faith in which I have been nurtured for so long lead to God anyway? Well, yes, I believe that it does, but the journey I find myself on isn't about what path works most efficiently, but, rather, it is about the adventure of exploring the wonder and the mystery of who God is. For me, nature is the way I am learning to be closer to God.

Through my engagement with nature I am learning to understand Jesus Christ, the centre of the Christian faith, in new ways. However, this is not just a process of accumulating more knowledge about Jesus, but of seeing the role of Christ, the essence of his life and work, from a different angle.

For example, those who come primarily from a nature-centred path draw parallels between the role of Christ and the figure of the Green Man, the symbol of the life force that runs within all living things. Indeed, many of the older churches and cathedrals in our land contain carvings of the green man over doorways, or in the ceiling decorations, and so this link is not a new one, but one which reaches us from the wisdom of the past. (What is more, it is agreed that such symbolism did not exist in Britain prior to Christianity, suggesting that the relationship between the Green Man and Christ was intentional from the outset.)

But aside from architectural and historical interests, this nature-church relationship can be enriching for those who seek to see the person of Christ in and though the created world. In her essay 'The Lily Cross and the Green Man' Maria Ede-Weaving suggests:

> ...it is clear that Christ's sacrifice reflects that of the Green Man's... As vegetation god, the Green Man offers his own body that others may live and flourish; he is grown up, cut down and reborn in the yearly cycle of his living and dying, and the deeper mysteries of his sacrifice bring hope and the possibility of renewal for all beings. Like Christ's story, we find in the Green Man's cycle our own cyclical and eternal natures.

The parallels in these stories have enabled me to reflect on my relationship with Christ as I observe the changing seasons of the year: in this way, my journey with God is enriched by my participation in nature. Maria Ede-Weaving goes on to say that as she reflects on the sacrifice of both the Green Man and of Christ she learns

'...to honour and trust in this process of shedding; of
releasing and transcending my old self that the life in me
might be reborn; that I might be more authentically myself.'

I then hear echoes of the words of Jesus in chapter 12 of John's gospel:

Very truly, I tell you, unless a grain of wheat falls into the
earth and dies, it remains just a single grain; but if it dies,
it bears much fruit.

And so, I find a rich growth of understanding taking place as I reflect on what I experience in nature and the faith which I have practiced for so long in the life of the church. The one feeds and is fed by the other.

This journey into the green is also about courage, and a willingness to have my beliefs challenged and transformed. For example, as I have travelled this path I have come into contact and conversation with those of other spiritual paths, many of whom walk far more closely to the earth than I ever have. Their beliefs are different to mine - they may not recognise the role of Jesus, and they might have a very different idea of who and what God is - but I have discovered them to have a very close relationship with God's creation and an intimate sense of what is sacred, which leads to a deep understanding of how that closeness leads them to live their lives.

To quote Matthew Fox once more:

We need a vital exchange between those who honour the
God of the Book and those who honour the God of the Book
of Nature. There need be no split. Union and communion
are beckoning us.

These insights and friendships have a central thread: the path of nature. And I have discovered real joy in coming to know these good folk, and learning that we can trust each other and help each other to travel our particular spiritual journeys.

Nature is my path

My journey into nature has taken me on an adventure filled with challenges, questions and connections. Over the last few years, I have taken part in outdoor rituals, full moon celebrations and pagan moots. At the same time I have worked as a Christian priest, trying to comfort, guide, inspire and serve a group of faithful people in a Church of England parish. Much of what I have learnt so far has enabled me to carry out my role in a fuller and more creative way, and to bring a greater understanding of God's world to the task. I love the ways of traditional Church: its stability, its presence in the community, its engagement with social issues and its calling to serve all people of all faiths and of none. And I have many good friends and colleagues there - people who understand and support me wholeheartedly.

And yet, at the same time, I feel the call of a spirituality based in nature, where the turn of the seasons, the mystery of place and the cycle of birth, growth and decay speak to something deep within me, and which I do not find reflected in the agendas, structures and liturgies of the Church to which I belong. Indeed, I even find myself uncertain of which spiritual label I should wear these days, as the ones I bore for so long do not take account of the person I now know myself to be.

Some of my friends and colleagues (for I am not the only one who feels this way!) who are on similar journeys suggest that the Church is on the brink of profound changes which could lead to new ways of understanding, living and worshipping in nature, alongside those from other spiritual paths. This is something I hope and long for, but we are not there yet. In the meantime, I feel that those of us from Christ-centred paths and those from earth-centred paths should continue to seek out and celebrate the places where our paths meet, and then have the courage to walk together along each other's paths as far as we can, without fear and in love and trust.

Simon Marshall is a Vicar, poet and liturgist and lives in the West Midlands. He leans towards an earth-centred spirituality, and helps to lead Ancient Arden Forest Church. He also grows herbs, practices yoga and watches the changing seasons from the tiny patch of woodland in his garden. When he remembers to, he blogs at barefoottree.blogspot.co.uk

Chapter 5 – Ruth Valerio

Paganism, Christianity and a Celtic Easter: Some Personal Reflections

An evocative sight greeted me when I reached the top of the winding path that led up the hillside with its tall trees and winding thick roots. As I looked to the right I saw Chanctonbury Ring – the hill fort based ring of trees on the top of Chanctonbury Hill in West Sussex - and about thirty people gathered there. Standing in front of them was my beautiful friend, Juliet, who had wrapped herself in a white blanket and was carrying a large stick on which she had attached a big white flag with a gold cross on it. The flag, the blanket and Juliet's hair were all fluttering in the north wind that blew up the hillside and I felt like I was entering a scene from Narnia.

It all seemed entirely appropriate, as I was there to celebrate the Celtic Easter, which happens on a different date to the Roman one that is customarily celebrated in the Western church, and which is the date that the first followers of Jesus in these British lands would have celebrated. As Juliet rang the bell she had brought with her, calling us to prayer, Greg (my husband) explained what was to happen, and off we went.

We walked round the circle of Chanctonbury Ring, stopping at each of the compass points, engaging in a different reflection at each point. At one we recited a Psalm; at another we sang St Patrick's great hymn, 'Be Thou My Vision'. At one point, Karen Lowe from Antioch Church in Llannelli led us through a reflection around a lit brazier and a meditation on what 'home' is and how our home is found in the risen Messiah. Finally, we went into the middle of the ring, where Dr Micha Jazz from the Axiom monastic community led us through communion, reminding us that as we have walked up to this high point on the Sussex Downs so we walk along our journey of life with Christ, and we are sustained in that through the bread of his body and the wine of his blood.

It was a truly beautiful experience, evoking a number of things in me that I would like to reflect on in this chapter and that I think are relevant to some of the discussions around Forest Church.

Some while ago – provoked by a good friend who left the Christian faith to become a practising Pagan – I did some research into Paganism and the different rituals that they do, particularly around the four equinoxes of our British year. What I discovered surprised me, and I was struck by the fact that much of what they do would actually give me little cause for concern. Let me tell you about one particular Beltane celebration (Beltane being an old Celtic celebration on May 1st, marking the mid-way point between the spring equinox and the summer solstice. In the calendar it stands opposite Samhain or Halloween, on October 31st).

The Beltane ritual I read about took place not far from where I live, in a wooded area with a cave. It had four main elements. Firstly, the group stood in a circle, saying words from a liturgy that welcomed everyone and drew them together. Secondly, the group then said words that welcomed the spirits of the North, South, East and West to their celebration and asked them to be present. The third, main, element focused on the cave. Each person was asked to take into the cave something that represented the darkness of the past year. They went in and said some words about that and then took time in silence to reflect on what they were wanting to leave behind. Then, when they were ready, they walked out of the cave into the light, leaving behind the object they had brought with them. Finally, they joined back together to say a liturgy about going out from there, leaving the darkness of the past year behind, walking into the new life and light of the year ahead.

I probably hardly need say how familiar this might sound to the kind of thing that is sometimes done by those of us reading this who are Christians. Certainly I can think of responses in the evening celebrations at the big Christian event Spring Harvest that would be very similar!

The key difference that I could see was in the Name/s in which these two rituals were carried out. The Beltane celebration might start off an evening by invoking the spirits of the North, South, East and West. At our Easter celebration we did something very similar, except – crucially – we invoked the One Holy Spirit and asked for her/his presence to be with us instead.

What struck me most forcefully with the pagan rituals that I read about was their earth-centredness. In comparison, my main act of corporate worship takes place in a bare building with concrete walls and shutters over the skylights in the ceiling, allowing no contact with the wider creation at all. Many churches around the country are like this and I'm not being unduly critical of my own. But, this lack of contact is a lack that I feel acutely and – if I can be honest here – there were elements of the pagan rituals that I researched that resonated with me strongly. That Easter evening, watching the sun set from Chanctonbury Ring and sharing communion with other believers, felt like the most authentic experience of corporate worship that I had taken part in for a long time: worshipping the Lord of All Creation, as a part of the community of creation.

The relationship between Christianity and Paganism has often historically been hostile, to say the least, and to suggest that there may be some similarities and resonances is to risk being hounded out of the Christian world and branded a heretic. I am interested in the history of this though.[69] One of the things I do regularly is teach on 'Transforming the Environment' to third year ordinand trainees at the St Mellitus college in London. St Mellitus was Bishop of London in the early seventh century and was part of the move to convert paganism to Christianity. I am struck by a letter to St Mellitus by Pope Gregory 1, encouraging him to undertake the conversion gradually and in a way that integrated the pagan rituals and customs, rather than obliterating them It is fascinating to reflect on how our understanding and practice of the Christian faith might be viewed differently to our experience of it today, in the light of that encouragement.

So what are we to make of what I am saying here?

Let me begin to answer that by highlighting two key differences (and no doubt there are others too). Firstly, there is a crucial difference between my faith and that of modern pagans, and that is the incarnate, crucified and resurrected Jesus (so, for example, a similar response at Spring Harvest would see people bringing their objects – or, more likely, bits of paper on which they have written – to a big cross and leaving them there). Thus, while there are similarities, I am not being naïve or overly simplistic: without Jesus taking a central place these celebrations would sit very uneasily beside my Christian faith.

---

69 A huge and complicated topic that I cannot consider satisfactorily here.

Whilst this particular Beltane celebration resonated with me, there are others that would not.

A second crucial difference is that, as a follower of Jesus, I worship the Creator and Lord of all creation, rather than the creation itself. One of the most helpful aspects of Celtic Christianity, with its emphasis on the whole of creation, is that it always maintained its Christ-centredness and never saw any part of the created order as divine in-and-of-itself.

So, I am not advocating Paganism. I am writing this chapter as someone who stands firmly within the parameters of historic Christianity. Nonetheless, having experienced my friend's involvement with Paganism, I have learnt that it is not something to be scared of and that it is unhelpful to take too rigid an 'us and them' approach. A lot of my church upbringing has taught me to take an adversarial and hostile position towards Paganism and I now do not consider this to be a positive way forward. I want to suggest instead that we might consider being humble enough to ask if there are things we can learn from them.

My reflections on the Easter celebration at Chanctonbury Ring and the Pagan Beltane ritual have led me to see two particular aspects where I think we might learn from our Pagan friends: two aspects that also seem germane to some of the discussions of this book.

The first is the bodily nature of how worship was celebrated. At the Easter celebration we walked, sang, prayed, reflected around a fire, stood in silence, listened, ate and drank. At the Beltane ritual they stood in a circle together, brought objects that represented their sentiments, walked into and out of a cave, and so on. In the Old Testament, too, alongside listening to and reciting the Torah and singing songs, it strikes me that the sacrificial system was an act of worship that involved the whole person, physically bringing something into the Temple.

There was a lot of dancing, and the playing of instruments, all in all giving us a picture of worship that was far from static and motionless. As so many of the key characters of the Old Testament show us, we encounter God through our whole bodies, so shouldn't our whole bodies also be involved in our acts of worship together?

I love singing and I love corporate sung worship. I also believe absolutely that singing is a fundamental part of being human – as was brought home to me strongly when sitting at Southampton train station once on the day they got promoted to the Premier League! I have friends who are involved in leading sung worship in church and I have no desire to disparage the good things that they're doing. It is also, of course, obvious to state with Romans 12:1 that we worship God with our whole lives.

But am I the only one who thinks it odd that the main way by which we conduct our corporate worship is by standing in rows and singing songs or reciting/singing a liturgy? We are, after all, whole beings, not just voices, so why do we use only our voices in our worship? The taking of communion is the one act that bucks this trend and it is a wonderful thing, making us move, walk, kneel, eat, drink, pray and embrace others (or at least shake their hands...).

I recently came across a quote from the eighteenth-century revivalist, Jonathan Edwards, who seemed to think something similar when he said, 'Some bodily worship is necessary to give liberty to our own devotion; yea though in secret, so more when with others . . . 'Tis necessary that there should be something bodily and visible in the worship of a congregation; otherwise, there can be no communion at all'. No communion at all? Wow, that's a strong statement...

The second aspect where we have so much to learn is that of worshipping the Creator in a way that celebrates and includes, rather than excludes, the wider creation.

One of the most noticeable features of modern Pagan rituals is that participants see themselves as absolutely integrated with the natural world around them: a feature that is almost entirely lacking from contemporary Christian theology and practice.

It needs to be said that modern Paganism, to my mind, comes from a false premise; reflecting a belief in the divinization of nature and collapsing the categories of Creator and created. Biblical theology, on the other hand, affirms that Yahweh alone is God and that the natural order is Yahweh's creation, and thus distinct from him.

Nonetheless, I would like to suggest that much of the contemporary Christian theology and practice with which I come into contact also comes from a false premise: one that creates too large a separation of human beings from the rest of creation. In one sense there is truth in this: it is only the human species that has been created 'in the image of God'. And yet in other respects – as we see in the Genesis creation narratives – we are an integral part of the wider creation. We were created on the same day as the other animals; we were given the same blessing (to be fruitful and increase in number), and we have the same breath of God within us (the breath of life in Gen. 2:7 is the same as that in 1:30).

One of the best ways by which we can recover our connectedness is to consider how we join with all creation in worshipping God. Psalm 148 is a wonderful celebration of this reality, as it works through so many features of the natural world – including human beings – exhorting them (us!) to 'praise the Lord'.

Richard Bauckham has written insightfully on how God's creation praises him.[70] He makes the point that it is only human beings who express praise specifically through voice, for the wider creation worships God simply by being themselves: 'they praise by being what they are, what God has made them, and by doing what they do, what God has created them to do'.[71] Surely this speaks into our worship of God too as we praise God, yes through our voices, but also with our whole lives?[72]

how do we know that?

I have found Bauckham very helpful on this issue of seeing ourselves as part of the whole creation's praise of God, and he lays out four implications of seeing things from this perspective. Firstly, it is a great leveller. In Psalm 148 humans join in with what Bauckham calls, 'the community of creation'. It is only God who is exalted. Secondly, it teaches us that the wider creation does not exist for us, but for God. As Bauckham says, 'all creatures exist for God's glory, and we learn to see the non-human creatures in that way, to glimpse their value for God that has nothing to do with their usefulness to us'.[73] Thirdly, it then enhances our own worship of God as we attend to the creatures around us. To quote Bauckham again, 'sharing something of God's primal delight in his creation (Gen. 1:31) enables us also to delight in God himself'.[74] The final effect of this should then be that we take on our role of looking after God's wider creation with a greater degree of humility and love than has often been the case.

As I said earlier, I struggle with the fact that my main act of corporate worship takes place in a concrete building that

....

70 R. Bauckham, *Living With Other Creatures*, chapter 7.
71 Ibid 149.
72 When I wrote a blog post on this issue, someone commented: 'why is so much of our Sunday corporate worship based on singing and our 24/7 worship based on serving? Should not one learn from the other?'. Indeed.
73 Bauckham, *Living*, 151.
74 Ibid 154.

contains absolutely no reference to the natural world, even to the point of drawing blinds over the windows so that we can see the screens better. Indeed, sometimes videos are shown during the sung worship of things like waterfalls and mountains, as if to prove the point still further!

Christianity all-too-readily takes on the characteristics of the culture around it. We live in a society that has divorced itself from the natural world, and our contemporary forms of worship reflect that, to our detriment. We are humans, formed from the humus; created as gardeners to serve the world that is around us. May our worship of the Creator God reflect that.

Some Questions for Reflection

1. Do you feel a disconnect in your corporate worship, if you are reading this as a Christian? How might we create more contact and connection with the wider community of creation?

2. What role do you think sung/spoken worship has in a corporate setting?

3. How might we begin to shift what we do when we meet together to worship so that it reflects our whole bodily reality? Have you experienced corporate worship done in this way?

Dr Ruth Valerio is Churches and Theology Director of A Rocha UK and author of, L is for Lifestyle: Christian living that doesn't cost the earth. Also a director of the fair-trade jewellery company, Cred, she is community activist, Christian, academic, eco-warrior, mum, author, veg grower, wife and pig keeper rolled into one. You can find out more about her at ruthvalerio.net.

Chapter 6 – Anne Hollinghurst

Franciscan spirituality & nature as sacrament within the Christian mystical tradition

St Francis and the first Forest Church?

Forest Church in some ways is nothing new. It gives expression to a contemporary resurgence of an impulse deep at the heart of Christian faith and our human nature - an impulse of wonder at the mystery and beauty of creation through which something of the beauty and wonder of the creator may be glimpsed. I am talking about the long and enduring, if intermittent, tradition of Christian nature-mysticism. It is a tradition that stretches back to the church's origins and the earliest centuries, but saw a period of particular flowering within strands of medieval spirituality in the thirteenth century. This was especially so within the phenomenon of early Franciscan spirituality and the traditions surrounding Saint Francis.

Francis lived from 1182 – 1226 and was born in Assisi, Italy, into the family of a cloth merchant. He grew up a good business man like his father but came to reject this early path in favour of a life of radical poverty and simplicity after a vision before a crucifix in which he heard God calling him to "rebuild his church". Seeking to imitate as closely as possible the life and teachings of Christ in the Gospels, he ran into conflict with his father, unsurprisingly, when he began to give away his father's goods to the poor and needy! He was a lively, deeply passionate and compassionate character who was probably not always very comfortable to have around, but his simplicity and poverty were accompanied by a world-affirming delight in the creation and creatures around him. This joy he frequently took up in song and music, in which he shows influence from the wandering troubadours of that period. The writing he himself has left us is largely in the form of the songs, liturgy and prayers that he wrote – some of the first to be written in the native Umbrian dialect. These include the well-known "Canticle of the Creatures" which we shall look at shortly. It was a period in which there was a growing disaffection amongst ordinary people with the uninspiring state the church was in. Although Francis initially interpreted his vision as being a call to physically rebuild the church at San Damiano where he had the vision, he came to understand it as a call to reform and renewal of the church's life. He soon gathered around him a new itinerate order of Friars, whose emphasis was on ministry amongst the ordinary uneducated people.[75]

Francis is receiving new attention in our own day and is proving an appealing figure. Not only has a new pope taken up his name and his message of ministry to and among the poor, but he is the saint associated strongly with peace-making and interfaith relations. He is also known for his legendary rapport with birds and animals. He is perhaps not so well known for how these stories sit within the broader picture of Francis's sacramental engagement with nature – as that through which he met with the living God. I am myself someone whose faith as a

----

75 St Clare was one of those attracted by Francis's spirituality and she was encouraged by Francis to start a new order for women which likewise sought to live out the message of Christ-centred simplicity.

child grew out of a sense of powerful encounter with the presence of God through my wonder at the earth beneath me and skies above me. Perhaps this is why I too am so drawn to Francis. In my adult life I have also remained deeply influenced by my own visit to the hills and woods around Assisi. They are still a wonderfully evocative place. It was there on Mount Vernon that Francis established a small chapel and humble hut dwellings where he and his friars could retreat for prayer and contemplation. It was there that Francis felt most at home and was the terrain that set the backdrop for many of the stories of his relationship with nature. Some of the accounts of Francis's life speak of how he and his friars were so at home in the forest that locals saw them more as indigenous denizens of the woods than ordinary human beings and there are accounts of how women sometimes fled from them – presumably unsure what kind of creature they actually were rather than due to the bad behaviour of the friars! They are described as lodging in caves or booths made of branches. Early Franciscan practice at this time also meant a rejection of grand church buildings and emphasised worshiping out of doors where ever possible. In one of the books about the life of Saint Francis, the Fioretti, we hear about Francis and his friars praying in the woods three times as often as in churches.[76] Another story relates how on one occasion "Lady Poverty", asked to see the brothers' cloister. Francis took her to the top of a near-by hill and pointed to the countryside that lay before them, saying "Madam, there is our cloister". These friars were serious and full-time Forest-Churchers!

I would like to suggest that in Francis and in the early Franciscan theological and spiritual tradition that followed him through his biographers such as Bonaventure, we may find a

....

76 Noted by Edward A. Armstrong in *Saint Francis: Nature Mystic – The Derivation and Significance of the Nature Stories in the Franciscan Legend,* University of California Press, 1976, p 24.

well of ancient wisdom from which to water the young sapling that is the Forest Church movement. I believe that Francis offers a particularly resonant source within the Christian tradition to speak to the wider contemporary search for nature-connection that we are witnessing in our day. Thomas Berry sums up well this contemporary mood and concern when he says:

"One of our urgent needs presently is a renewal of our primordial intimacy with the natural world. Alienated from the land, from the mountains, the meadows, the rivers and coastlands, the woodlands, and from all the flora and fauna of the natural world, our souls shrivel, our imagination becomes confused, and our psychic energy dissolves. …. We must be clear about the issue we are dealing with. Renewal of our human intimacy with the planet Earth is the deepest imperative of our times".[77]

Sometimes we can think that it is only in our own era that we suffer from this nature-disconnect, but Francis emerged at a time when theology had moved by and large to the scholastic schools and the cities where it had become rather abstract and philosophical. Francis' passion to live the Gospel radically, simply and to worship not in grand churches but amongst the trees of Mount Vernon, led him to a new sense of connection with nature and a new sense of vital connection with God. In a similar way, many Christians today are discovering that this renewal of our intimacy with nature leads to a renewal of intimacy with God. It is not a new discovery, but a rediscovery of nature as "the simplest and oldest way… in which God manifests himself" as Richard Foster has expressed it.[78] It is the secret that not only Francis discovered, but the Christian nature mystics who went before him. It is a way of faith as old as the hills.

....
77 *Befriending the Earth*, Twenty-Third Publications, 1991.
78 *Celebration of Discipline*, Hodder & Stoughton, 1980, p.25.

Christian Nature Mystics within the Tradition

"My book, philosopher, is the nature of created things and it is ready at hand whenever I wish to read the words of God" (St Anthony of Egypt, ca. 251–356, in one of the stories of the desert fathers).

Francis is sometimes seen as a charismatic and original individual whose form of spirituality rose up as something quite new and seemingly out of nowhere as a challenge to much of medieval church practice. In many ways he was indeed something of a one-off. Certainly bishops were not always sure what to do about his often unorthodox behaviour, such as when in dispute with his father before the bishop, he stripped naked to demonstrate his utter commitment to a way of radical poverty! But he also stood within a tradition. Whilst the quickly-spreading phenomenon that was the Franciscan movement would burst upon the scene and be developed with greater sophistication after Francis's death by his great admirer and biographer, Bonaventure, Francis was himself influenced by saints and forest-lovers before him. It is not straightforward to trace an unbroken and unambiguous trajectory since the Christian witness would not seem to be always nature and world-affirming in its entirety. And yet, the thread of theology and spirituality that recognised the forests, mountains and meadows as holding the imprint and presence of God, runs long and broad and deep as an ancient, albeit sometimes underground, river. The influences at work on Francis arose from a trajectory rooted in the scriptures and stretching back to some of the earliest great Christian writers and teachers, through the desert fathers and mothers, near medieval contemporaries, and quite probably it has been argued, most directly from the wandering Irish monks of the Celtic peregrini tradition. So were there "Forest Churchers" even before Francis? How does Francis's spirituality sit within the wider tradition of the church and within both the promise and ambiguity of the tradition's reflections on the natural world?

From the Early Church to the Medieval Church

Shaping Christian thought and practice in the earliest centuries of the church, theologians and spiritual writers were soon busy interpreting scripture and tradition in response to the concerns and challenges of their own day. These may not have been quite the same as contemporary concerns framed by ecology and interest in faith and earth-connection, but some of the unhelpful philosophies and spiritualities which they sought to engage with are not a million miles away from similar attitudes to nature which keep resurfacing in our own century in differing forms. One of these was that of Gnosticism, an ultimate form of dualism which taught the evil and prison-like nature of all created matter. This strand of thought and spirituality also crept into the church at times and from here comes the idea that the purest form of religion is all about the soul ultimately trying to escape from the body and the world of nature. In this way of thinking, the physical creation is not the place of encounter with God and has no eternal worth.

Figures like Irenaeus in the early second century wrote against the backdrop of these nature-denigrating attitudes. He taught instead a unity of all things in God the creator and spoke of God as the source of all things. He wrote against the speculative theology of his day, affirming the Divine purpose for creation as being its renewal and fulfilment at the end of time - a new heaven and a new earth. But God's activity in creation was not just restricted to the last days in Irenaeus' view, he also saw God as ever-present in creation, at work blessing and renewing it. Clement of Alexandria in the second and early third centuries meanwhile saw nature as sanctified by the incarnation. The divine Word which took flesh in Jesus of Nazareth pointed indisputably for Clement to the essential goodness of the body and the holiness of all created life and matter. Origen, writing mainly in the third century, and building on Clement and others before him, refined classic Christian thinking on the practice of the presence of God and meditative prayer by identifying three stages. Within this he refers to "physics" as involving the contemplation of nature - the seeing of God within nature and indeed within all created things. A similar three-fold map of the Christian life can also be found in the writings of later spiritual guides such as Evagrius of Pontus, a Desert Father of the late fourth century, John Cassian a disciple of Evagrius, and in the writings of other holy desert dwellers, including in the seventh century those of Maximus the Confessor. It was Evagrius in particular, who in expounding "natural contemplation", drew out yet more fully the idea of reading nature as God's book and seeing each created thing as a sacrament of God's presence.

There are many others who might be regarded as being in some way forerunners of Francis in terms of his love of nature and forest-dwelling instincts. Amongst them in the medieval period St Bruno of Cologne, (1030 – 1101), founder of the Carthusians, an order that began when Bruno inspired a group of followers to form a community living in the craggy terrain near Grenoble. The Cistercian order too traces its origins to a small community established by Stephen Harding on a wooded slope at Molesme in 1075. Then there is the intriguing order founded by Blessed Robert of Arbrissel (1117), who initially lived something of hermit's life in the forest of Craon. Here he is reputed to have lived for a while in the hollow of a tree with the animals of the forest as his companions. It is thought he may have influenced the Humiliati who in turn are thought to have been a source of inspiration for Francis.[79] Then there was Hildegard von Bingen amongst the Rhine-

---

79 *Humiliati* means "humbled ones". This was an association of laymen formed in the 11th century in Lombardy,

land Mystics, (1098 – 1179). In earlier Christian centuries the writings and voices of women nature-mystics that have come down to us are sadly few and far between, writing and education being largely the preserve of a small number of privileged men through much of our world's history. However, in Hildegard we find not only the writer of three theological works based on her visions, but artwork, musical compositions, along with other medical and scientific writings. She was a formidable Abbess in her day. Her visions of God have particular potency and many are mediated through images of the natural world. They speak of the interconnectedness of the whole cosmos, of the elements and the seasons, in a way that has contemporary resonance.

Influences on Francis and legends of the Irish Saints

In terms of possible direct influence on Francis, the lesser known Joachim of Fiore, (1145-1202), has been pointed to as a particular candidate. There was no personal meeting but it is likely that he would have been known to Francis by reputation.[80] He lived high in the mountains of Calabria and in his vision of a new world order he stressed voluntary poverty and pacifism. He had an awe for nature that is recounted in stories such as that which tells of how when the clouds cleared from above the church in which he was officiating, he would hail the sun, sing the Veni Creator, and lead the people out of doors to wonder at the light-bathed landscape and continue their worship there.

Another possible direct influence that has now been recognised as being entirely plausible, is that of the wandering Irish monks of the Celtic tradition, who in turn continued something of the tradition of the Desert Fathers. Although

....

Italy. They wore simple clothes and took special vows which were
lived out very much "in the world" in their ordinary day to lives.
80   O. Engelbert, *St Francis of Assisi*, London: 1950, p. 88-96.

we do not know as much about historic Celtic Christianity as we sometimes like to think we do, it is clear from the art work, symbols, stories and texts that we have, that nature was extremely important to them and was imbued with spirit. It is known that Irish monks travelled widely in Europe, making pilgrimages to Rome, living in the open air, embracing poverty, doing the work of wandering itinerant preachers, and founding monasteries – all of course conspicuous marks of the spirituality of Francis. Stories of the Irish missionary Saint Columbanus (543 - 615) would have been familiar to Francis, the founder of the monastery at Bobbio in present-day Italy. The site, along with the cave that was Columbanus's retreat, was a place of pilgrimage in Francis's day and long after. Stories associated with Columbanus spoke amongst other things of his love of nature and encounters with animals in a way that resonate with the stories of Francis. It is also notable how close in spirit are the Columban rule and that of the primitive Franciscan rule. Meanwhile, one of the most important Irish foundations on the continent was at Ratisborn in Germany, and from here in particular it is thought that other stories of the lives of the Irish saints were circulated widely, including across Italy. Ratisborn was indeed visited in 1221 by Franciscan friars, including Celano the writer of Saint Francis's Life. Travel through pilgrimage and trade in medieval times was opening up more generally and there was a flow of thirteenth century Irish travellers passing through northern and central Italy also bringing their tales of the saints with them.[81] All of this suggests not necessarily that Francis modelled himself directly on Columbanus or any other Irish saint, but that the mythologies and nature stories surrounding them had permeated the culture and region that produced him.[82]

---

81 Hundreds of churches, chapels and shrines there were dedicated to Irish saints.
82 This argument is made well by Armstrong, ibid. p. 34 ff.

This somewhat speedy canter through the Christian centuries offers but a sample of names and traditions, but suggests that Francis, innovative as he was in many ways, was not alone in seeking to glimpse the wood through the trees - the loving creator through the creation. Not only Franciscan spirituality, but the broader mystical tradition of the church, offers many treasures to those who are rediscovering the great outdoors as a God-filled setting for ritual and revel. Whilst the Franciscan strand does not stand in isolation therefore as the sole bearer of a sympathetic Christian engagement with nature and one that chimes positively with the ecological and spiritual perspectives of our current day, it does have particular inspiration as well as challenges to offer. It would still seem to have the power to capture imaginations and influence spirituality in our own day. It is true that neither Francis, nor the traditions which influenced him, are always immediately accessible in the sense that we cannot jump straight from twenty-first century concerns and read the ancient mystics of the church as starting with the same viewpoint. However, as we explore them with minds open to understand the context and worldview within which they forged their faith and spirituality, then we will find riches to fertilise the soil in which new Forest Churches up and down the land are currently being planted and which will enable strong roots to be established.

The way of Franciscan spirituality

What especially do the legends and spirituality of Francis have to offer those who today seek a greater connection with the mystery of nature, and through nature the mystery of the divine?

As we begin to explore this, it is important to start with a note on sources as these are very different from the kind of popular "spirituality book" that we might pull off a bookshop shelf or Amazon listing today. Medieval hagiography was an art form in itself with its own conventions and norms, and it is on writings in this genre that we are predominantly reliant. This offers particular interpretative challenges in terms of looking for the man beneath the legends. Francis, however, did leave us at least some writings of his own, not least some fine poetry which was the first of its type to be written in ordinary Italian language and dialect. Thomas of Celano, who has already been mentioned, was a contemporary and disciple of Francis, and he produced the first "Life" in response to a request from Pope Gregory IX with the particular aim of establishing Francis' sainthood.[83] Bonaventure, a scholastic theologian and philosopher who entered the order founded by Francis about twenty years after his death and became the seventh Minister General of the Order of Friars Minor, is the other major writer who provides us with a source on Francis. His writings are sophisticated works of mystical theological which further developed the Franciscan vision. His Life of Saint Francis was approved by the Friars Minor as the official biography of their founder.

It will be clear from this brief description of the nature of the major sources about Francis that we should be careful not to over-romanticise him or claim for him an eco-spirituality that may be more a product of our own day and way of thinking than his. Nevertheless there is much to draw upon and it is clear that Francis's life and spirituality was something quite remarkable. It inspired greatly ordinary men and women in his own day, as well as intellectual theologians in the Franciscan tradition that followed him. What was it that set him apart along with the movement he gave rise to, in a way that means we still today associate Francis in particular with a lighter way

83 Thomas was asked by Pope Gregory IX to write a biography of Francis, perhaps at the time of Francis's canonization in 1228. The life was completed in 1229. Thomas composed a second, revised life of Francis around 1246. Thomas also composed a collection of the miracles of St. Francis, a biography of St. Clare of Assisi (d. 1255).

of treading on the earth and a reverential, harmonious relationship with creation?

The Sacrament of Nature

Francis's deeply sacramental relationship with nature as well as his sense of solidarity with all creation are at the heart of the answer. Whilst he was not the first to hold a view of nature as sacrament, he did so with a rare intensity difficult to find in the western tradition prior to Francis, except perhaps amongst some of the Irish saints to a greater or lesser degree. He was a charismatic and colourful example of one who sought to actually live out his day to day life in light of this understanding, and to follow radically in the footsteps of the one who had nowhere permanent to lay his head.[84] It was his cheerful embrace of both simplicity and poverty that meant he was free to delight in life and creation as utter gift and see within them the mystery and goodness of God. Such poverty of Spirit he knew to be a prerequisite for intimacy with God. His was also a spirituality focused very much on the human face of God in Christ, and on the mystery of incarnation. Francis, like Clement of Alexandria and others before him, saw nature as sanctified by the incarnation. For Francis this led to a lived spirituality that saw all creatures as his brothers and sisters. In Celano's first biography he writes – "who would be able to express the very great love which he had for all things that were God's? Who would be able to tell of the sweetness he enjoyed when he contemplated in creatures the wisdom of the Creator, together with the Creator's power and goodness?" He goes onto describe how "even towards small worms he burned with a great love"! He tells of how hailing even these as brothers,

----

84 Matt. 8.20; Luke 9.58. Both Celano and Bonaventure report that Francis took up this Gospel text as a blueprint for his own life.

Francis would "remove from the road little worms, lest they be crushed under foot ...". [85]

There are some wonderful stories amongst the legends of his encounters with the world of creatures from birds and furred beasts to reptiles and fish, and indeed including insects. In many of these stories he exhorts creatures to praise and give thanks to their creator. His sermon to the birds is a story that especially caught the imagination and is depicted in much Franciscan-inspired art. Sometimes it is he who is taught by other creatures to give unceasing praise, such as the occasions when he sings duets with birds and cicadas. He gently cares for bees and ensures they do not go without food; he releases creatures that have been caught and these are reported to be reluctant to leave his side until he prays a blessing on them; a falcon serves him faithfully as his alarm clock to get him up for matins; and in another of the most famous legends he even converts to gentleness an aggressive wolf who had been terrorising the residents of Gubbio. He is also capable of silencing noisy swallows and banishing ants so that they don't bite and disturb the people he's preaching to! As noted above, the special nature of medieval hagiography means that these stories are filled with meaning and symbolism and not simply to be taken at face value, but behind them, beyond a doubt, is a man who impressed his followers with such a reverence for the mystery of his fellow creatures that he was led to seek relationship with them, and a man who took seriously the biblical idea of all creatures sharing in the vocation of worship. [86]

It wasn't just animals he addressed. Celano records: "when he found many flowers growing together, it might happen that he would speak to them and encourage them, as though they

....
85 Book II of *St. Francis of Assisi*, by Thomas of Celano, Franciscan Herald Press, 1963, 1988, Chapter CXXIV, p. 124.
86 See for example Isaiah 43.19-21- "The wild animals will honour me, the jackals and the ostriches".

could understand, to praise the Lord. It was the same with the fields of corn and the vineyards, the stones in the earth and in the woods, all the beauteous meadows, the tinkling brooks, the sprouting gardens, earth, fire, air and wind – all these he exhorted in his pure, childlike spirit to love God and to serve him joyfully".[87]

Such stories make me reflect that my grandmother was perhaps not quite so strange after all in talking to her plants – which did seem to always thrive as a result!

Francis's sense of nature as sacrament and his sense of family unity with all creatures, finds most beautiful and poetic expression in his most famous of prayers, written in the last year of his life – the Canticle of the Creatures as it's often called.[88]

> *Most High, all powerful, good Lord, Yours are the praises, the glory, and the honour, and all blessing,*
>
> *to You, alone, Most High, do they belong, and no human is worthy to mention Your name.*
>
> *Praised be you, my Lord, with all Your creatures, especially Sir Brother Sun, who is the day and through whom You give us light. And he is beautiful and radiant with great splendour; and bears a likeness of You, Most High One.*
>
> *Praised be You, my Lord, through Sister Moon and the stars, in heaven You formed them clear and precious and beautiful.*
>
> *Praised be You, my Lord, through Brother Wind, and through the air, cloudy and serene, and every kind of weather, through whom You give sustenance to Your creatures.*

87 Cited by Armstrong, ibid, p. 9
88 Or the Canticle of Brother Sun

Praised be You, my Lord, through Sister Water, who is very useful and humble and precious and chaste.

Praised be You, my Lord, through Brother Fire, through whom You light the night, and he is beautiful and playful and robust and strong.

Praised be You, my Lord, through our Sister Mother Earth, who sustains and governs us, and who produces various fruits with coloured flowers and herbs.

Praised be You, my Lord, through those who give pardon for Your love, and bear infirmity and tribulation.

Blessed are those who endure in peace for by You, Most High, shall they be crowned.

Praised be You, my Lord, through our sister Bodily Death, from whom no one living can escape. Woe to those who die in mortal sin. Blessed are those whom death will find in Your most holy will, for the second death shall do them no harm.

Praise and bless my Lord and Him give thanks and serve Him with great humility.[89]

The canticle holds together the two great affirmations of God found within Francis's spirituality – the awesomeness and the intimacy of God. It extols the beauty and majesty of creation, which reflects in turn the beauty and majesty of God. Creation for Francis is filled with the Spirit of God – the planets, the elements, all creatures, and even death itself which is part of the mystery and the reality of nature and of our own nature.[90]

....

89 Translation taken from *"Francis"*, by Brother Samuel Double SSF, in Journey to the Heart, ed. Kim Nataraja, Canterbury Press, 2011, p.185/186. Francis is said to have written this as song for his brothers to sing and was in fact blind by the time he wrote it.
90 Sister Bodily Death is part and parcel of the gift of life which God has given and there is nothing to fear from her for those made holy by God This verse was added later by Francis as he faced illness and his own death, and

All mediate divine grace, providence and blessing and speak of God's goodness, fruitfulness, beauty, abundance and love. So God is in all things but also, and importantly, all things are in God. This is sometimes referred to as a form of panentheism.[91] The natural world and the creatures which fill it are a locus of encounter with the divine, but they are also held in life by the divine breath - held in being in God. Further, they are not passive in this encounter, but themselves, along with us, give praise to God each in their own way through simply doing what they were made to do. Therefore for Francis, when we give praise to God, we in fact join with the eternal hymn of the universe. In this Francis draws on not only the traditions of the church but the scriptures and psalms which in turn have formed them.[92]

The Nature of Sacrament

It is through Bonaventure that we have a more developed theology of nature as sacrament as lived out in the life of Francis and where a more articulate Franciscan spirituality emerges. It is worth first being reminded of a classic definition of a sacrament as an understanding of something being an outward, visible sign of an inward, invisible grace. Even where there is a very high doctrine of sacrament in the church today, such as in the tradition of adoration of the blessed sacrament, (a spiritual practice often misunderstood by those of a more protestant / evangelical persuasion), the intention is not that we fix our gaze so completely on "the sign" as the bearer of presence, (in this case the consecrated host), to the extent that we cannot see beyond or behind this to the immensity it points to. To do this would render us unable to glimpse the vastness and

he is purported to have recited this canticle on his own deathbed, expressing his sense of solidarity with all of nature – even in the experience of death.
91 As opposed to pantheism – i.e. all things are God.
92 See for example Psalm 104

beauty of God that even the universe cannot contain, let alone a small piece of bread.

Likewise, a sacramental view of nature in the Franciscan tradition does not ask us to equate any material conveyor of God's grace with the full immensity that is God, rather it invites us to encounter the gift and presence of God in a way that points us to and connects us with the immensity. Bonaventure employs a number of images to explore this. Creation and creatures all hold "vestiges", (literally footprints of God); they are like stained-glass windows onto God;[93] and they are like mirrors that reflect the goodness, wisdom and glory of God to different degrees, with human kind as created especially to reflect God's image most strongly. It is not that we can look at an individual creature or aspect of creation and fully see God. Indeed Bonaventure, (perhaps more clearly than Francis), declares creatures to be a mixture of darkness and light - though all bearing something of God even if the reflection appears distant. Creation is also described by him as a book of God, but it is a book which we have lost the ability to fully read and hence our need of another book in addition, the scriptures, or rather more importantly, the one to whom the scriptures point - Christ as The Word of God, the book of God incarnate.[94] Hence Bonaventure is not content to leave us simply gazing at nature or the wonderful creatures who along with us are a part of it. He urges us to see through to the very source of life and mystery behind creation – the creator whom Francis exhorted all created things themselves to praise.

....

93 He writes - "Just as you see that a ray of light entering through a window is coloured in different ways according to the different colours of the various parts, so the divine ray shines forth in each and every creature in different ways and in different properties". *The Soul's Journey into God, (Classics of Western Spirituality)*, Trans. by Ewert Cousins, Paulist Press, 1978, p. 26.
94 For a helpful exploration of Bonaventure's use of these images see for example Zachery Hayes, *Bonaventure – Mystical Writings*, Crossroad Publishing Company, 1999, chapter 2.

A Franciscan sacramental view of nature hence sees contemplation of the natural world not as an end in itself, but through wonder at the beauty of the tree and the divine presence and reflection it holds, we are invited to glimpse the much greater glory of the cosmic and eternal forest that is God. If we are in danger of not seeing the wood for the trees, then our focus of wonder is too narrow and our understanding of God too small. To encounter God as immanent within the natural world is the thrill and joy of the soul, but this divine presence whilst in creation, is not confined to it, thus enabling mystics such as Mother Julian of Norwich to catch a vision of the world as a hazel nut in the palm of God's hand – God as indescribably intimate, and yet also encompassing the world in a way that means it is held in God's encircling palm of love.

The sort of imagery Bonaventure uses to articulate this great sacramental mystery has sometimes given rise to a suspicion of it being too aligned with the idea of spiritual ascent within the Christian tradition. This has been seen as potentially problematic language in terms of affirming an ecological theological vision of the goodness and value of the physical creation. Is Bonaventure leading us back to a strand of Christian spirituality that would posit a dualism between pure spirit and the material world of nature? I'm not sure this is a fair criticism of Bonaventure if his writings are taken as a whole and he is correctly understood. Being able to "look through" the creation to the creator and source of it all does not have to mean we leave nature behind – discarded as if only a ladder which we put to use in climbing to a more direct encounter with God. Where Bonaventure appears to speak in a negative way about the created order in encouraging a certain detachment from it, this is ultimately so that we may approach creation with a right spiritual attitude. This involves not wanting to hold to or possess any of the creatures and beauty we see around us, so that our relationship with these may not become distorted and destructive of either ourselves or the creation. We are rather to learn to hold-lightly, and to rejoice in the free gift of it all, respecting creation's own freedom to fulfil its purpose in God. Here Bonaventure's mystical theology is reflecting on the poverty of spirit which was such a part of the quintessential message of Francis and to which all things return. As Zachery Hayes argues, Bonaventure, (and Francis), are concerned that we should not just love the world of God's creation for its own sake, nor seek in creation alone fulfilment of our human desires. He writes of Bonaventure's mystical theology – "when all the exhortations about the world are finished, we do not really leave the world of God's creation. But we do try to resist a certain ethos of the human world of society and culture. This involves a way of relating to the world that is concerned excessively with sensual pleasures, or with money, control or power."[95]

There is a story of Francis which speaks of this in parabolic terms. The story tells of how Francis one day climbed the holy mountain of God, and then from the heights turned back to embrace in overflowing wonder and love the whole of the created world spread out below. The soul's journey to God does not involve for Francis leaving creation behind, but coming to love it all the more as he learns to see it through God's eyes. Hence Francis's spirituality does not leave Christ on the margins in its celebration of God encountered in nature, rather it places him right at the centre. For it is in coming to know Christ as our brother that we can enter into a true relationship with all created reality and know our own connectedness. Within the medieval worldview of his time, Francis glimpsed a vision that all things are related. This is something which we are re-discovering within the new frameworks of knowledge in our own day. The Franciscan way of being in the world is

....
95 *Bonaventure Mystical Writings*, ibid. p.72.

not just for our own sakes, and certainly not just about having warm, romantic feelings about creation. The world about us is a wonderful and precious gift of which we are a part within the fellowship of all creation. This perspective is a vital one in relation to how we treat the environment and respond to its sacredness. As Brother Nicholas Alan puts it - "We need to inhabit the world and the environment not as tourists or exploiters but as brothers and sisters".[96]

Life from the parent tree - root and branch reflections

Francis and the spirituality he inspired, was neither entirely new nor entirely wacky - a little wild and extreme as Francis himself appears in some of the legends! There is a chord of continuity with voices that sung nature's hymn before him, and an especially strong affinity with the traditions of the Irish Celtic saints. Of course Celtic spirituality has been much drawn upon in our current day amongst those seeking what is perceived as a more nature-aware stream of spirituality. But it does not stand alone in Christian tradition as representing a greener source of inspiration for faith and practice, and indeed on some aspects where the known history is sparse or ambiguous, contemporary romantic imagination has in any case filled-in the gaps. In comparison, Franciscan nature-mysticism has perhaps been a little overlooked as offering a further sacred well from which we can draw deep. It too does not stand alone within the Christian tradition, but it does catch the eye as a particularly fruitful and attractive branch within medieval spirituality. The move of the Spirit in our own day which is inspiring Forest Churchers and others who seek a renewed intimacy with creation, is likewise in continuity with that same tradition - the latest shoot from the ever-green tree of life. Francis was at times misunderstood and accused

....
96 "St Francis", in *Journey to the Heart,* ibid., p. 188

of pantheism, even though his sacramental view of nature was something rather distinct from this, and no doubt those who today are drawn to enter profoundly into the rhythm of nature's seasons and celebrations may be misunderstood. But we are in good company with those who stand in a tradition that reaches directly back to the scriptures and to one of the very first mystical theologians of the church – even St Paul, who could celebrate with both Pagan poet and Christian prophet that "in him we live and move and have our being" (Acts 17.28).

And of course it is not that the river has run entirely underground since the thirteenth century. Whilst early Franciscan spirituality is offered here as having a particular resonance with the contemporary mood and as a source of wisdom that is earthed, the trajectory of nature-inspired mystics did not halt abruptly in the thirteenth century. One might think of Julian of Norwich who spoke of God as the "ground of all things" and "nature's substance"[97], or of Teresa of Avila whose works are permeated with images from the natural world through which the nature and presence of God are recollected. In more recent centuries there is William Blake who saw "heaven in a wild flower"[98], or the more recently re-discovered Thomas Traherne who knew creation to be a gift from God which God intends us to enjoy and delight in – but more than this, the place where we encounter God and the bearer of the infinite and eternal. A theologian of the twentieth century also worth revisiting is Teilhard de Chardin, who in the light of ever expending scientific knowledge and understanding about the cosmos could write that the great mystery of Christianity is not "the appearance" of God in the universe but the

----

97 *Showings of Divine Love,* trans. E. Colledge and J.
Walsh, Paulist Press, 1978, p 290, 302
98 From *Auguries of Innocence*

"transparency" of God in the universe.[99] Again, there are many others who could be cited. But Francis and the traditions surrounding him do open up a particular and poignant conversation with our own age.

Alongside the affirmation, inspiration and wisdom that early Franciscan spirituality has to offer forest-lovers today, it also raises some important questions for those of us seeking a more nature-based spirituality. One of those is on the place of creatures within this spirituality - whether animals, birds or indeed insects. It would be good to see more serious theological, mystical and spiritual writing, as well as praxis, arising from reflection on the mysterious encounter that the animal kingdom peculiarly offers us.[100] It is also noticeable how in much poetic sensibility, verses extolling the glories of flora and fauna proliferate rather more than for example those extolling the glories of brother worm! In our present day revival and re-invention of ancient rural festivals celebrating the turning seasons, the stories of Francis challenge us to keep before us a vision of the place of the creaturely world. How do we celebrate the light of the sacred in our fellow creatures as well as in the earth and its green fecundity? What part might the birds of the air be invited to play in our rituals and how do we engage reverently with whatever wildlife happens to be in our neck of the woods? How do they reveal to us something of God? If we are serious about developing a spirituality that enables us to more authentically connect with the creation of which we are a part, then surely animals occupy a very significant place in that creation. We are re-discovering the natural world as sacrament

....
99 P. Teilhard de Chardin, *Le Milieu Divin*, trans. R. Hague, Collins, 1967, p111
100 Andrew Linzey's book - *Animal Theology*, is a rare example of a serious attempt to theologically engage with the nature of the animal world and to raise important questions for our treatment of and relationship with God's other creatures. Professor Linzey is also Director of the Oxford Centre for Animal Ethics which is an independent Centre with the aim of pioneering ethical perspectives on animals through academic research, teaching and publication.

and filled with God's presence, and as part of this, the witness of Francis invites us to discover in a more conscious way, God's indwelling of all our fellow creatures. As a result, there will also be important ethical things to say about the implications for how our society in turn treats animals.

Whilst Francis saw in creation and in all creatures a spark of the divine glory and knew himself to be standing on holy ground, this in itself was not, however, what effected his own initial transformation from business man to man of God. The story from the life of the saint which tells of the powerful moment of faith ignited, is that of his encounter with a leper on the road – an encounter with a human face and human need. Both the law of the land and the law of the church at that time forbade physical contact with such a person, but Francis felt an urge, a God-urge, to get off his horse and embrace the leper. It was this transgression in the name of compassion that had such a profound effect upon him that he dedicated the rest of his life to Christ whom he understood to be the source of that compassion and the source of all life - the very tree of life himself. His was a very Christ-centred eco-spirituality.

This story relates closely to the Jesus we encounter in the gospels, who tells us that as we visit those in prison, as we minister to the sick and support the weak, as we give a cup of cold water to one who is thirsty, we discover that we have offered these acts of compassion to Christ himself. And here we must be clear to add to our sacramental view of nature the human species as the creature most singly created in the image of God according to the Jewish and Christian scriptures. Within the mystery that is each human being, we therefore encounter something of the God who was in Christ – something of the very likeness of God, something of the Spirit of God that animates and gives breath to the spirit of the human person. It is not that we stand outside the mystery of creation seeking to encounter it, we are part of that creation and part of that mystery. Reverence for each other and compassion for human need should have a high priority in any genuine creation-focused spirituality. This is what incarnation means. It would be easy to simply use Francis as one more resource amongst others to give legitimacy and mystical aura to a romantic spirituality of the natural world developed in reaction to all that we might feel is bad in the crowded, modern, urban, consumerist world about us, or in reaction to what may at times have been neglected or worse demonised by the church. But true Franciscan spirituality demands something more from us, for Francis taught radical gospel living, simplicity and poverty of spirit – a rejection of the grand and glorious, whether in terms of wealth, success, status or reputation. We cannot with authenticity live largely according to our culture's rule of self-centred consumerism, and swap it just occasionally for the rule of Saint Francis when we come together for seasonal rituals and celebrations. Pope Francis is right to see that our age needs not just the witness of a Forest Church, but of a Poor Church – a church with deep compassion for the poor and for the face of the human forest, a church committed to global justice for people and planet alike.

The challenge to those seeking to keep in step with the irrepressible Spirit of Life in our own day, the Spirit who inspired Saint Francis, is to place transformational compassion at the heart of our response to the whole created order ... to the forests and fields, the mountains and moors, the birds and beasts of the animal kingdom, and to one another as precious and mysterious brothers and sisters of God's kingdom in which no one is to be left outside, but all embraced in the love of the one in whom all things have their source and their fulfilment. This is the invitation and the challenge of Francis.

***Anne Hollinghurst** is a vicar and a co-founder of St Albans Forest Church. Her journey has taken her from inner-city youth ministry to Higher Education chaplaincy, cathedral ministry to city-centre parish, where she continues to work out how to be both a contemplative and an activist. Her post-graduate research is in the traditions of the Christian and Jewish mystics and she enjoys walking the Cumbrian fells for inspiration.*

Chapter 7 – Simon Cross

Alien Nation: The Rise And Fall of the Green Men

"And some things that should not have been forgotten were lost. History became legend. Legend became myth... Much that once was is lost, for none now live who remember it..."

The Lord of the Rings: J.R.R. Tolkein

Around our countries, in cities, towns, villages and out-of-the-way places, many mysteries are to be found.

One such mystery is abundantly present in the old stone work of church buildings across the West of Europe. Usually above a doorway, guarding an entrance, is the face of a man – leaves and branches protruding from his mouth and curling up around his face. He has no written name, his identity has been lost in the passage of time but he is now widely known as The Green Man – despite the fact that he is almost always grey.

The Green Man is so commonly found, that he is said to be second only to the figure of Christ himself in the canon of Christian architectural iconography. Look closely and one may find him in cathedrals, parish churches, and ruins, throughout Western Europe, but particularly in the British Isles.

The now mysterious Green Man is in fact so common that he simply cannot always have been unknown. At some point his meaning – indeed his name, must have been clear. But somehow, as these things do, the meaning became lost to us.

What's more, he must surely have been important – culturally significant somehow, so much so that he was appointed to stand guard over the doorway to innumerable ecclesiastical buildings – perhaps to remind congregants of the reason for their assembly – or to ward off unclean spirits.

As much as we understand the carved figure of Jesus today, so much we have lost the meaning of the Green Man.

Many attempts have been made to decipher the code of this symbol. Some resolve around the idea that the Green Man is a carry-over from one form of pre-Christian symbolism, possibly as a form of fertility symbolism. Others point to an ongoing fascination with 'foliate faces' and 'men of the woods' which characterise cultural figures from Robin Hood and Jack in the Green to stone carvings in Hindu temples – suggesting that perhaps like the labyrinth the Green Man is some kind of universal trope.

It may be that (in part) the Green Man served in part as a semiotic reminder of the forests in which worshippers used to gather, like the pillars and stained glass which subtly mimic trees and remind us of light flooding through wooded glades.

But there are also lots of other 'green men' carried over from the past – faeries, sprites, leprechauns, elves, mythical woodland figures who, while they may seem fanciful now, were part of a diverse belief system for many centuries.

The idea of a Green Man or green men, seems to tap into something deep in our psyche, something primal which serves as a connection between us – like the ancient idea of 'the deep' for instance – the dread of the dark depths of water, or the fascination with fire, and the way that it flickers in the darkness.

I believe that the Green Man is a symbol of the creative energies of the beginning of the world – much of what we humans do revolves around trying to solve questions like 'where do we come from?' 'Are we alone?' And 'what happens when we die?' In coming to terms with the origins of life, a profound mystery to all regardless of their world view, we give ourselves a starting point to come to terms with these things.

Where the Green Man symbolism may come from, we can reconsider shortly – but first let's note that with the demise in understanding of who the Green Man is, a widespread fascination with a different mysterious green men has arisen.

> *"The chances of anything coming from Mars are a million to one… yet still they come…"*
>
> *Eve of the War (War of the Worlds): Jeff Wayne*

Around the end of the 19th century references began to appear to 'little green men' – referring of course to visitors from outer space. By the time the 1950s had rolled around the concept of the green men from Mars was well established – appearing in pulp fiction and making its way into TV, radio and film.

The first clear reference to green skinned aliens comes from the 1890s, not long after the end of the Industrial revolution – the period of history which, while it began in the 1700s took until the 1830s to be fully felt. Today the idea of 'little green men' has grown in popularity to almost ubiquitous status as a cultural icon, despite the fact that these 'aliens' are often pictured as grey.

These fascinating extra-terrestrials are – I would suggest – another attempt at answering the same old questions, who are we? Are we alone? What happens when we die? By exploring space, it seems, we may find new ways of understanding our origins, and perhaps our eventual destination.

In this way aliens form part of a continuum of Creation mythology, they represent a way in which one part of contemporary society attempts to reconcile the mystery of our existence. They are perhaps the most current form of 'green men' – but they aren't the only ones to have made a mark on the popular psyche in the last few hundred years.

Stick with me for a moment as we have a quick skip through social, political and psychological history.

The Industrial age was one of great psychological turmoil – everything that had been done manually became mechanised. Labour saving devices came into being – most famously perhaps the 'Spinning Jenny' which dramatically changed the way in which cotton was spun by British workers, and in so doing altered the face of the world.

Change of this nature is profoundly disturbing, it unsettles and causes fear, often panic in those who feel its effects – this is compounded by the fact that technological change often goes hand in hand with societal change of another sort.

In the early years of the Industrial revolution another invention came into being, really an improvement on an older, much less efficient machine, which was to make an important task much less onerous. In France you must understand, the Spinning Jenny wasn't really in use – one reason for this was that the social class system was different there. In Britain there were enough middle class cotton buyers to make the adoption of this expensive new technology profitable, while in France society was dominated by a top tier of wealthy aristocrats and a large bottom tier of poor peasants.

Given this gross level of inequality, the radical societal change which became known as the French Revolution was perhaps inevitable – but it was its adoption of the afore mentioned invention, a highly efficient industrialised decapitation machine known anthropomorphically as 'Madame Guillotine' that was to be its most iconic legacy.

This labour-saving death bringer enabled the revolutionaries to put an end to thousands of their enemies, and caused terror in the hearts of the wealthy across Western Europe.

> *"Nothing is so painful to the human mind as a great and sudden change."*
>
> *Frankenstein: Mary Shelley*

The 19th century was certainly a time of great upheaval, along with the industrial revolution, the French revolution and other political turmoil, this was the time of Marx and Engels, just as it was the time of Charles Darwin – in short, it was also a period of rapid philosophical change. In a sense it could be considered a last gasp of the renaissance, a direct continuation of the changes in thinking which took place three or four hundred years before hand.

But the changes that had been brought those centuries before, both through the enlightenment thinking, and the Protestant reformation, were to suffer a backlash, as 19th century romantics began to resurrect and reinvent superstitions and ways of belief that were thought to have passed out of the public consciousness.

The rise of occultism in the 1800s is a good example of this, and I would suggest that this phenomena, which led in later years to form a platform for the 20th century religion of Gardnerian Wicca, was really a (justifiable) kick against the pace and nature of change going on in society.

But whatever their underlying motivations, individuals such as Swedenborg and Mesmer certainly helped to usher in a new era of belief in the unknown. They also stoked the fires of imagination in poets and writers across Western Europe and beyond.

So it was during this 19th century new wave of Occultism that, ensconced in a villa in Switzerland, a group of young romantic poets and writers managed 'one dark and stormy night' to create some of the finest literature of their time. It's hard not to see the twinned fear and inspiration of the Industrial revolution and the French Revolution in the text of Mary Shelley's Frankenstein – the first ever true work of 'Science Fiction'. It is also intrinsically linked with the climate of occultism which led to talk of necromancy and 'dark arts'.

Subtitled 'The Modern Prometheus' Mary Shelley's book traces the story of Victor Frankenstein and his tragic creation, creating what was to become one of the most powerful modern fables of all time. (It's interesting to note, although very much a side issue, that despite the fact that Frankenstein's monster is often pictured as having green skin, having been made from Cadavers he would probably have been more grey.)

There are many interesting aspects to this story, Shelley named the Monster 'Adam' in a hark back to the first man of Genesis, and in a literary reference to Milton, whose epic poem Paradise Lost finds the biblical Adam pointing out that he never asked to be created. Shelley the Romantic is pointing to a new dawn of grotesque scientific creation, where technology takes the place of the creator God. The monster also spends much of his life living in the forested mountains - but finds himself drawn to human habitation, in an echo of the way people of that era were moving from the countryside to urban environs.

Among the various more or less explicit spiritual references is that subtitle, 'The Modern Prometheus' which refers back to the Greek Titan Prometheus, who was the creator of humankind. Once they were created, the humans threatened to become as powerful as Gods, so Zeus withheld from them the secret of Fire, preventing them from becoming a true threat. Prometheus however steals fire, and gifts it to humanity – a crime for which he earns a gruesome punishment.

All this is to say that Frankenstein is something of a 'coming of age' story for the Industrial age: a new 'Adam' myth, a fable of fear and crucially a new creation myth, a tale of the dramatic power of electricity and the danger of humans becoming as powerful as God. It is a literary foreshadow of what Foucault would much later write about as 'bio power', the use of humanity as a kind of raw material for society.

So in a sense this new story was another retelling of the Creation account, blending mythologies as it went to create something fit for the modern age. It represents a powerful urge to understand where we come from, and crucially who we are. The story of Frankenstein urges us to examine ourselves, and learn what it means to be human.

During this industrialisation period and time of societal transformation, yet another revolution was taking place – mass literacy. For centuries the ability to read had been growing steadily throughout the population, but it was during this time that it became very widespread. Notwithstanding the fact that there are pockets of illiteracy within Western Europe today, we who live here are now a generally literate people. With this growing literacy came an industrialisation of printing technology, which made the production of books, pamphlets and newspapers even more widespread. This growing combination of the ability to read, and the ability to disseminate written information widely made a real change in the way stories were told and myths were shared.

In some cases, powerful new myths were created, and new histories written – in other cases stories were lost.

One such lost story was the Legend of the Rood, a story popular in Medieval times, which drew loosely from the Old Testament, and from non-canonical sources. In times of pre-literacy the learned clerics who taught from the pulpits of the stone churches around Western Europe, would have been well versed in the Legend of the Rood, and would surely have used it in their preaching, or to inform the way they understood the Bible.

Aspects of the Legend continue today, but usually only as shadows in our consciousness.

The story goes back once again to the time of the beginning, and tells of a dying Adam, who asks his son Seth to return to the garden of Paradise, to fetch an elixir which would make him immortal. Seth's attempt is thwarted however by the Angel who guards the garden, and will not allow him entry.

The Angel doesn't send Seth away empty handed though, for he gives him a seed from the tree from which Adam and Eve ate the fruit.

Upon his return Seth finds his father dead, and so he buries him, with the seed under his tongue. The tree which grows from the seed is, eventually, to provide the wood for the cross, to which Jesus was nailed. In pre-reformation times pieces of the true cross commonly changed hands as relics, and to this day churches and other buildings remain named after the 'Holy Rood'.

The relationship of this story of a tree which grows from the mouth of the first man, or the primary 'Alpha' male, to the Green Man symbolism found in church architecture looks obvious, and it may indeed be the 'root' of the myth. But while we remain comfortable with Jesus, the second Adam, and the 'Omega' of the Christian story, we seem to have become alienated from this Alpha story of leafy beginnings.

The way that this has happened seems clear too – with the reformation purge, and then the growing process of industrialisation and urbanisation, we've lost both our own connection with the natural world, and the oral story telling culture which allowed myths like that of the Green Man to flourish and eventually become literally embedded in our architecture.

Urbanisation and industrialisation has largely left us alienated us from the natural world. We no longer understand plants in the way that we used to for instance, and ways of eating, catching food, treating illnesses, making fire and building shelter among other things have been lost from the common consciousness – to be known by a few who call it 'bush craft' or 'survival skills'. Only a relatively short time ago though, people still regularly fished with Hawthorn thorns, used comfrey to heal broken bones and worked their own leather. For them this was not 'bush craft' but everyday life.

We are fortunate enough to have custodians of many of these skills, herbalists, TV survivalists, and the like and as such it seems unlikely that this knowledge will disappear entirely any time soon. But the same can't necessarily be said for spiritual and religious knowledge – much of what we now call Paganism (the beliefs and practises of the 'Pagani' or countryside dwellers) has been somewhat dubiously translated into the 21st century – how much of it really stems from the practises of Ancient Britons and how much is really a 19th Century invention is something of a 'moot' point.

But here in the UK our connection with the spirituality of the natural world and its symbolism has faded significantly – hence the mystery of the Green Men.

Meanwhile we have moved on in our myth making, from a green man made from cadavers in a scientific laboratory, to green men from Mars, walking among us, taking our shape, becoming like us. It is as if our internal preoccupations and beliefs have moved on, taking us from a long held spirituality which was closely linked to the earth, to one which found meaning in science, and then in the universe beyond. In each movement, we have taken with us the trope of the Green Man. The issue becomes though, as our 'green men' change in nature, is this a sign that we have lost something important?

"Sometimes dreams are wiser than waking..."

Nicholas Black Elk in 'Black Elk Speaks': John G Neihardt

In 1863, or 'the Winter when the Four Crows were killed on Tongue River' a baby boy was born to the Oglala Lakota people in Wyoming, USA. His name was Black Elk and he went on to become a warrior, medicine man, and prophetic visionary.

The books of Black Elk's life, as written down by the poet John Neihardt, chronicle a way of life which even at the beginning of the 20th century still remained in touch with the land which gave it its being. It was a way of seeing the whole world as being sacred.

At the age of 12, many years after first experiencing vivid visions of a spirit world and already a seasoned warrior and hunter, Black Elk fought in the battle of Greasy Grass Creek – a fight known by the non-indigenous Americans as the battle of Little Big Horn, or 'Custer's Last Stand'. At the age of 17 he became a Medicine Man, carrying out miraculous healings using powers given to him by Wakan Tanka (the Great Spirit). A decade later, in 1890, he was one of the few survivors of the Massacre of Wounded Knee which saw a terrible slaughter of the Lakota people.

But despite these experiences, Black Elk remained interested in the ways of the Industrialised 'Wasichu' (white man), and travelled to Europe as part of Buffalo Bill's Wild West show. He found the time difficult and missed home dreadfully. When he eventually returned to America, he pondered the meaning of the things he had seen.

Not long after this, Black Elk became a Catholic convert and enthusiastic Catechist, at his Baptism he took the name Nicholas. This conversion notwithstanding, he remained a tribal leader and vision keeper, maintaining a truly ancient way of looking at the world which measured time in terms of natural occurrences (September for instance is 'the Moon when the calves grow hair') and recognised the spiritual nature of all things, rather than the objective value. To Black Elk, his ancestors and his people, the earth was a person, sacred, and worthy of deep respect.

One of the remarkable things about Black Elk is that his story is from an ancient oral culture (he himself was illiterate) but it was captured in a book. This means that today we see through his eyes, a direct link between the people who saw the world of the Green Man, the people who saw the changes of Frankenstein technology, and the generation who began to fear the arrival of green men from Mars. The ability of Black Elk to forge and articulate a link between modern and ancient times is key, he brought to the table a way of looking at our environment as spiritual and created, and looked at our presence on the earth in that light. He recognised the way that humans were becoming increasingly alienated from their surroundings, speaking at times of grim prophetic visions of people living in 'square, grey houses.'

It is not a surprise that Black Elk was embraced by the 1960s counter culture movement as a prophet, even if he was arguably widely misunderstood. The hippies were, as Crosby, Stills, Nash and Young pointed out, generally trying to get 'back to the garden'.

And just as the symbolism of the Green Man was drawn from a time when people spent more time in natural surroundings than they do now, Black Elk used a great deal of natural symbolism in his teachings.

He spoke of the way grasses show 'tender faces' to one another, talked about the earth as a grandmother and a mother, recognised the virtues and humility of small animals, and listened to the voices of trees.

acknowledged or not, that without checking ourselves we will destroy the capacity of this fragile planet to continue to provide for us as has been our wont. The word fragile is a misnomer. The earth itself is not fragile per se, it is a complex interweaving of life and relationship built for continued life. It is the intervention of humans that makes it appear fragile to our way of existence. With this relationship to our planet we grow yet further away from mother earth.

Psalm 24 opens with 'The *earth is the Lord's*' though our behaviour does not reflect this. We behave on the whole as if the earth belongs to humans, that we are the Lord over creation, that humans were the crowning achievement and have every right to deal with the earth as we see fit. You might need to go and reread the creation narratives in Genesis 1 and 2. While you are at it, read Leviticus 25. Whether you hold these accounts as scriptural matters not, they are accounts of a people's relationship with the land as they saw it. It should by now be clear that the creation narratives are not to be interpreted literally - no one can suggest plants, trees and vegetation can come before the sun and the seasons. The crowning glory of creation in Genesis 1 is in fact the seventh day - the day of rest, the hallowed day. Sabbath becomes an integral part of the biblical story for all parts of life, human, slavery, financial, and land. In Leviticus we find that even the Land is allowed a year off, one in every seven years. During this year all farmed land was to lie fallow and the people were to eat only what the earth provided naturally. I want to suggest the idea of Sabbath Space, where not only do we as humans find rest, but also the economic rests, and what is more important the earth rests honoured as the basis for all life. A space where we loose our control over the earth. Whether in scientific terms of carbon life-forms or in terms of God shaping 'adam from the 'adamah (the human one from the earth) our life and our death is with the earth, we are bound together so too is it natural to rest together.

It is possible already to catch a glimpse of this way of life. Places where the balance is either restored or human intervention is held back. A window into another world, or, another way of seeing and being with this earth. There are places on this earth that have not yet been contaminated by the human desire to control and they are seen as very special indeed. To some they are known as sacred spaces. To others they are known as thin places. To others they are simply places where the mind is able to rest without competition from outside. Perhaps we should begin to see them as Sabbath Spaces, places where we loose our control. Some of these places are natural, some have had intervention from humans, but are significant for their meaning. Some are places of struggle and pain. Other places are those which have been carved out by humans to create such a space. These spaces are able to teach us about our connections with the earth, but also through a deeper connection with the earth we can learn more about our desire and need for such places and the desires and needs of the earth itself.

The Isle of Iona, a small remote inner Hebridean Island off the Ross of Mull where in 563ce St. Columba is said to have landed from Ireland and established the first monastery on the island. Iona is one of the most visited sacred places on earth with many very different groups claiming an attachment to the island.

Pennant Melangell, situated at the head of the Tanat Valley in the Berwyn Mountains in Mid-Wales where in the 7th century St. Melangell is said to have come from Ireland and lived as a hermit. She was given permission to stay by the Prince of Powys and established a small religious community.

A burial ground, perhaps any maintained cemetery or church-yard where bodies or cremated remains of those who have died are placed and visited by families.

Roadside flowers at the scene of a car accident in remembrance to the young man who died.

All of these four places have a threefold connection. First they commemorate the lives of humans who have gone by. Second they have a strong draw for the living to visit. They are all known as thin places or sacred spaces because we as humans venerate them as such. In religious language they can be described as places where the veil that separates heaven and earth is thin. They can simply be places where our minds are brought to focus with few distractions. The third connection is that of geography, they are all distinct places that cannot be replicated. There may be similar places, but ultimately they are unique. A common complaint of modern shopping centres is that they are all the same. This is what those who build them are asked for, so that we are familiar with them wherever we go. The testimony of the places above suggests that uniqueness is a priceless quality. We go to these places with no less of a desire to get 'fed'. I would suggest that we also now need to acknowledge how we regard these places and declare them Sabbath Spaces. Spaces where we begin to loose control so that our soul can rest and where the earth itself is regarded once again as partner, 'adam to 'adamah.

Certainly each of these places has something to say to us about our connection to the earth. However it is possible that the corollary is also true, that through being in closer connection with the earth we might learn something about our relationship to such places about the earth and perhaps even about ourselves.

A journey to Iona might take any number of days depending on your starting point. But even from the closest mainland port Oban it is around two hours away by ferry, bus and then a second ferry. The journey itself can be an important part of the visit especially for those on pilgrimage. Its remoteness is often claimed to be one of its drawing features together with the history of St. Columba and those who followed in his stead. Its distinctiveness does not only stem from the Christian history of the island, it was known as the Island of the Druids from pre-christian times. The rock of which it is formed is some of the oldest in the world, perhaps 1500 million years. Many groups have marked the island as a 'spiritual' place and it is regularly visited as a place to retreat from the world for healing and wholeness of body, mind and spirit, to connect to something beyond ourselves. The Iona Community who have a presence on the island use the remote nature of the island to allow a reflection on the rest of the world from which we have 'retreated' and encourage those who visit to engage with issues of justice, peace and reconciliation on their 'return' to the mainland.

So what might a visit to Iona say about our connections to the earth?

And what might the reply of the earth be to these thoughts?

Perhaps a visit here might satisfy in us a desire for places that are out of the way, unspoilt wilderness locations, the beauty of the natural.

You say that I am beautiful, unspoilt, and that I am for
the most part, yet if you truly believe this is desirable,
what have you done to the rest of the world and why
when you leave here do you continue to be destructive?

The wild and rugged coastline viewed standing on the north beach looking out over the wide North Atlantic reminds us of how small and insignificant we are on this earth.

You might seem small and insignificant standing
on my shore, but your footprints on this world
are neither insignificant nor small.

Reflecting on the journey the significance of relying on others for our connections to the rest of the world may be brought home to us.

If your journey here was significant then reflect
on what you take from this earth in order to
fuel your so called comforts of travelling.

If we become stranded on the island due to stormy seas we might recognise our own fragility at the mercy of the elements.

What you describe as fragility is an obsession with your
own health and death. Do you govern the patterns of
the waves or the delicate balance that is the earth?

The geology of the place, a random rock of Lewisian Gneiss reminds us of great shifts in climate of the past, ice ages that literally moved mountains.

You marvel at the geology of my rocks and the make-up
of my hills which were formed with the beginning of the
world itself before you were even slithering in the mud - so
that small stone you take to stand on your mantle reflects
the beginning and the end of all that is. I have seen a
thousand climates change - each one brought healing and
restoration. Are you prepared to live in the come-what-may?

Reflecting on the blood spilt on its beaches we might feel somehow the power of such a place to connect us to those who have trod its paths before.

Those who trod and died on this hallowed earth
walked a martyr's path, be careful for what you
wish, you may end up walking their path.

Sitting in the ancient 'hermit cell' amid the hills we reflect on hospitality and our journey of life through this world, that we are just passing through.

As you sit leaning against the wall of my hermit cell I am no more hospitable to you than to any other life on this planet that chooses to visit. Make of me what you will, but hospitality is reciprocal. Am I at fault if your heel breaks on my ancient rock?

This far off place may allow us to recharge and reconnect away from the distractions of the world.

You say that I am far off - Yet I am where I am - It is you who are far off dreaming of distant galaxies and stars. You come to me to recharge, to use my eternal energy, yet do not expect me to help your healing if you are not ready to face the demons you have brought with you and the ones that are awaiting your return.

Pilgrims and visitors arrive at **Pennant Melangell** in a variety of ways and for a variety of reasons. Some who arrive as walkers or visitors leave as pilgrims. Some walk the last mile from the village of Llangynog on pilgrimage, often with some difficulty. Unlike Iona, its location is not well known; off a B road in midst of the Welsh Berwyn Mountains. Yet to those who know this ancient space the hiddenness adds to its uniqueness nestling as it does towards the end of a valley between two hills. Being hidden away means that people often turn up unexpected and unprepared for what they find. It is recognised as a place of great spiritual power of healing and restoration. Travelling the last road from Llangynog the dead end road sign really need not be there, the mountains up ahead suggests that there is no through road, at least not for vehicles. As the valley deepens the rusty heather on the hills is contrasted with the dark slate in the bright sun. Trees line the road on both sides creating a funnel towards the destination. This is not a new path. Arriving at Pennant Melangell, which is little more than a clearing, it is a place full of noise, yet full of silence. The silence of the man-made world, the noise of the natural. There is no mobile phone signal, no traffic sounds, no hubbub from an urban street. Yet the trees sing in the wind, distant water echoes in the valley as it falls over rock and the birds chatter endlessly. Walking through the lych gate you are entering an ancient space. St. Melangell's church stands in the centre of a circle of yew trees. A new silence is apparent. The same sounds are still present yet there is a silence here made by humans also. It is the silence of a graveyard. Hundreds of stones litter this space, ancient and new. People have come here to be buried for centuries to be close to this place perhaps in the belief that this is a gateway to heaven similar to the dream of Jacob in Genesis. It is believed to be a bronze-age burial site and these stones hold their secrets closely. The present church building stands quietly at the centre, testament to the past 800 years, a relative newcomer in this place. One of the oldest stones, set into the floor of Cell y Bedd (cell of the grave) is reputed to be the grave marker of Melangell herself, maybe the first Christian to venerate this place in the 7th Century. She dwelt here, a visitor from Ireland. What drew her to this place? What encouraged her (other than the Prince of Powys) to stay and establish her small monastic community here amongst the mountains, water and trees? Though the stones of this place hold their secrets tightly the world outside the small church is awake, bright, vibrant with life. Four of the yew trees are ancient, some say one is 2000 years old. What have they witnessed over those years? Perhaps they greeted Melangell on her arrival and bid her to stay? People come and pray here because Melangell was here, that is certain. It is clear that some also find answers to their requests. Do we ask this place to change us or should we ask for the energy to change ourselves as Gandhi suggested: 'Be the change you want to see in the world'. The question remains: Is Pennant important because Melangell came here, or did she set her dwelling here because it is an important place? The answers to that may well still be here in the stones, the yew trees, grasses, flowers and in the earth. There is indeed a power to be felt standing in the deep shadows of the yew trees and there are those who come to be in their presence. It is a sense and feeling of protection as if nature is on our side. A feeling of never wanting to leave the shadow of these trees. Those who visit places such as Iona or Pennant Melangell speak of being drawn back time and time again. Is this what Melangell felt - a home coming, a hiraeth? For these same trees, mountains and valley were here in her day also.

Characters like Melangell and Columba add something to a place, they add a human element. Both left Ireland and ended up in the places we now associate with them. In order to open up the power of natural places to humans, someone must first recognise their importance. Not all places are the same and not all possess the ability to affect everyone who visits. Or perhaps not all humans are so ready to recognise these connections. Perhaps that is the beauty of Iona and Pennant Melangell. As we leave distractions behind, the natural power of the earth is able to somehow break through our defences. At such places our tenure as humans is broken and we must loose control. We must come to realise that we cannot claim ownership to such places, that 'this is mine' makes no sense in terms of 'The Earth is the Lord's'. How do such thoughts transfer to more ordinary places?

Traditional **Burial grounds** are places that are hallowed and revered, yet at the same time shied away from and feared. Surely there is nothing more natural than death? The moment we are born our death stands before us. Having sat with many who are near to their death it comes easier to some than others, but the inevitability of it is clear in their eyes. Every life comes to an end at some point and others are born, the cycle continues. We lay those humans and even some animals who have died to rest with ritual reverence and dignity. A family grave in a traditional graveyard or ashes scattered or strewn at an appropriate place. Wherever it might be, the location is important. Burial grounds tend to be very regimented places often with all the headstones facing the same way, for religious reasons, or simply to keep order. Grass predominates around graves in the UK and in the majority of cases is kept short mown, especially around new graves. Short grass and neat edges reflect a sense of respect for those who have died and show outwardly that we still care even though they have gone from our sight. We can do no more for them but keep their final resting place in good condition, the stone that marks the grave their final mark upon the world. Human life has been elevated to such a position that even after death nothing must violate what remains. In a western Christian culture this may be a reflection of the religious expectation of resurrection as depicted in the Revelation to St. John. The idea of full bodily resurrection at the end of the world is a theology and belief that is still held in some conservative Christian churches. For the majority maintaining a burial ground is a duty out of respect and an extension of our understanding of the sanctity of human life. Graveyards are known sometimes as hushed quiet places for reflection and contemplation. They can be places for remembrance, for tears and laughter at the memory of those who have gone. A place to go, perhaps, to say what was never said in life. A place to be angry, to accept or reject the feelings of loss, or to be swallowed up in the grief. Then, after the visit, such emotions may even be left behind. As the gates of the graveyard close behind it can be possible for some to leave these raw emotions in this space and move on with the rest of living. They are thin sacred places to the dead, but also for the living. The living in this context should include all that is alive.

The charity *Caring for God's Acre* has taken a bold step forward in challenging attitudes towards burial ground maintenance claiming burial grounds for nature. In some cases returning the whole space over to nature with minimal management, in others reserving areas for nature to take control and humans to take a step back.

This is an important consideration and brings us once again to the question of control. Questioning those who frequent graveyards the answers seem to point to the needs or requirements of those left behind, not those in the graves. Somewhere to visit and pay respects, to keep headstones in good order so that they can be read by future generations. These requirements are for the living, not for the dead. So what about the rest of the living world?

Every parent expects to watch a child grow into adulthood, but equally, every grass would flower. Every small shrub wants to be a bush. Every sapling tree yearns to fill out its crown. Each frond of Ivy seeks to mature and flower. A dandelion wants to set seed into the wind. The redwood to reach into the clouds. Human needs and desires often deny them becoming what they are meant to be. From the point of view of the rest of nature - looking at a burial ground, it is as if we are looking at a scene of starvation and deprivation. Standing in the midst of our local managed and heavily maintained burial ground it is possible to feel a sense of the struggle for life. There is also that sense of peace that it is possible to feel in such places and the feeling of time gone before, so many lives stretching into the past. It is not really peace, but lack of activity. Even the grass is relatively dead compared to grass that is allowed to grow. The feelings of struggle for life comes not from the graves or the lives of the humans buried, but from the land. Here is a piece of land which is controlled beyond all reason, like the well-manicured front lawn of suburbia. The last vestige of control over lives to which we cannot any longer lay claim. Dust thou art and unto dust though shalt return. *(Ash Wednesday Liturgy)* Earth to earth, Ashes to ashes and Dust to dust. *(Funeral*

Service) Are these just convenient liturgical words or do we truly mean them? If we are children of the dust and our bodies are returned to the earth, is it not ironic that in the majority of places we lay our dead, the land is not allowed to flourish with the nutrients from natural biological decomposition. Here we feed the land a rich fertiliser, then refuse to allow it to grow. 'No', is the word which we say to the land with mowers, strimmers and weed killer. Not here, stay back, keep out, get down, stop growing, this is a place for death. Signs placed in graveyards mock this behaviour: *'no litter, no plastic flowers, no graffiti - respect this place.'* For the land, it is frustration, groaning with the weight of well fertilised soil unable to achieve its potential. The visual order, neatness, which is associated with such places is contrary to what nature would do naturally. The order of nature is to allow each grass, plant, flower, shrub and tree to have its turn.

The more we continue to perpetuate the idea of a controlled graveyard the more these feelings of not being in control and needing to control will dominate our lives. We feel the frustrations of being restricted in our daily lives and these are reflected back to us by our traditional burial grounds. No wonder some do not always find visiting a grave a useful and easy process. It is because it is not natural, it is against the run of nature to control these sites in such a way.

We lead busy compartmentalised lives and it is seen to be better to have a section of our life or a place which is for bereavement and pain and death, rather than to allow each feeling to pervade our whole being. If this is the case, then should not these places be ones of healing and restoration, true Sabbath Spaces. Our attempt to control life after death either with religious ideology or extreme gardening is contrary to the poetic vision in Genesis and contrary to a deep understanding of the natural world.

We desperately need to loose our control, our taboo, inhibitions, traditions, social pressures, anything that stops us allowing the natural world to be what it can be, for then it will teach us in its natural rhythms. All burial grounds could be Sabbath Spaces - if only we would let them. Perhaps they would teach us that those who have gone before us, have gone. And yet they still remain in each tree, plant and flower that grows up and around the place where they are buried. Such places exist. Green burial sites restore this natural order. The best of them are truly Sabbath Spaces where humans have loosed control and nature is allowed to order itself with minimal interference.

Roadside flowers marked the spot where, very early one morning, a young man lost control over his car which slipped on ice. It crashed into a wall and he died at the scene. It was the terrible, tragic death of a young man full of potential. It is always unnatural and heart wrenching to be burying our children, for this is not the natural order. His funeral was attended by many local people, families, friends and well-wishers as one might expect. The outpouring of grief however, began the day of the accident on social media sites and directly at the scene. Flowers and other tributes were, perhaps naturally, left at the site of the crash. It didn't stop. For a number of years there was always at least one bunch of flowers stuck into the wall and on birthdays, Christmas and the anniversary of the death cards flowers and even presents were left at the scene. Finally a bench was placed in his memory close to the scene of the accident. This account could of course relate to any number of places in the UK. These memorials to accidental, often violent deaths are creating new places of remembrance. There is a link here, whether articulated in any real sense or not to the blood spilt on the earth. This physical place is important as it connects the family to the violence which removed the life of the person. However, one wonders if this was how ancient burial grounds began. A significant death in a particular place, others buried there, then begins a tradition. Before long people are venerating the space and even planting yew trees to mark it lest future generations forget. The roadside sites are sacred, thin spaces for the families of those who have died, yet for others they are little more than reminders of the violence of someone's death. These places were not chosen for burial, nor are they in particularly geographically special places. The link is that of a human death, but perhaps that is enough to open our eyes to a new place.

It could be said that for a true Sabbath Space, a place of healing and restoration for body, soul and mind together with the earth, it is the geography that must come first. That these so called 'thin' places must be special in some way in their own right and those who have recognised the importance of a particular place become signposts to others. However, I am not convinced that this is necessarily true at all.

To build a true nature connection with such spaces and perhaps all places is to have compassion, to suffer alongside nature, to understand her ways. It is the rare individual who can for themselves see all places as sacred without someone to point the way. Those places that become the well-known sacred sites similar to those mentioned above are often out of the way, hidden or hard to get to. This sense of journey towards the place is important for our ability to connect upon arrival, that and the need to be cut off from distraction to focus our attention. However it should be possible for any place to become a Sabbath Space given the appropriate conditions. How often is it that we stop to marvel at the simple miracle of a small plant pushing tarmac out of the way in search for the light? Nature is teaching us in ordinary places, if only we are ready to listen.

It is said that both Melangell and Columba shared a close connection with the earth so deep that the veil has lifted slightly and the spiritual realm is allowed to penetrate the physical. Is this way of speaking true or is it romanticising an era of the saints? To be sure there are those who have been signposts for others in terms of our connections to nature and to other humans. The testimony of George Macleod and Iona Community which he founded is that the island of Iona, though important was not the central mission for the early community. Urban Glasgow was of central importance for Macleod. Iona served its purpose, it allowed new connections and allowed old prejudices to be broken. Members were then sent out restored and healed to work for the kingdom. Melangell established her small community in the Berwyn Mountains, yet all who come for healing, transformation and reconciliation are naturally sent back to where they have come from for there is no healing without facing the issues that instigated the visit. Our connection with graveyards and places of burial is real, but it is flawed in that they could mean so much more for us and perhaps be even greater places of peace, reconciliation and healing if only we could recognise the importance of allowing nature to take its own course and loose our control over them.

In these interactions with the earth, we become closer to specific places and begin to learn, perhaps even subconsciously about them so much so that they get under the skin. Given time to begin to connect to recognise we may finally say that 'The Earth is the Lord's and all that therein dwells' rather than 'This is mine'. The temptation is still to say 'The Earth is the Lord's' but this land is ours. However if we change our being with closer connection to Sabbath Spaces treading in the footsteps of those who would show us the way we might instead of 'the land belongs to us' rather, as Fr Elias Chacour would say: 'We belong to the Land' the 'adam to the 'adamah'.

When not tending to his 'flock', you'll often find **Stuart Elliott** *scything meadows or running* *mountains. An Ordained Priest and member of the Iona Community; he is passionate about regenerating community with fresh bread and home grown food.*

Chapter 9 – Steve Hollinghurst

Liberating The Land: Recovering The Human Priesthood of Creation

I consider that the sufferings of this present time are not worth comparing with the glory about to be revealed to us. For the creation waits with eager longing for the revealing of the children of God; for the creation was subjected to futility, not of its own will but by the will of the one who subjected it, in hope that the creation itself will be set free from its bondage to decay and will obtain the freedom of the glory of the children of God. We know that the whole creation has been groaning in labour pains until now; and not only the creation, but we ourselves, who have the first fruits of the Spirit, groan inwardly while we wait for adoption, the redemption of our bodies.[101]

With these words St Paul finishes his initial exploration of what God does in Jesus Christ to overcome what Paul refers to as sin, death and the devil in the opening eight chapters of his letter to the church in Rome. This starts with a declaration of how all of creation reveals God's nature to a humanity that is

....

101 Romans 8. 18-23

damaged and blinded by what Paul calls sin and thus becomes bound by death and the power of the devil. Much of the discussion in the following chapters is about how this applies to all people Jewish or non-Jewish and how it is through Jesus they are all set free. Finally this liberation becomes something not just for people but for all creation. But why is this linked to the revealing of the sons and daughters of God? Paul's statement implies a relationship between human liberation and the liberation of creation. This may not at first sight seem an obvious conclusion. We have in recent centuries often portrayed God's liberation as something related to human individuals and lost Paul's emphasis on the liberation of creation. Further, in what way might creation be seen to be in bondage to decay in the first place? I believe Paul makes this connection because he understands the rituals of the Jewish Temple and the service of its priests as a way of representing the relationship of humanity to creation. An understanding in which Adam and Eve were made in God's image as priests of creation; a priesthood that has been lost. The restoration of this human priesthood will therefore in his view enable the whole creation to be set free and the Kingdom of God to come in all creation as it is in heaven.

It is the imagery of this human priesthood I want to explore through an examination of biblical texts and show how it is intimately linked to how we can view salvation as something for all of creation. There are also implications for how we live with creation now if we are to be priests within the world that this imagery helps us uncover.

East of Eden: the lost clothing of Adam and Eve and the subjection of creation

The service of nine lessons and carols has become a staple of many Christmas programmes both in the church and on TV. The lessons begin with the story of Adam and Eve in the

Garden of Eden and their temptation and fall. The story that is told through the further eight lessons is thus laid out as God's unfolding plan to rectify the situation of humanity expelled from Eden. Paul's schema in Romans follows a similar path. Indeed for Paul, Jesus is a new Adam and his bride the church a new Eve.[102] Yet the Jewish Scriptures don't refer to Adam and Eve outside of the opening chapters of Genesis. So why does Paul, and later Christian tradition, have so much more to say about the story of Adam and Eve?

Much recent scholarship on Paul is being aided by the use of Jewish writings closer to Paul's day than those in what are now the accepted Jewish scriptures. These writings are found in what is known as the Pseudepigrapha, a collection of Jewish literature from the time of the Maccabean revolt up to the first centuries after Christ. Our knowledge of these has also been helped by the discovery of the Qumran library which contained versions of several of these works, especially apocalyptic books. A number of these refer to Adam and Eve and offer a background to Christian references to them.

Jewish Apocalyptic typically features the ascent of someone like a prophet into heaven where they are re-clothed and enter into God's presence in a heavenly temple. The book of Revelation is a Christian version of this genre. There has been considerable discussion of why Apocalyptic burgeoned during the inter-testamental period.[103] I agree with Russell[104] that the priestly tradition is key to the development of this literature, and hence it emerges at a time when the Kingship is no more and the Temple and the Priesthood are central to the life of Israel. Further to this, many of these texts are concerned with a threat to the Temple, either from outside forces or internal

....
102 See Ephesians 5, Romans 5 and I Corinthians 15
103 For a discussion of these see Himmelfarb M,Ascent to heaven,Oxford University Press 1993pp95ff and Russell D.S,Divine disclosure,London, SCM 1992 pp5ff.
104 1992 as above

corruption. Thus it surfaces in Jubilees[105] at the time of the Greek king Antiochus Epiphanes, who desecrated the Temple, and in the books of Enoch and the Testament of Levi at the time of the Hasmonean Priest-Kings whose priesthood was questioned because they were not of the line of Aaron. Whereas the discussion of these themes in 4 Ezra and 2 Baruch are attempts to understand how God could have allowed the Temple's destruction by the Romans in AD 70., Himmelfarb suggests that it is the distance from God created by the effective removal of the Temple that necessitates the narrative of ascent to a heavenly Temple to stand before God's throne.[106] She further claims that: -

'The destruction of the Temple is intimately linked to larger questions of God's expectations of humanity and human failure from the beginning of history. It is no accident that the sin of Adam figures prominently.'[107]

In addition to this, or perhaps because of this, I would like to suggest that the discussion of Adam is also present because of a typological connection between Adam and the High Priest and between Eden and the Temple.

4 Ezra seeks to explain the destruction of the second Temple in AD 70 by arguing that the Temple was in fact not the true Temple at all. The true Temple the writer argues is in heaven. So 4 Ezra 4:3-6 says of the true Temple,

> 'It is not this building that is in your midst now; (i.e. the earthly Temple) it is that which will be revealed, with me, that was already prepared from the moment that I decided to create Paradise. And I showed it to Adam before he sinned. But when he transgressed the commandment, it was

---

105 Ch 5 1-11.
106 1993 pp69-70.
107 Ibid. p66. She is particularly referencing 4Ezra, the Apocalypse of Abraham and 2Baruch.

taken away from him-as also Paradise. After these things
I showed to my servant Abraham in the night between the
portions of the victims. And again I showed it also to Moses
on Mount Sinai when I showed him the likeness of the
Tabernacle and all its vessels. Behold, now it is preserved
with me-as also Paradise.'

This passage is written on the basis that Eden and the Temple are linked and Adam is in effect therefore the first to see the Temple. Similarly it views Moses as seeing the Temple/Eden on Sinai not just being told about its construction. I Enoch draws parallels with the Holy of Holies in the Temple and the Garden of Eden. The tree of life and the tree of knowledge of good and evil are viewed as being in the Holy of Holies in the true Temple. The barring of Eden in Genesis 3 by angels with flaming swords is thus compared to the prohibition on entering the Holy of Holies.

3 Enoch Chapter 5 tells us that after Adam was banished from Eden, the Shekinah (God's Glory) remained in Eden, resting on a cherub beneath the Tree of Life. Adam and his first descendants remained at the gate of Eden from where they could gaze upon the Shekinah and as a result were protected from sickness and demons. The Shekinah was understood to have dwelt in the Holy of Holies in the Temple, which, like Eden, had its entrance in the east. Adam and his first descendants are thus acting as priests before the Holy of Holies. However, in the generation of Enosh, the sin of the people leads to the withdrawing of the Shekinah. The Shekinah goes to dwell in heaven, where there is a curtain before God's presence like the veil of the Temple. The idea seems to be that Eden was the earthly counterpart of heaven and the design of the Temple in Jerusalem was a representation of both heaven and Eden. Hence both heaven and Eden are described in terms that reflect the Jerusalem Temple

An unusual text in Jewish literature is the History of the Rechabites. Original Jewish elements perhaps as early as first century AD have been edited into a much later Christian document. The text tells the story of a boat journey to the isle of the blessed and this may well be the basis for the Christian 'Navigation of St. Brendan'. In 5:2-4, the traveller having reached the island of the blessed, initially thinks that the blessed ones are naked but is told that he is seeing wrongly. He then gazes at them and sees their faces blaze like an angel's and falls down in fear. Later the book declares the island to be like the Paradise of God and the blessed ones to be like Adam and Eve before they sinned. Indeed later the blessed ones confirm they are not naked, saying 'for we are covered with a covering of glory; ..... a stole[108] of glory similar to that which clothed Adam and Eve before they sinned'.[109] For the writer of this text Adam was clearly clothed with garments of glory which were like the High Priest's vestments - usually described in Greek or as here in Syriac as a stole. The blessed in Paradise will clearly wear these again. This interestingly makes them at first sight appear naked. This may be an attempt to connect the story of the loss of Adam's garments with the text of Genesis 2 & 3. Here we are told that when Adam and Eve were created they were naked but knew no shame. The realisation of nakedness follows the fall, but significantly, whereas the text from the fall onwards uses the normal word for 'naked', a unique word is used for the pre-fallen state. Those who saw Adam as 'unclothed' by the fall might well use a device like that used here to pick up on that strange word usage. They had not been naked in the way that was normally understood but in fact

....

108 The Syriac Stl' is a loan word from the Greek stolhe used in the Greek old testament of the long robe of the King or High Priest. The angels are said to wear the same 14:4. This Greek word is now used in English to describe the sash Catholic, Orthodox and Anglican priests wear at communion.
109 The history of the Rechabites 12:3

had worn garments of glory like those worn by the blessed ones and this was in fact high priestly clothing.

What the texts we have explored show is that a number of Jewish writers understood Eden to be like heaven and both to be represented by the Temple in Jerusalem. Further, that Adam and Eve were clothed in garments of glory that marked them out as High Priests in Eden's 'temple'. We cannot be sure if the original writers of Genesis understood the text this way. However, what does seem to be the case is that this was a common, though probably not universal, approach in the time of the New Testament writers. This helps us to understand how they saw the place of Adam and Eve, and also Jesus and the Church as the new Adam and Eve. But if so, what are the implications of this for humanity's relationship to creation today? We need to go back to Genesis and explore it in the light of these apocalyptic texts but also in its own older context.

It is easy to forget that the ancestors of the Jews were near- eastern pagans. Walter Moberly[110] notes how Genesis charts the story of a people from a pagan faith into a new monotheism that is often quite different from the post Mosaic understanding of Judaism. Much of the Genesis text is a record of some of that transition and in many cases a reappraisal of the ancient near-eastern paganism that someone like the person called Abraham would have been raised in. In many cases Yahweh is written about in the language of Canaanite mythology, hence like Baal, Yahweh has a home in Zaphon[111] in the north and rides the storm clouds; like Ashteroth, Yahweh gives children to the barren and gives growth to the crops, and like El, (the word indeed used for God in Hebrew scripture), Yahweh is the ancient of days seated on the heavenly throne. The growing

....

110 *The Old Testament of the Old Testament* Augsburg Fortress 1959. See also F. R. McCurley *Ancient Myths and Biblical Faith* Augsburg Fortress 1981 and T Frymer-Kensky *in the Wake of the Goddess* Ballantine 1993
111 Isaiah 14:33. Ps 48:2 Job 26:7

reflection is that whilst the stories that had been familiar to the early Jews from their pagan roots are at least in part kept, they are re-interpreted to be the stories of one God not many.

In this tradition, Genesis 1-3 are written with the Canaanite creation myth in mind. In this myth the life of the gods is threatened by the seven headed chaos serpent Lotan who dwells in the sea. El summons the gods and Baal and his sister Anat are sent to kill the monster. This they do and divide his body to make the earth arise within the sea. There are numerous references to this in Jewish writing with Lotan appearing under the name Leviathan. A good example is Psalm 74 which makes the link to the creation myth explicit.

> *Yet God my King is from of old,*
> *working salvation in the earth.*
> *You divided the sea by your might;*
> *you broke the heads of the dragons in the waters.*
> *You crushed the heads of Leviathan;*
> *you gave him as food for the creatures of the wilderness.*
> *You cut openings for springs and torrents;*
> *you dried up ever-flowing streams.*
> *Yours is the day, yours also the night;*
> *you established the luminaries and the sun.*
> *You have fixed all the bounds of the earth;*
> *you made summer and winter.*

This fills in the Genesis 1 account in which God divides the waters to make the land and makes clear how that story is understood to have drawn on the Canaanite myth. Yet the biblical accounts are ambiguous. Psalm 104, also about creation, has a far more peaceful understanding in which Leviathan is made by God to sport in the sea. Whereas both Isaiah 27 and Job 41 return to the combat theme but suggest that God's battle with Leviathan is ongoing and that Leviathan will not be overcome until the final day of the Lord. Later Jewish Midrash (a commentary tradition which goes alongside the text) would address this problem by arguing that there were two Leviathans, one of each gender, created by God. The prospect of them breeding was too much of a threat for God to allow it so he slew one as in the creation myth and the other awaits death at the final day of the Lord.[112]

I would suggest, however, that something else is going on in these Jewish texts; a debate about the nature of evil and suffering in creation. In this debate Psalm 104 reflects the Wisdom tradition of the book of Proverbs among others, in which God has created a peaceable and orderly creation and the world runs according to the orderly rules of God seen in nature. Only good can exist in creation in such a view unless evil is brought in by the weakness of humanity. Suffering in this approach is seen as God's punishment on those who do not live by God's rules. Job however, offers a very different understanding. Job's 'comforters' offer the Wisdom viewpoint and ask Job to admit his wrong doing so God will take away his suffering. Job protests his innocence and we the reader know he is right. Finally God appears to Job and addresses his call for vindication and his bafflement at his righteous suffering. God does this in two great speeches. In chapters 38-39 God points Job to the wonders of creation and God's intimate knowledge of it way beyond that of a human being, by implication highlighting Job's ignorance of the world as perhaps a source for an unfounded complaint about his suffering. Job admits he cannot answer God but is not fully satisfied. God then in chapters 40-41 talks of fighting the chaos monsters Behemoth and Leviathan and how no human can overcome them. This answers Job and seems to offer understanding. God then turns on Job's 'comforters' and chastises them for not speaking the truth about God as Job has done.

---

112 See for instance Rashi's commentary on Genesis 1.21 where he offers this account and applies to the Genesis creation myth.

Within the wider picture of the creation and chaos imagery the argument of Job appears to be that, unlike the image of Psalm 104 and perhaps also 74, God's battle against the chaos monsters is ongoing and their continued presence is the reason for suffering in creation. So in Isaiah 27 God declares he will defeat Leviathan on the final day. Similarly in Christian scripture in chapter 12 of the book of Revelation we again meet this sea monster identified as the same as the Devil and Satan the accuser. At this point, the monster is defeated and thrown out of heaven by the Archangel Michael. Yet the chaos serpent still has power to lead nations astray and cause suffering for those who follow Christ. It is not until the final chapters of Revelation that the sea monster is finally destroyed.

This language, like that in Genesis, is mythic. It conveys a truth about a power of chaos in creation that threatens creation and leads to suffering, but doesn't intend us to expect a real giant monster to emerge from the sea. But it does allow us to read the Genesis story with greater insight and perhaps understand some otherwise strange details in it. At first Genesis 1 looks like a version of Psalm 74 in which the chaos monster is defeated and we are left with a good ordered creation. But there is a disturbing detail that has often raised questions about the ecological standpoint of this chapter. These appear in the account of the creation of humans in Genesis 1:26-31

> *Then God said, 'Let us make humankind in our image, according to our likeness; and let them have dominion over the fish of the sea, and over the birds of the air, and over the cattle, and over all the wild animals of the earth, and over every creeping thing that creeps upon the earth.'*
>
> *So God created humankind in his image, in the image of God he created them; male and female he created them.*
>
> *God blessed them, and God said to them, 'Be fruitful and multiply, and fill the earth and subdue it; and have*

> *dominion over the fish of the sea and over the birds of*
> *the air and over every living thing that moves upon the*
> *earth.' God said, 'See, I have given you every plant yielding*
> *seed that is upon the face of all the earth, and every tree*
> *with seed in its fruit; you shall have them for food. And to*
> *every beast of the earth, and to every bird of the air, and*
> *to everything that creeps on the earth, everything that has*
> *the breath of life, I have given every green plant for food.'*
> *And it was so. God saw everything that he had made, and*
> *indeed, it was very good. And there was evening and there*
> *was morning, the sixth day.*

The problem lies in giving humans dominion over the earth and commanding them to subdue it. It is understandable both that some have used this passage to justify a human 'conquest of nature' or an idea that it is there for our benefit and equally that others have seen here a Judaeo-Christian justification of human ecological damage.

The Hebrew here uses the language of kingship and war; 'radah' is used in Hebrew for the rule of kings and 'kabash' for the conquest of ones enemies in battle. These are indeed words that might raise ecological concern and need exploring! However, this understanding flows directly from the making of humans in the divine image and what God has done in creation. God has subdued the chaos monster and blessed the land and made it fruitful. Yet in spite of the impression given by Genesis 1, later writers would come to see this task as begun but not completed by God. Indeed the imagery of Genesis 3 does not have all of creation as paradise but only a garden outside of which is still chaos. Humanity in God's image is in effect told to continue to subdue the chaos monster and continue to bless creation and make it fruitful. Or in terms of Genesis 2, enable the spread of the Garden of Eden until it fills all creation.[113]

This raises some important questions about nature itself as well as humanity's relationship to it which we will continue to explore; but at this point it is important we put out of our thinking the notion that the Garden of Eden is like that of an English house with a neatly mown lawn and flower border! Though it may also be worth noting that the human draw to gardening and working with nature is in fact God's image stirring within us calling us to our true purpose.

From here we can proceed to the second creation account in Genesis 2 and what is called 'The Fall'. If the vocation of the 'one from the earth', Adam, and the 'mother of the living', Eve, is to subdue the chaos serpent and enable all creation to become the Garden of Eden, in fact what happens is that the serpent masters them. A whole other piece could be written about the role of the two trees in this narrative. There is only space for a few comments. It is hard for us in an age that exalts human reason to find the tree of the knowledge of good and evil as anything but good to eat from. Many commentaries today assume this must be so. However, it is usually a mistake to read other contexts into ancient myths. God clearly gives humanity moral imperatives and understanding. The knowledge the tree represents is something that is only for God. Other passages using this phraseology would suggest this is not about understanding but authority; it is about who decides what is good and evil. When humans place themselves in authority over creation and dictate morality in place of God, things go wrong and vital relationships are damaged. Men dominate and abuse women, humanity dominates and abuses creation - which gives food only after struggle, humanity is

---

113 Indeed a number of Jewish Midrash note that on the seventh day God does not in the Hebrew text cease from creation or from what is made but from creating and making, that is the task is not complete on the seventh day.

estranged from God, the land is damaged and produces weeds and thorns in abundance. This is the situation described in Genesis 3 when humanity fails to live up to its calling and as a result is shut out of paradise. This story does not see this as only a human tragedy but one that causes all creation to suffer too.

I am not an expert in ecological systems, but I was reminded of the situation beyond Eden when recently hearing someone talk about the effects of intensive farming and artificial fertilization on local plant life. This I gather leads to areas of land in which the natural plant life are replaced by weeds, nettles and thorns which thrive in the artificial environment. Very much the imagery of Genesis 3 when humans no longer live as priests of creation.

Humanity's priesthood restored through Jesus

The importance of Adam and Eve and the Genesis story for a Christian understanding of how humanity is related to suffering in creation is brought into focus through understanding Jewish Apocalyptic. This has used the imagery of the Jerusalem Temple to depict both the Garden of Eden and Heaven as if they were temples too. The loss of paradise and the breakdown of relationship between humanity and God, between humans and between humans and creation is in this writing viewed as a loss of humanity's priesthood in creation, represented by the loss of high priestly garments of glory. It is then not surprising that, as St Paul claims in Romans 8, the salvation of humanity and creation are linked and that this will be depicted as a restoration of humanity's priesthood shown as a re-clothing of humanity in the glorious robes of the high priest.

The Qumran community in its own writings viewed the Jerusalem Temple as corrupt and in response to this they had withdrawn into the desert and lived as if they were the priests in another temple. These texts, like other Jewish Apocalyptic, spoke of the Jerusalem Temple as 'made with hands' indicating it was corrupt earthly. They went on to say this earthly temple would be replaced by one from heaven 'not made with hands' at the coming of a messianic prince of righteousness. We cannot know if the early church had a direct link to the Qumran community, but similar ideas are present. So we see Stephen in Acts 7 using this language and having an apocalyptic vision of the ascended Jesus in the heavenly temple. It is this speech that leads to his death. Similarly Jesus speaks of the Temple's destruction in texts like John 2 and Mark 13, and at his trial he is accused of saying "I will destroy this temple that is made with hands, and in three days I will build another, not made with hands."[114]. Yet it is clear from John 2 that Jesus saw himself as the new Temple coming out of heaven, the one that would be raised up in three days at the resurrection. This is the language of Jewish Apocalyptic, but given a new twist.

When one realises this, it becomes clear that when Paul speaks of Jesus as the new Adam, or the writer of Hebrews speaks of Jesus as having entered the Holy of Holies in heaven as our forerunner and as priest for ever in the order of Melchizedek,[115] they both draw on this apocalyptic tradition. In this tradition the one entering the heavenly temple is re-clothed in the way the high priest of the earthly temple is on the Day of Atonement on the one occasion he can enter the Holy of Holies. If so this clothing is likely to be a representation of that which Adam and Eve lost. If the church is to be a new Eve as Paul claims, or to follow him who is our forerunner into the Holy of Holies as the writer of Hebrews claims, might we too be so re-clothed and regain our lost priesthood?

114 Mark 14:58
115 Hebrews 6:19-20

The High Priest's garments on the Day of Atonement are themselves a representation of humanity's calling to bear God's image and overcome the chaos monster. The robe is depicted as made of material that would make it look like the veil of the Temple behind which God dwelt. The High Priest thus goes behind the veil dressed in a white robe and comes out as it were wearing the veil. We may relate this to the language of Jesus' incarnation as 'tabernacling' among us.[116] Jesus puts on the tabernacle and comes among us just as the High Priest does on the Day of Atonement, becoming as it were an incarnation of God. 3 Enoch also develops this theme. We learn that Enoch has become Metatron, called by the name of God and as such is called 'the lesser YHWH'. The title seems to follow from speculation about the Angel of the Lord of whom Exodus 23:21 says 'my name is in him'. 3 Enoch also clearly depicts the process of Enoch's transformation into Metatron as that of being clothed with the eight garments of the High Priest. The naming of him as the 'lesser YHWH' follows the crown being set on his head, a further allusion to the High Priest who had the name of God inscribed on the frontlet worn on his head.

Crispin Fletcher-Louis[117] has connected the chaos myth with the clothing of the High Priest by noting how the account of Daniel 7:1-14 is based on the imagery of Baal's defeat of the sea monster, his approach of the throne of El and his enthronement. He notes how the description also fits the coming of the High Priest before the earthly throne in the Holy of Holies on the Day of Atonement, dressed in white linen and shrouded in incense.[118] He further notes that in Josephus[119] the High

....

116 John 1:14 often translated as dwelling among us but the Greek has him being a tabernacle in our midst
117 Fletcher-Louis C 'the High Priest as divine mediator' Atlanta, SBL seminar papers 1997
118 Ibid. p. 167.
119 Antiquities 3:154-6.

Priest's sash is described as like a 'serpent' and as 'twisting'. These are the same words used elsewhere to describe Leviathan.[120] Fletcher-Louis thus suggests that the High Priest is depicted as a conqueror of the sea monster, wearing a belt that is an image of Leviathan.

The Christian apocalyptic of the Revelation of John also draws on the imagery of the High Priest at the Day of Atonement. The opening chapter has a vision of Christ standing in the Temple setting with seven lampstands reminiscent of the menorah giving seven messages to seven churches. Each message alludes to Old Testament passages about the restoration of Israel and the Temple and each describes Jesus' appearance according to different aspects of the High Priest's clothing. So there are references to Zechariah 3 and 4, which supplies the vision of the lamp stands. This text is about the restoration of the Temple and in it we also see Joshua[121] re-clothed in the High Priest's garments. In Zechariah 4 Joshua is describes as one of the two olive trees, along with Zerubbabel the restored King, seen by the lamp stand. Here however we see one person, fulfilling perhaps both roles as 'Priest King'.[122]

That the 'High Priestly' Jesus of Revelation 1 is supposed to also be seen as fulfilling the role of Davidic Messiah is further suggested by another text alluded to in the vision when it describes Jesus as having a two edged sword coming from his mouth. This comes from the account of Zion's restoration in Isaiah 49-52 in which the Lord's Servant is described in this way.[123] Following this passage about Zion's restoration, the Lord's servant's sacrifice is described in the famous suffering

....

120 E.g. Is. 27:1-2
121 In the Greek Old Testament he is of course thus Jesus, but on its own this should not be taken as significant. It may however have strengthened the linkage in the writers mind between the risen Christ and Zechariah 3 and 4.
122 As argued by Farrer. Farrer A. The Revelation of St. John the Divine Clarendon. Oxford. 1964, p65
123 Is. 49:2

servant passages. Margaret Barker has noted that these passages probably relate to the treatment of the scapegoat on the Day of Atonement.[124] Such a linkage is also present within the Apocalypse of John in which Jesus is revealed not only as High Priest on the Day of Atonement but also as victim of the sacrifice, for instance as a slain lamb in Rev. 5.

Other events in the schema of Revelation also contain the intervening events depicted in Is. 49-52; that is Zion adorned as a bride, a new creation, and the defeat of the chaos monster. The latter part of this sequence is also part of the context of Psalm 89 that also supplies some of the opening titles of Jesus in the book of Revelation. Here the Davidic Messiah is cast as 'Baal to YHWH's El'[125] in a passage used to support the idea that the festivals of the Jewish month of Tishri, of which the Day of Atonement was the climax, contained an enthronement ceremony in which the king was viewed as fulfilling the chaos monster battle myth.

In such passages, interpretations of the Day of Atonement from Jewish Apocalyptic are connected to Old Testament texts of the messiah and applied to Jesus. But Jesus is not the only person whose clothing is referred to as that of the High Priest. The same in the end is also true of Jesus' bride as she comes dressed for the wedding feast in Revelation 21. What is at first confusing about this vision is that we are told we are seeing the Bride of Christ clothed for their wedding but what we see is the New Jerusalem coming out of Heaven. But there is a precedent for this also in Jewish Apocalyptic. In 4 Ezra 9:26-10:59 Ezra is sent to a field to live on wild flowers and await God. Whilst he is there he has a vision in which he sees a woman

---

124 *Atonement the rite of Healing,* Scottish Journal of Theology Vol. 49 no.1 1996 pp 1-20., she sees this passage reflected in 1Enoch, and cites the Mishnah tradition, M.Yoma 6:4, in support of the details of Is 52&53 relating to the Atonement ritual.
125 Fletcher Louis, ibid, p165. He is quoting from P
Mosca's identification of psalm 89 with Daniel 7.

mourning with rent clothes. She tells him of how she had an only son who died on his wedding day and that she is beyond consoling and will die. Ezra replies that Zion, the mother of them, all has more reason to weep because the sanctuary is in ruins, the Temple destroyed and the people in exile. The woman however is transformed before his eyes.

> 'While I was talking to her, behold, her face suddenly shone exceedingly, and her countenance flashed like lightning, so that I was too frightened to approach her, and my heart was terrified. While I was wondering what this meant, behold, she suddenly uttered a loud and fearful cry, so that the earth shook at the sound. And I looked, and behold, the woman was no longer visible to me, but there was an established city, and a place of huge foundations showed itself.'[126]

An angel tells Ezra that the woman was indeed Zion and she has become the city of God.

Many of the statements about the New Jerusalem in Revelation 21 and 22 are references to passages in the second section of Isaiah about the suffering servant and the restoration of Zion. These sections are also full of imagery about the marriage of Zion. So Isaiah 61:10 tells us that 'God has clothed Zion with garments of salvation and a robe of righteousness as a bridegroom decks himself with a garland and a bride adorns herself in jewels'. Similarly Isaiah 54 tells us that 'Zion's maker is her husband, the Lord of Hosts is his name',[127] and that God will 'set her stones in antimony and her foundations in sapphires, make her pinnacles of rubies, her gates of jewels and her walls of precious stones'.[128] Finally Isaiah 51:3 tells us God will 'comfort Zion and make her wilderness like Eden and her desert like the garden of the Lord'. Whatever Isaiah's

---

126 4 Ezra 10:25-27a.
127 Isaiah 54:5
128 Isaiah 54:14-15

intention, Revelation also links these images, showing Zion as the bride of Christ clothed in jewels as well as, like the vision of Ezra 4 a city. It also gives a concrete portrayal of Zion as Eden, with the Tree of Life open to all at its centre. Isaiah's prophecy links the restoration of Zion as God's bride with the clothing of that bride and further links this with a restored Eden. Revelation shows this prophecy being fulfilled through God's people as his bride.

The description of the New Jerusalem thus needs to be seen as also a description of the Bride's dress. 21:11 shows the radiance of the city is like that of God in the throne visions, not surprising if God has become her light. The city has twelve gates named with the tribes of Israel in common with Ezekiel, but twelve foundations named after the twelve apostles. This is similar to Ephesians 2:14-20 in which a new Temple is built on the foundation of apostles and Prophets and welcomes the gentiles. Having been told of its cubic nature we are then told its square foundation is bedecked with a list of twelve jewels. The list seems likely, bearing in mind the mention of the names of the twelve tribes,[129] to be that on the High Priest's breastplate, also square. The problem is making an identification because the same stones are called by different names in different times and places. Trying to relate the list in Revelation written in Greek to the Hebrew Scriptures is thus even more difficult. The Greek Old Testament, the Septuagint,[130] however is quite promising and was of course the text the New Testament writers were using. This not only lists these jewels in Exodus 28 when the High Priest's garments are described but also in Ezekiel 28:11-19 about the fall of the king of Tyre, in

---

129 Noting it is the apostles who form the foundation, they are the new Israel and thus on the new breastplate.
130 A reference to the idea that it was miraculously translated by 70 independent scholars hence the Roman numeral LXX for 70 is also used to denote the Greek Old Testament.

which he is described as wearing the High Priest's breastplate. Intriguingly he is also said to be in the paradise of God,[131] Eden in Hebrew scripture. This in itself is interesting because it may be that the tradition associating these jewels with Adam, and thus Adam with the High Priest, may be especially prominent around the time the Septuagint was written. Revelation's list is nearly identical to that in the Greek Old Testament with four variations. Of these the likely descriptions and colours of the stones suggest they are the same stones even if they don't match in name.[132] The Bride of Christ shines with the glory of God and 'wears' a square adorned with jewels identical to the High Priest's breastplate on the Day of Atonement because she emerges dressed just like her bridegroom Jesus, herself High Priest on a cosmic Day of Atonement, finally transformed into the likeness of Christ.

The ancient conflict between the serpent and Adam and Eve is connected to the architecture of the Temple, and the rending of the Holy of Holies linked to the defeat of that serpent. In the Day of Atonement liturgy one goat is killed, the sacrificial lamb, here Jesus. The other is sent into the wilderness. That goat was 'for Azazael'. This is the name given by the Jewish apocalyptic writers to the fallen angel who is elsewhere Satan and the Dragon. Thus in his final banishment into the abyss In Revelation 20 the eschatological Day of Atonement is complete. The wedding feast can begin as the new Adam and new

....

131 This is the usual rendering for Eden in Septuagint which does not use the name used by Hebrew Masoretic Text. There is thus no problem with the lack of the name here, the identity of the place is the same as the Hebrew text.
132 Calcedon in Rev. 21is a green or red stone often viewed as Agate in the Sptuagint. Sardonyx, Rev 21, varies only from Onyx in the Septua-gint, in that it is a slightly streaked version of the same stone. Chrysophrase is either a green or fiery gold form of chalcedony, this makes it very simi-lar to Athrax, the name means 'burning stone' but it appears to have been green. Jacinthas is translated sometimes as Ligure, or Ligurion in the Septua-gint, and seems to have been a yellow stone once called Jacinth as here.

Eve adorned once more in their lost glory become one. Christ and his church are joined for eternity.

Both the apocalyptic and Old Testament texts that Revelation alludes to, see the New Jerusalem as a restoration of Eden. And so John's vision of a new heaven and a new earth in which the former things are no more and there is no more crying or pain goes back to Isaiah 65. Isaiah 65 goes on to tell us there will be no more early or violent death, people's life spans being that of trees, and also tells of how animals will stop eating each other and shall do no harm on God's Holy Mountain, and with reference to the Genesis story that the serpent will eat dust. The animals have returned to their state in the Garden of Eden. The Greek Old Testament takes the Eden link further by saying that people's life spans will be as the Tree of Life. In Revelation by this point the serpent has been thrown into the lake of fire which is the second death and is thus returned to dust, and people appear immortal not just long lived, indeed they live as long as the Tree of Life. Isaiah also goes on to highlight Eden imagery, telling us of the whole creation rejoicing as the thorn is replaced by the cypress and the brier by the myrtle; the curse on the land that produced thorns and briers has been removed.

However there is an important difference, the New Jerusalem has no Temple. It does however conform to the cubic measure of the Holy of Holies in Ezekiel's Temple,[133] save that it has expanded to an impossible size, filling the world. The New Jerusalem, the new heaven and the new earth are all the Holy of Holies from the Temple, all dwell with God in the place once beyond the Veil. Like the vision of Ezekiel a river flows from the Temple,[134] from under the tree of life with leaves for healing.[135] Significantly Revelation adds that they are for the

....

133 c.f. Ez.42:20
134 Ez.47:1 & Rev.22:1
135 Ez.47:12 & Rev.22:2

healing of the nations. Nothing could be further from Ezekiel's vision which places further exclusions on Israelites entering the Temple, let alone allowing non-Israelites access. Here all people are welcomed in, but not just humanity, all creation is included.

Jesus the Great High Priest has restored the priesthood of humanity and in the end Christ's Bride is also, like him, a High Priest. Revelation depicts this High Priest having gone into the Holy of Holies in white robes now coming out in full apparel; the eschatological Day of Atonement to end all others is completed. The Church as the Bride of Christ is a new Eve to his new Adam. If a fallen Adam wore the High Priest's jewels in the first Eden,[136] then a new Eve wears them as High Priest and bride of the new Adam and is the new Eden. Finally it is worth remembering that this marriage tradition cited in the epistles goes back to Genesis 2 where the man and woman are separated and thus told they will be joined together in marriage so that they become one flesh. We may also note that the Jewish commentary on this story, Genesis Rabbah 8:1 and the Jewish philosopher Philo in his Questions on Genesis 1:25, both cite a tradition in which this is linked to the dividing of Adam and Eve by stating that the original Adam was both male and female, this being re-created at their joining. In Revelation we note that Eve/Zion has married God, shines with his light within her, becomes his dwelling place, and wears his garment of glory, the two have become one flesh and Eden is fully restored. Creation too is finally freed from bondage to decay.

---

136 Ez. 28

Living towards the new creation as priests of creation now

When exploring the idea that humanity has a calling of priesthood within creation, people often assume this places humanity in a superior role. Yet as the writer of the letter to the Hebrews points out, Jesus' priesthood of humanity is based on his becoming like those who are his brothers and sisters.[137] Humans can be priests of creation precisely because they are part of creation and not superior to it. Indeed that priesthood was first given to Adam the one whose name reminds us he is of the earth. Embracing our calling as priests requires us to identify with creation, indeed all things become our brothers and sisters just as Jesus identifies with us as brothers and sisters.

Humans can act as priests because like Jesus they are also made in God's image. They bridge the worlds between creation and creator. This is not to suggest that God is not otherwise connected intimately with creation apart from humanity but that humans represent creation to God and God to creation in a unique way. Indeed we should understand God become human in Jesus as not only essential to setting humanity free from bondage to decay but also through his humanity creation also. It is interesting to note therefore that the animals are brought to Adam to name, an act that reflects his ability to give voice to creation and an act in the image of the creator, but also to see if any will be a partner to him. That the idea is explored shows the affinity between Adam and the animals, yet only another like him in God's image is a suitable partner.

The psalmist[138] sees all of creation as full of voices praising God of which humans are one among many, yet the priestly role here is also a calling to help creation give voice. This can

---

137 Hebrews 2:17
138 Psalm 148 especially

be a speaking up for creation when humans fail in their care towards it, but also a giving voice to creation in our art and worship. It is perhaps the call of priesthood buried deep within us that means the world around inspires worship within us. There is also a calling in this to learn the languages of the world around us, to let animals, plants and soil speak to us. Many ancient peoples saw this as part of the priesthood offered by the Shaman. I think such an image is just as relevant to a Christian recovery of humanity's priesthood within creation.

This speaking about creation is also what leads to the very understanding of creation humans have developed that means they can not only manipulate it destructively but also nurture and save threatened species, help preserve particular environments, offer medical care to animals and stable management of crops, and indeed have an environmental debate at all. Creation clearly works without us, but it is interesting to note how our care for creation causes us to intervene to help protect all life and the very planet itself from harm that would otherwise be part of that natural cycle. In the past we have often been too cavalier in doing this, too confident of our ability. We are learning to be cautious in our interventions many of which have unintended consequences. But would we feel it ethical to stop such interventions entirely? We have much here to learn, but our calling is to work with God's guidance and strength to set creation free from the power of the destructive 'chaos monster'.

The approach this offers to creation therefore does not envisage it as complete without human intervention. This is not so that humans can treat creation as a giant food and minerals supply, nor turn it into an English country garden. Rather the fulfilment of creation is something humans acting in the divine image are called to enable to happen. That final destiny of completed creation is not the ecosystem as we know it. As with all these things it would be unwise to over interpret the poetic language of the diet of the animals or humans in Eden, nor that of Isaiah in which lions turn vegetarian. But this is pointing to an idea of an ecosystem in which nature is not 'red in tooth and claw'. Sometimes ecological views of humanity treat humans on the one hand as 'just another animal' or on the other as a deadly parasite that might destroy the planet. Both may be true of humanity as it is; alienated from God, each other and creation. But the vision of God as expressed in Jewish and Christian scripture is not of a creation best off without us, or with us operating as simple hunter gatherers like any other animal. God's vision for the ecosystem recognises that humanity made in God's image has indeed a great destructive power and thus also a much higher level of responsibility for creation. However, it also sees a developed and interventionist humanity as essential for nature to flourish at its best.

This is on the one hand very challenging. Humanity as it has developed has not got a good track record of living well with itself let alone its brothers and sisters in animal, vegetable and mineral kingdoms. Yet it is also realistic. Humans bear a unique responsibility within creation and thus also a unique calling. Creation is suffering because we have forgotten who we are in God's image. We have allowed our pride and self-interest to dominate us and we have believed the world is ours to use and not God's to love. For this reason the great high priest Jesus broke the power of destruction, pride, selfishness and death in facing them in his own suffering and death. Through his coming back to life he has offered each of us a new way forward so we can become the people we are called to be so that all of creation may be set free from bondage to decay and suffering and pain will cease because the former things are no more. On the seventh day of the week, God in Jesus rested in death in the tomb, on the eighth day a new creation was begun which would offer life not just to us, but to all God's creatures. Our calling is not just to be transformed but to be key workers in that transformation, the forgotten priests of creation, God's co-workers in banishing chaos and bringing in paradise.

Steve Hollinghurst *is trainer, consultant and researcher in contemporary culture, mission and new forms of church and also a part-time tutor for Church Army. He has an academic background in social science and theology, looking at culture and spirituality in today's world. He helps coordinate Communities of the Mystic Christ and runs Christian stalls at Mind Body and Spirit fairs. His publications include Mission-Shaped Evangelism Canterbury Press 2010, New Age Paganism and Christian Mission, Grove 2002, and Starting, Assessing and Sustaining Pioneer Mission Grove 2013 along with a number of chapters and articles in others.*

Chapter 10 – Dan Papworth

Rewilding the Soul

The call to prayer

We went to the woods. By the standards of my watch it wasn't late, not even 3pm, but grey clouds brought a wintry gloom and we encountered no one on the road. Autumn had come late again and the fallen November leaves retained a crisp freshness, a warm mosaic that quietly received the misty rain. It is not a wild wood, this place by Hatherley Brook, surviving in the corner created by Willersey Road and the railway, although I sense something wild there. The hard packed ground beneath the trees testifies to frequent use by humans and management by the local authority. It is a place with no name, as far as I can tell. People locally call it "Benhall Park", and I guess that name will eventually stick, but I want to call it "Athelai", the medieval name for the area, literally "hawthorn-clearing", from which the district name of Hatherley derives. It is not a large space, but big enough, I think, to warrant a name. Our naming of places and things – in this case our failure to – says far more about our priorities than it does about the places themselves. To many this would simply be "waste ground", as if such a thing is possible.

Growing up in North London such places were my first experience of nature, something that in this country is generally limited to "reserves". As I grew they became favourite playgrounds to be sought out and explored. Around the age of eleven, with one or two others, I donned wellies and old clothes and sloshed along the Yeading Brook, crawling under bridges, peering into water outflows and delighting in the sparse wildlife that occasionally showed itself. I dreamt of seeing otters and of journeying across the UK without using roads at all. As a campaigning teenager I wrote to the Council to try to prevent a local woodland from being built upon, and I still believe we need these "in-between" places, and that they are too small and too few. Like prayer they seem all too often to be squeezed to the edges. Indeed they are often defined as "marginal", on the periphery.

For the past few years prayer has become an experience I can only describe as "spacious". Where at first there were many words now there is silence, a silence of unknowing, even of myself. Instinct rather than pragmatism takes me outside in winter, when most other people seem to be dreaming of sunshine in other places. Standing beneath the swaying branches in that cold hour of the sun's setting my spirit was moved to prayer but my mind was robbed of words. A prayer of being, of presence. The wind, deep breath of the earth, gusted in the treetops, causing them to sway darkly against the cold afternoon sky, graceful, calming, but not altogether safe, not "bound to be kind." We watched. Time passed. Birds, solitary or in small family groups, streaked above the canopy. The light faded. My companion, not yet two years old, also listened, was also still. Whoever thinks children have no attention span should try this. I don't think he needs me to tell him how to pray. He comes alive outside and is completely at home, not yet schooled enough to love the woods and hate the traffic, to know why we must tread softly and be awake and alert for signs of grace.

A new humility

"God made us in his image...male and female", so we are told in the first chapters of Genesis.[139] In recent times this sentence has, quite rightly, been a rallying cry for change in how women and men work together. In the past the suggestion that Eve was brought forth not only after Adam but also from him[140] has provided proof-enough text for theologians wanting to establish a male hierarchy. But who has questioned the notion of hierarchy itself? There seems to have been an assumption that it is implicit in creation. So we speak about "orders" in the natural world, not least because the theory of evolution implies an order, and increasing complexity.[141] As we begin to revise our thinking about particular, human, hierarchies, is it not also time to look at the whole concept of hierarchy? There was a time when theologians were preoccupied with the "pecking order" of the Trinity: "is the Son subordinate to the Father?" and so on. Even a cursory reading of Scripture[142] shows this to be an irrelevance to God. Where love abounds there is no need for domination. And yet domination has been the principle way in which we have looked at, and related to, the created world. There are some who have sought to lay the blame for this at the Church's door,[143] but the reality has been that the rise of capitalism, and capitalists, has driven

....

139 Genesis 1:27
140 Genesis 2:21-23
141 I have never believed there is a serious conflict between the theory of evolution, which is about a century old and so far remains unopposed (although Intelligent Design theory seems to be a valuable counterpoint to it) and belief in a creator. Were ancient people merely imposing an idea or responding to revelation? It seems a supreme act of arrogance to claim we can answer that either way.
142 The arguments have been set out far more competently and comprehensively than I have space for here. Suffice it to say that "God is love" trumps a lot of other things that can be said about God, since it refers to God's nature whilst other attributes (justice, power, knowledge and so on) are in God's possession.
143 Lyn White's much-cited lecture, "The Historical Roots of Our Ecological Crisis", delivered on 26 December 1966, proved to be a rallying cry for those who wanted to distance themselves from responsibility as well as from Christian faith.

the machine of human "progress". In a relatively short time humans discovered, and then developed, the means of mass production (which is mass consumption), and the standard of living improved vastly and rapidly. Today we enjoy wealth unimaginable to former generations, as wealth has traditionally been assessed. But we have also gained awareness, and it this that requires us to think again.

Has the Church been to blame? That would seem to be a popular view. Strangely it is most often held by people who have chosen not to be influenced by the Church. You cannot really have it both ways. But there has been a tendency among Christians to fill in the blanks. The Bible provides quite a surprisingly large number of these, suggesting that God wants us to move freely and be creative. It is interesting how many people, especially those in leadership, feel the need to supply what seems to be lacking. So, for example, we are told that God made humanity in the divine image. I remember being told this when I was a child, but somehow the word "alone" crept in where it doesn't appear in the text. On the strength of this addition, a whole world view of human superiority seems to have been built. Is that really necessary? Are we so insecure that we need to insist upon our uniqueness, our separation from "the rest" of creation? In fact the idea that human beings alone carry the divine image is not explicit anywhere in Scripture. But we are one expression[144] of the immense variety of nature, or to put it another way, we are made in nature's image, in the image of life. Looked at in this way the cosmos can also be said to be made in the image of God, and we as a significant part of it have a particular honour, not in exclusivity but through our God-given awareness.

----

144 That is to say one species, because the various expressions of humanity are similarly multiple and diverse.

Mind the gap

In Britain there are almost no truly wild landscapes. Everywhere belongs to someone and is affected by human "management". There was a time, though, when we were the ones who lived "in between", making a clearing in the trees that stretched as far as the eye could see, even if we found a vantage point on a hilltop or climbed one to help us choose our direction. Surrounded by life we took it for granted. The world was limitless and we were so few. But we had this advantage, and have it still: that we are "super-co-operators", able both to imagine and to plan, enlisting the work of many individuals to a shared cause.[145] So now we have to do something never done before. We have to *intentionally* change the paradigm in which we live, first because we know about paradigms and how powerful they are, second because we know our present paradigm is taking us at a frighteningly rapid pace towards a global catastrophe that could result in the deaths of millions.

Be aware

"Be still". It is an extraordinary command. Nothing in nature is still, although some things, like continents, the growth of trees and the digestive tracts of three-toed sloths, move more imperceptibly. Whatever stillness we can achieve is only partial. Like so many aspects of the divine, what we know, what we *can* know, is limited. And yet stillness is an experience available to us, as it is to every living animal. It is associated with alertness, and listening.

....

145 I am grateful to Howard Rheingold for the word "super-co-operators". He states; "Those of us who live in urban, industrialized societies all know the old story – a narrative taught to us by our parents, schoolteachers, and (outmoded) [sic] scientific theories: biology is a war in which only the most fiercely competitive can survive....I see the outlines of a new narrative emerging...Competition is still important, but its place on our map of the universe has to shrink to make room for what we now know about cooperative arrangements and complex interdependencies in ecosystems, economies, and societies". Netsmart, pp.148-9

Consider a gazelle, grazing at the edge of the herd. There is a tiny movement several metres away. Its head comes up in an instant, every sense alive. The movement, or noise, was slight, little more than an irregularity in the air. The gazelle *felt* it, as much as seeing or hearing. Now its body knows stillness, as every personal movement is set aside to allow the senses to do their work. Only the beating heart, whose task of distributing vital adrenaline, retains priority. In the camouflage of the gently swaying grass the lioness is also still. She has come to this point painfully slowly, belly to the ground. She too is *feeling* as much as seeing, hearing, smelling the herd and those at its edges. The wide pads of her feet reduce the vibration of her footfall to almost nothing. Through them she can sense the movement of the animal she is hunting. For both of these creatures, the hunted and the hunter, everything depends upon their ability to be still, and to move. Could this be the stillness, and the movement, to which we are called?[146]

Be still and know. When we go "into nature" (when are we ever out of it?) beyond the safe confines of our structures, by which I mean more than buildings, we open ourselves to rediscover this capacity within ourselves. For too long we have thought it meant only to sit, or to kneel, in a room. Those who have explored this way have indeed discovered a deep inner peacefulness, and a challenge to face the self. But as creatures of the earth we do not exist in isolation. The solitary cell is an illusion. Without the green plants outside it the room would be devoid of life. Encountering our fellow creatures, animal, vegetable and mineral also confronts us with ourselves, and draws us towards a deeper communion, a deeper trust.

---

146 A friend is fond of the following saying: "At the appointed time I shall move quickly". I have not yet managed to find the source of this important piece of wisdom.

A destructive creativity

Perhaps alone of all creatures we have been able to invent a category which we call "synthetic", "unnatural" or, more crudely, "man-made". It is a bizarre ability. If you can bear it, try switching on a television at peak viewing time. How "natural" are the colours you see? Why are the presenters shouting? Consider straight lines, something you almost never see in nature (even light is bent by gravitational fields), but which are so useful to us. We have imposed them everywhere, and even incorporated them into our language, referring to something as "true" if it is straight. We live in structures that attempt – and often fail – to keep "nature" out. As a new homeowner I have been impressed and dismayed in equal measure by the way water in particular manages to penetrate and do damage, and I wonder why it is that we have made an enemy of something that is almost impossible to defeat. It is time to grasp the nettle of our own creative power and accept that "synthetic" is all too often another way of saying "unhealthy", out of balance.

Rewilding ourselves

For too long we have lived within a story in which human beings are something separate from, and somehow above, nature. The time has come for a personal, and group, "rewilding", that enables us to locate ourselves properly within God's creation, and live in harmony and balance as part of it.

If we are to be those who affirm that God made us both *of* nature[147] and *in* nature, that nature is our home, and not just a pet project or some kind of responsibility, we need to recover a sense of the wild. There are instincts that lie within

---

147 It is significant that the Genesis account speaks of nature created through God's Word, but of humanity being created out of the "dust of the earth".

us that lie dormant but which can be revived.[148] We need to nurture, in ourselves and our children, the awareness that we rely completely on the rest of nature for our lives. We need to retain the deep self-knowledge that has developed through the reflections of millennia, the ancient wisdom accrued by many cultures, and a vast body of knowledge about natural phenomena, including other species, compiled in the past several generations. The project called "Rewilding" is intricately linked to this. We are intimately connected to our environment. If we are to change then we must bring about change, and allow this change to change us. Rewilding is the latest in a series of steps that I have observed in the past decade. Hugh Fearnley-Whittingstall's TV series *A Cook on the Wild Side* and his better known follow-up *River Cottage* came at a time when people were just beginning to realise how separated they had become. Mark Boyle's *Moneyless Man* project is another step. Although Mark's starting point was living without money he ended up living in touch with nature too. These things are connected. Of course there have been pioneers of this way of thinking, naturalists such as Roger Deakin and Richard Mabey, as well as journalists like David Attenborough, who have pointed us to the natural world for decades now, but I sense we are seeing a far more popular movement arising, one that ought to tear us away from the profit-driven culture of capitalism towards a greater humanity, a greater wholeness. After all, what do we make this money for, if it is not for life?

Little and often

I would love to be Ray Mears, Hugh Fearnley-Whittingstall or David Attenborough. These people seem to "live the dream".

---

148 Howard Rheingold suggests that reading, for example, may have begun with an ability to "make use of deeply embedded perceptual mechanisms that probably evolved in order to track predators and prey by deciphering their footprints". Netsmart, p.59

You can't see the cameras, so the impression you get is that these people live outside, in touch with creation all the time. The reality is that they, like most of us are bound by important relationships, obligations and therefore limited time, little and often is where we have to begin.

Is there a place where you go? For some it is a hilltop, for others a wood. It can be a nearby park or garden, where wildness is kept at bay but can still be seen, pushing upwards where others have failed to look. I was privileged for two years in my twenties that I lived at Lee Abbey in Devon. As a member of the community there I had a half hour every day for contemplation and would invariably walk briskly to "Upper Jenny's", as it is known, where a flat rock provided a seat and a view across the estuary. It was not long before a half hour was insufficient, and I would touch the granite with my hands, and feel the branches of trees on the way back down the hill, wanting to be connected to it and to stay. I remember one occasion the words came to me "Treasure it. It will not be yours for ever." and, towards the end of my time there, preparing myself to leave, I said to God from my heart; "When you judge the earth, judge me here, for here I am myself". It was only later that I discovered, that that high rock overlooking the sea is also a place within me.

Action

As a human being you will have been imagining things. This book may well have appealed to you because your imagination takes you outside. To go outside in this time in human history is a spiritual act and, like most spiritual acts there is a discipline. If you have ever tried to develop a regular prayer life you will know that the biggest obstacle is getting started. You will also know the tremendous gift of finding others who want to pray with you. I have no doubt that the Spirit of God is calling forth a new community of those who go outside together to meet with God, to be transformed and to bring about transformation.

On Ash Wednesday 2012 a group called *Operation Noah* released a declaration[149] that I believe is a template for how Christians are to go forward at this time. It speaks about our relationship to God, the poorest communities in the world, future generations and other species (I would include non-living "creatures" here too, such as the rocks, the streams and so on). The "Ash Wednesday Declaration" gives us seven actions to apply in our lives. They are: 1. Find joy in Creation, 2. Listen, 3. Repent, 4. Take responsibility, 5. Seek Justice, 6. Love our neighbours, 7. Act with hope.

We began in one place, a vestige of "nature", doing what nature does – living and persisting despite our worst efforts. We have looked at how humanity has also forced itself outwards and relegated "nature" (in this country at least) to the interstices of our increasingly urban, consumer-dominated geography. I believe we, as human beings, have all we need to bring about significant, positive change, reversing the damage we are doing to the climate and living in a healthier, happier and more sustainable way. But it begins with you who are hearing this call. It is a call to rediscover the God-given one-ness, communion, we have with Creation, which we have for too long thought of as "other". So go outside. Go now. Don't delay.

For further reading: Boyle, Mark, *The Moneyless Man: A Year of Freeconomic Living*. MacFarlane, Robert, *The Wild Places* (2007). Rheingold, Howard, *Netsmart: How to Thrive Online*

Dan Papworth, *45, is ordained in the Church of England but left parish ministry in 2013 to concentrate on family,*

149 http://www.operationnoah.org/read-the-declaration

writing, spiritual accompaniment and stacking shelves.
He lives in Cheltenham and would love to hear from
anyone there who wants to explore Forest Church further.

Chapter 12 – Helen Bradley

Selfhood in the Community of Nature

Many people have sought to identify 'who' nature is so that they can have a personal relationship with 'her'. I think this is vitally important and something I have explored. However, the question of nature's identity raises the question of human identity and we need to explore that too within a developing theology of nature and how this affects our community.

I recently ran a research workshop in order to explore some of these themes of identity with many faith paths. The group consisted of a number of Pagans, Christians, those who follow Native American traditions and mystics. All have, to some degree, incorporated earth based spiritualities into their path. We explored three themes; 'Self', 'Spirit' and 'Other'. This workshop has enabled me to look at the wider implications of these themes and how they relate to different worldviews.

Attempting to develop a participatory relationship with the earth around me has vastly improved my relationship with the spiritual. In many ways I have grown further away from established religion, but in others I have been drawn almost involuntarily to ritual and rhythm, particularly in relation to the seasons. I am discovering the soul in nature, discovering divinity in the smallest and most exuberant moves of nature and choosing to commune with God in it. This has been revelatory to say the least. It would be tempting to continue looking outwards at this amazing cosmos so wonderfully woven and to continue to look less and less at myself. This is tempting, instructive, helpful and honouring, considering the many years I have ignored her. However, I want to pause and look back at myself and my identity and explore some of the changes in my identity because of this shift in my worldview.

I am going to use the term 'her' as I refer to nature, not because I have a distinct theory of nature's femininity, but because for me the term represents kinship and balance. There are many items and concepts with no distinct gender which we refer to as 'he' because in the west we are part of a male oriented society. I chose 'she' because I am a human with little other language to cope with the overarching and expansive concepts I am exploring and this allows me to personify nature from within a feminist worldview.

From a human perspective the universe appears to revolve around us. We have an unavoidably anthropocentric view. We have crowned ourselves as the pinnacle of creation. It is difficult to get away from this viewpoint. Even with a developing biocentric view of the world, in which all living things hold equal value, we will still find ourselves coming back to 'I'. I think this is important. If we are to change the way we see the earth, I think we also need to change the way we see ourselves.

The question 'who am I?' is one that has bothered humans for millennia with a variety of theories, some related to thought, or responsibility, or individuality, or flesh and blood, and the list continues. A year or so ago someone asked me what made me feel like a woman? For me the answer couldn't be based on having children, or my relationship status. I am single and without children. It struck me how much we define our identity by our relationships. For a while, I considered how I could define myself without these things. I settled on something quite surprising and a little tongue in cheek. Doing my tax return makes me feel like a woman. I settled on responsibility and individuality. In the research group we began by talking about our humanity and we settled on similar attributes, 'Responsibility' being the key attribute. That Responsibility however stretched beyond our immediate selves to the rest of humanity, to all life and to the earth. The group considered it human to care and have compassion and feel a sense of responsibility towards others. We often talk of being 'humane' as having compassion or acting responsibly towards others. By others we also included a whole realm of non-human persons; nature, animals and spirit. With Responsibility we must feel a connection somehow to the things we feel responsible for. Responsibility however is not dominating, on some occasions we have a responsibility to get out of the way, rather than to intervene. One person in the group saw 'spirit' as trying to reach into the suffering on earth, which he saw everywhere. He saw his role as a human to be an aid to this connection; connecting spirit with earth, and stepping into suffering himself, alleviating it any way he could. His responsibility was to connect and care.

I am connected, directly and indirectly, to a plethora of entities, each of which might operate as the centre of their own universe. A bug, a tree, an entire wood, a town, a country, the earth and the entire cosmos. Each of these aspects holds its own sphere of influence that I am just a part of, inhabiting briefly the space next to it, two individuals on a path together. A tree and I. So if someone in a relationship redefines their identity, even the slightest bit by their intimacy with another human, how might I do the same with an aspect of my surroundings? This may be easier to understand in a relationship between two humans; but for me to redefine my identity in relation to a tree, what would it take?

Miroslav Volf asks the vital question; "What kind of selves do we need to be in order to live in harmony with others?"[150]

It is my hope that as we think of 'others', we are thinking in both human and non-human terms. So if we are to live in harmony with the entire universe, including nature and including the divine, what could that look like for our self-identity?

I am still me, with all my thoughts and gifts and flaws, but I wish to see myself in a different context, which will hopefully enable me to walk more gently on the land and interact more freely with my surroundings and my God.

Charles Taylor suggests that, "the identity of a person is inescapably marked by the particularities of the social setting in which he or she is born and develops".[151] Our identity is shaped by our identification with the social surroundings.[152]

We all have different 'lenses' through which we see the world, reflecting our 'worldview'. Being aware of the bias our own lenses give to our perception of the world is a good place to start when considering our perception of our identity within the world.

What are my lenses? My own formative western Christian worldview tells me that to be in God's will is to be successful as an individual. Modern Capitalism defines for me what that success looks like. It tells me I should seek material gain and that I should dominate creation so that the land serves me and my success. Though I may be quite uncomfortable with some of these assertions, I have to acknowledge that this is my background.

---

150 Volf, Miroslav (1996) *'Exclusion and Embrace: A Theological Exploration of Identity, Otherness and Reconciliation'* Nashville, Abingdon Press, p20
151 Volf, 1996, p 16
152 Redhead, Mark, 2002. Charles Taylor: *'Thinking and Living Deep Diversity'* Rowman and Littlefield Publishers; Oxford, p 97

But my lenses are also ones of compassion. A love for other humans instilled by my mother's example, drumming into my mind the concept of fairness and justice for all on a global scale; awareness of others and a willingness to take a stand for others. If this had not been her passion I am unsure whether it would have been mine.

My lenses are also those of a young woman. These are not insignificant lenses. I am negotiating the world at a tipping point in feminist history.

My lenses are those of someone who is comparatively affluent. I don't know poverty and I am privileged to be educated, I have work and the time and space to explore more of the world and think philosophically.

All these lenses, and there are many more, at once define and cloud my sense of self. They make up how I have interacted with the world, but also frame my world and dictate the way I see it.

The philosopher Heidegger[153] talks of finding a 'clearing' in which to find your sense of self. This is a call to authenticity, being fully aware and present; our awareness comes from challenging the view our lenses give us and seeing ourselves more and more clearly.

You might look on Jesus' 40 days in the desert as a 'clearing'. The time, space and questions asked of him that defined his identity were significant in establishing how he continued to relate to others and the earth. This was a time when his world-view was challenged.

For a follower of Jesus attempting to live as God created them to be; in the image of God and therefore both more God-like and more human, it may be that the very idea of who they are

153 Heidegger, M. (2002) 'Heidegger: Off the Beaten Track' Cambridge; Cambridge University Press

created to be is a distorting set of lenses we wear as we enter the clearing. It could be that our time in the clearing is a time of honesty where our false image of what it is to be made in God's image is revealed.

To be fully aware and present, we must inhabit that exposed sense of self all the time and carry the challenge of the paradox of Jesus within that.

Heidegger's observation may suggest that we don't need to fast for forty days in the desert to find this clearing, but that we can be aware of it within us.

> Zizek, taking on board the motto of Irenaeus said 'God made Himself man that man might become God who made himself man'. In other words, our task of emanating the image of God within us is to emanate both God and humanity simultaneously.[154]

This concept tells us that all reflect the image of God (Imago Dei), and then may explore the realms of reflecting Jesus (Imago Christos) as Romans 8:29 suggests. Through this journey of following Jesus we enter into the 'Gloria Dei', whereby we are transfigured and entirely redeemed in a future reality. This instils a sense of eternity, a motivational factor in restoring identity.

Our core identity, the way we see ourselves in relation to others is going to be instrumental in the way we relate to the earth.

One way of knowing our self is through biology. I am not a scientist, but I am consistently amazed by the intricacies and complexities of our bodies. Recently I was told that we have six types of bacteria that only live in the crook of our elbow.[155]

154 Brewin, Kester, (2011) 'Other' London, Hodder and Stoughton p 30
155 Wade, N, (2008) 'Bacteria Thrive in inner elbow, no harm done' published in the New York Times on May 23 2008. (Accessed via www.nytimes.com on 3/2/14)

Just there. That is their home. They are part of us, and because they live there, we are healthier. We've all heard of the 'good bacteria' in our gut thanks to pro-biotic drinks adverts. Just knowing this instantly widens my sense of self and includes others within it. We are complex multi-species organisms. In relation to my identity, I become part of nature rather than walking on nature. We could extend this even further and look at Lovelock's theory of the earth as a single complex organism, named Gaia.[156]

When we work out what sort of people we need to be to live in harmony we become "capable of responding to the Other-human or non-human with immediate relevance and reverence. It is humankind in sustainable relationship with his environment."[157]

My journey of knowing myself has grown deeper and more profound alongside my connection with nature. As I have explored the forests and hills close by, as I have eaten the vegetables grown in our garden (not by me, I hasten to add), as I have looked at my consumption and addressed the cost to myself and the earth, I have come to know myself deeper. Like the psalmist such experiences stir my soul, 'awake my soul to sing! Come on my soul! Praise the Lord, O my Soul!'[158] Stir it for this earth. And I am stirred more and more as I become more and more aware of the changing seasons, the changing earth and the changing spirit within me. I talk to the trees and I capture God in the blinking moments stood still.

As I seek to know the earth, I know myself and I know God. I am intertwined. I am participant, I am not central.

156 Lovelock, J. 1989 *Geophysiology, the science of Gaia.* Published in Reviews of Geophysics 17, 11 May 1989, pages 215-222. American Geophysical Union. (accessed via www.jameslovelock.org on 1/3/2014)
157 Restall Orr, Emma. (2007) *Living with Honour, A Pagan Ethics.* O Books; Ropley, p 198
158 Psalm 103

The way I have come to love myself is to love the other. It is only when I have seen myself in the wider context of this huge cosmos, or when I have viewed myself as a multi-species organism that I have accepted this. I have bought myself down in rank and with that have come awe and inspiration. We really are like a speck of dust.

Looking again at Jesus' commandment; 'Love one another as I have loved you'.[159] I feel I have only grasped the second half by embracing the first. Until I rooted myself as part of 'one another', I found it very difficult to love, or know myself and therefore grasp what it is to be loved by another. I had a limited view of what that could be. I saw myself through distorted lenses, rather than within a clearing which integrates me with others.

This expanding relationship with all life and nature, and within that God, is a slightly heady experience. But how does it affect my interactions with other humans? How do I see and value them?

We must recognise that we can only really grasp how we see ourselves and others from our own perspective, however much we seek to understand; we will always be viewing people through our own lenses. In our identity workshop there were people who felt they were a human spirit, here for one life only and only present in human form. There were others who felt they were purely spirit, not specific to a creature and could easily have become an animal. Others felt they were animal in essence. Yet as has already been mentioned, the common thread was our responsibility to step out and intervene in suffering. However we perceived the identity of our core spirit, the common experience of our human bodies creates compassion and a responsibility towards the hurting. This went beyond human suffering to an experience of the earth as

---

159 John 13:34-35

suffering. Even with differing worldviews concerning whether life on earth is fundamentally good or bad, the overarching theme was this sense of compassion.

What happens in community when this is the overarching theme and we see nature as part of our community? How do we respond to a hurting earth, remembering we are part of that earth?

Within the research group we all instantly noted our only option was; we work with her to heal. We adapt our practical life to walk gently, love mercy and seek justice.[160] Easier said than done; but in this change of identity brought about through my relationship with nature, there have been instinctive changes in practice. Some have come as a result of educating myself on the issues affecting our earth, others have arrived more intuitively. Yet even with a change in mind-set, not every change in practice I might see as necessary has automatically followed. I have for some years been vegetarian and only bought fair trade or recycled clothes and advocated for fair trade. These decisions have been a result of a deep conviction that it is better for the earth and the people in it. This is a result of being educated in the issues and these values being instilled in me by my mother. However, I still use my car regularly and am not very good at recycling consistently. I seek to walk gently on the land and to make changes, but sometimes these changes go beyond what I am currently willing to embrace and I find myself asking what it would take to make these changes? This may not only come down to my own motivation and organisation but also dramatic shifts in whole communities and governments. The environmental crisis is very real. Even taking into consideration new realisations from scientists such as James Lovelock who now admits climate change is happening slower than expected; it is still

---

160 Micah 6:8

happening.[161] Will a change in perception help us to adapt to this reality and live and breathe alongside the earth, rather than in competition with her?

The community dynamics of nature fascinate me, the way one part speaks to another. We can so often be separated from this. What would it look like to include her in our conversations? If you follow a spiritual path you may be used to allowing space for spirit to be involved and have their say. Your ears and minds are readily attuned for that voice.

Are we attuned to including nature in our worship? Luke 19 tells us that if people stop crying out, the rocks will cry out. People often use this as an admonishment to either be louder or more visible in their worship. However, might it also be the case that regardless of whether humans are praising and worshipping, the rocks will be, the trees will be, the animals will be crying out?

Psalm 148 portrays a picture of co-worshipping with the whole of nature. The Psalm is a call to worship for all creatures. It is human centred but simply because of the human perspective of the psalmist. But are humans mentioned last because they are perhaps the most reluctant to worship? It is certainly true from the psalmists' point of view that not all kings of the world were following his God however, he calls them just as he exalts the mountains and the sea monsters in their worship.[162] This and many other calls to worship with all creatures animate and inanimate[163] gives us a beautiful picture

161 Johnston, I. (2012). *'Gaia'* Scientist James Lovelock: I was 'alarmist' about climate change. Published 23 April 2012 on MSNBC. com (accessed via www.jameslovelock.org on 1/3/2014)

162 Bauckham, R (2010) *Bible and Ecology; rediscovering the community of creation*. London: Darton, Longman and Todd Ltd, p 78

163 Psalm 69:34; 89:12; 96:11-12; 97:7-8; 103:22; 1Chronicles.16:31-33; Isaiah 35:1-2; 43:20; 55:12, Philippians 2:10; Revelation 5:13

of co-worshipping with nature. We come alongside nature, not in competition with her.

Looking at these concepts practically for a moment; it might be useful to look at theories of community dynamics to help us negotiate the personification of nature. We currently negotiate a postmodern western society. We are told that thought and experience is relative. With this relativity, we deconstruct our thoughts and systems, and challenge concepts of truth.

This deconstruction has us question whether the concept of nature is even real, just as postmodern society has questioned and deconstructed God into ideas. Perhaps our society has projected our own image of nature onto it in order to feed our own agenda? Do we only believe nature is fundamentally 'good' because we desire a baseline moral structure to judge ourselves against?

There is plenty of evidence in ecology to suggest that this isn't the case, that nature really does work together well in community and the natural structures on the earth are 'good', but equally we look at the destruction that's possible in an act of nature and mourn. It's an interesting thought which I think is important to consider when communicating with nature. Are we merely projecting onto and personifying nature into our ideal image?

When we look at the idea of animism in community we are bringing together two worlds, the ancient world of tradition and text, through poetry, scripture and ancient philosophy, as well as the world of science mapping out our natural history and our current philosophies that expose our religion and thought to be social constructions. This itself is a picture of post-modern art and architecture, fusing the old with the new.[164] We have a romantic and poetic view of nature twinned with our material experience.

When we play with ideas of nature, it is difficult to draw ourselves down to examine the social background we inhabit because it feels as though we are watching an entity that is at once the oldest on the planet and disconnected from the intricacies of modern society and at the same time entirely present, to be felt and touched and seen and experienced in context.

I think it's important to recognise this may be another set of lenses. When we include nature in our community, are we personifying her and incorporating her into a construction she is not really a part of? Or are we including her, an equal partner in our discourse?

Perhaps both are true. Indeed it may be that we are allowing ourselves to become part of her community.

I am continually surprised and sometimes baffled by the experiences I am having in nature, but I can't deny the benefit this experience is bringing to my own life. This is really the only measuring block I have; how is it affecting me and how am I affecting the world as a result.

I could look at my own faith development, and that of others exploring nature connection from a human development perspective. It would be possible to view my journey in reference to Fowler's theory of faith development,[165] and indeed, such a theory is built on an assumption from Piaget[166] that the whole of nature consists of logical structures and connections which progress and evolve in patterns that can be observed

164 Wallace, M.I. 2005. *Finding God in the Sing-ing River.* Minneapolis; Fortress Press
165 Fowler, J. 1976. *Stages in faith: the structural-developmental approach. In Values and Moral Development,* ed. T. Hennessy: NY: Paulist Press.
166 Piaget, Jean. 1970. *'Piaget's Theory'* in Carmichael's Manual of Child Psychology, 3rd edition, ed. Paul A. Mussen; New York, John Wiley and Sons

and followed. This theory might be attractive when we talk of Gaia as a single complex organism. However, this theory tends to ignore our own individual 'meaning making'. It is in essence a modernist theory which does not sit well in the post-modernity which we inhabit. Fowler's theory has become so popular in the last few decades that many people measure their own and others journey against his hierarchical, invariant and sequential stages of faith. When someone begins to incorporate new aspects into their faith, or to reconsider the universality of their faith, it would be easy to look at that as maturation or a 'step up'. This suggests a question of whether I am simply moving through a natural progression of faith development in my own life, or is something wider happening among those who are looking at nature connection. Is what I am taking part in part of a paradigm shift towards a human identity that participates with nature?

So with the stripping down of many lenses, where do we find ourselves? I find myself both small and yet significant. I have purpose and a role and responsibility, and within my little world I am vitally important. But I am within a greater cosmic ecosystem and I am but a tiny part of this. This inspires the divine in me. It lifts my eyes to the other that is bigger and more infinite than we can know. I finish with this passage from Jergen Moltman's lectures on 'God in Creation'. For me it sums up the identity of human, spirit and nature and my place within its rhythms.

'Through the spirit we are bound together with the natural environment. This association is a system comprising human beings and nature. We might describe it as a spiritual ecosystem. Through the spirit, human societies as part-systems are bound up with the ecosystem 'earth' (Gaia); for human societies live in and from the recurring cycles of earth and sun, air and water, day and night, summer and winter. So human beings are participants and sub-systems of the cosmic life system, and of the divine Spirit that lives in it.'[167].

Helen Bradley *is a youth worker living in Wiltshire and facilitator of Avalon Forest church. She is also studying for an MA in youth and community work with practical theology and basing her research around nature connection.*

167 Moltman, J. (translated 1985) *'God in Creation, An ecological doctrine of creation. The Gifford Lectures 1984-1985'* SCM Press Ltd: London, p 18

Chapter 12 – Nick Thorpe

An Oceanic God

ONE day in the late sixth century an Irish friar called Cormac clambered gingerly into his leather coracle and pushed off from the shore. He was soon drifting upon the unknown depths, with no firm idea of where he was going. Nowadays he'd be ticked off by coastguards for being irresponsible. Back then he was following a long-established spiritual practice.

Peregrinatio, or religious voyaging, was a Celtic discipline which the holy men undertook as a kind of sea-borne pilgrimage. There was something about offering themselves to the whims of the elements - particularly the untameable, seemingly limitless sea and sky - which connected their mortal bodies to eternity. Some deliberately navigated vast distances, St Brendan famously crossing the Atlantic. Others simply cast themselves off, trusting God to guide them to their pre-ordained "desert in the ocean': a holy island or outpost from which to contemplate their Creator. The most famous of the *peregrini* was St Columba, a miscreant warrior-prince who sailed to Iona in penance for lives sacrificed in battle, and subsequently converted wide tracts of pagan Scotland to Christianity. His experience seemed to show that if you kept your eyes and heart open you would know your destination when you found it. It was called *seeking the place of your resurrection.*

But what if you never arrived there? Cormac of the Sea appears to have struggled a little in this regard. Born into a Cork family of mariners, he was a likeable but seemingly frustrated man, who 'not less than three times went in search of a desert in the ocean, but did not find it'.[168] Little has been written about this third-division saint, save what is preserved in Columba's rather airbrushed biography (by Adamnan),[169] in which he features mainly as a troubled friend sorely in need of direction. But I rather like the sound of him, and identify with his very human struggles to find his place within the natural world. I am both attracted and frightened by the untameable, dangerous enormity of nature. I seem to need the perspective that it brings, the reminder that forces much bigger than me are at work. I wonder if Cormac felt the same inner pull.

In one typically colourful incident, the friar was fourteen days into a dogged northward sail in search of his place of resurrection when Columba (based on Iona) obtained 'prophetic knowledge' that his friend was in danger. As Cormac and his crew battled against swarms of "loathsome and annoying insects" which stung them, clogged their oars and battered the leather hull, Columba called the faithful to prayer, and – hey presto - the wind changed and blew the boat back to Iona. When I first read this story I couldn't help feeling a little irritated on Cormac's behalf. Might he not have preferred simply to carry on without the attacking creatures rather than come back to base and start his search all over again? Instinctively siding with the spiritual underdog, I felt sympathetic to his impulse to go on travelling away from institutional religion, like a naked hermit crab scuttling around in search of a roomier shell.

---

168 St Adamnan, *Life of St Columba* (Penguin Classics 1995)
169 Ibid

Postmodern Peregrinatio

Or perhaps that was simply *my* agenda. I was undergoing a *peregrinatio* of my own when I first heard of Cormac, having set off from Edinburgh on a sort of spiritual sabbatical, hitching around the canals, rivers and coastline of Scotland on other people's boats. It was an attempt to get to know my adopted country a little better, to create some space and perspective, and work out what remained of my rather dog-eared faith. Crossing the Sound of Jura in a steam puffer I had visited a tiny uninhabited islet that bore the name of this lesser-known saint, and excavated what little there was to know about him in the ship's library. I liked the sound of him almost immediately. He seemed my kind of mystic, a lover of wide skies, bracing winds and rolling ocean: the Patron Saint of Wanderlust.

As things turned out, less than a week later I was invited to join a crew of Christians trying to reconstruct Columba's journey to Iona in a canvas-skinned curragh. It was exhilarating to feel the flexing and twisting of the wooden frame against the muscular waves, to pull hard at the oars as we shot through tidal races knowing that only millimetres of oiled cloth separated us from the deep. A humbling, visceral, holy experience of our vulnerability in the natural world.

And yet the voyage had a certain presumption about it too. The expedition leader, an Americanised Scot called Donald, felt that God wanted us to preach to the inhabitants of islands we briefly visited. On a couple of occasions he beseeched Jesus confidently for a change in wind and weather, just as Columba had done (though in the end the emergency outboard motor proved a better bet). I felt much closer to Cormac than Columba as I wrestled with the oars and questioned the cheery certainty. I was reminded uncomfortably of my own missionary days as a teenager, and the domesticated God I espoused back then. I struggled with the idea of a Creator who was willing to be at our beck and call while somehow omitting to step in and halt famine or natural disasters.

"It's not that I don't believe in God," I explained to Donald. "But I don't see how you can be so sure He's personally sponsoring the expedition."

"Of course He is," said Donald, impatiently.

Cormac and Columba continued to experience similar tensions. Cormac, an early embodiment of the refrain "I still haven't found what I'm looking for", launched repeated trips into the Atlantic and up towards the Orkney Islands, while Columba waited confidently to inform him why God hadn't yet revealed his destination. On one occasion his failure was apparently due to a crewman's omission to ask his abbot's permission – which seemed to me a disappointingly bureaucratic quibble from the creator of the universe. Increasingly, Columba was convinced his itinerant brother should simply go home to Ireland.

'Though thou travel the world over,' he warned in a typically finger-wagging prophecy, 'it is in Durrow thy resurrection shall be.'

Fingal's Cave

Working my own way northwards on different vessels, I often thought of Cormac and Columba and their different journeys. Why did one find spiritual fulfilment, the other only wanderlust? Was it simply a personality thing? Or had Cormac's perpetual travelling indeed become a way of avoiding going home? The thought haunted me: perhaps the traveller's itch, the impulse to "find oneself", was simply, as the US writer

Wendell Berry has suggested, "the easiest form of self-flattery - a way to construe procrastination as a virtue."[170]

Yet I identified strongly with Cormac's determination to keep scanning the horizon, to stay connected with the vastness of the natural world, instead of rushing back to the safe harbour of pat explanations and theology which never quite rang true. A boatman I met after our arrival on Iona made me more hesitant than ever to accept easy answers, or the idea of nature benevolently mirroring divine will. Davie had lost both his father and his son at sea – one killed while unloading wood for Iona Abbey, the other drowned when his rowing boat overturned - and was understandably sceptical about Donald's assertions that God had guided us safely to the island. 'To be honest with you," said Davie, "if anyone says to me they're a Christian, I look at them and think: *what are you hiding?*"

We were circling the island of Staffa at the time, passing the gaping mouth of Fingal's Cave, its hexagonal basalt pillars of sixty-million-year-old lava amplifying the boom of the sea. Davie looked at me suddenly. 'What do *you* think?'

'I struggle to believe,' I said, hesitantly. 'I think it's complicated.'

He nodded, swinging us back round towards the landing stage, ready to pick up the passengers for the return leg. 'It's this honesty thing: you have to be honest about what's there,' he said, a whimsical look in his eye. He throttled back, nodding towards the cave. 'Some folk look at Staffa and tell you those are vertical columns. But if you look more closely, a lot of them are subtly twisted or slanting. Truth is rarely a simple thing – it's all about perception.'

170 Berry, Wendell: *The Unsettling of America: Culture and Agriculture* Sierra Club Books (1997)

He had a point. The columns weren't straight, though the mind corrected them almost automatically. It was a shame really, because when you looked carefully, their kinks and slants and cracks were what made them interesting, hinting at vast pressures and tectonic shifts below.

Wolves At The Door

Dare we allow ourselves to be wooed by a natural world that is both beautiful and dangerous? A world which brings death as readily as life? Or is our default role as humans always to tame it or resolve it or somehow shut it out?

I had worked my way around to Fraserburgh on the corner of the Moray coast before I managed to find out whether Cormac eventually followed Columba's advice. Googling in a public library while awaiting a lift to Shetland, I was discouraged to learn not only that had he returned to Durrow as instructed, but – if two folkloric websites were correct – that his love of the natural world had been shattered in a quite spectacular manner. He was barely back in his old Irish parish when a fellow cleric had issued a prophecy: that Cormac would be torn to pieces by wolves.

As an evocation of nature red in tooth and claw, it's an image difficult to forget, and the fable records its devastating psychological effect on the man once fearless enough to push northwards into slate-grey seas. Now terrified, he erected a strong round stone tower and retreated inside in panic, pulling up his food and drink through a hole or window at the top, hoping to keep the wolves at bay. Yet it was all in vain. 'One day,' ran the fable, 'upon looking out he saw two black snails crawling up the side of the tower, slowly changing shape.' As they slid inside, they morphed back into the form of wolves, chased him out into the fields and, with somewhat wearying inevitability, tore him to pieces.

It was "only" folklore, of course – the martyr's spilt blood had miraculously become springs of healing holy water – and yet such tales often carry a deeper psychological truth. As a classic bulwark against the natural world, the tower also seemed to me a powerful metaphor for the kind of belief that is based on fear, and the need to preserve purity and certainty. How could a man famed for his seagoing bravery and navigational skill have allowed his life to shrink to such a tiny frame of reference? How did someone who took on the uncertainty of storms and sea monsters and ever-changing horizons become this cowering wretch, walled in by his own private war on terror?

Seafarers' Faith

By contrast, the danger and uncertainty of the sea seemed to me to inspire a more honest form of faith. After five months of travelling on ships I had met many wheelhouse philosophers, all well aware of the provisionality of life on the undulating surface of the deep. I had hitched aboard a fishing boat whose nets had recently crushed and killed the skipper, and shared lunch on a cargo boat with a terminally ill man who had attended the Piper Alpha disaster. The sea never let you forget we are only ever potential moments from death. My nautical acquaintances adopted various strategies for facing this fact. Some went in for lucky charms, banned words or talismanic Gideon Bibles at the helm. But the ones I really admired seemed somehow to balance the complex truth of human frailty with a primal joy in the moment - and a navigational skill that interacted with the dynamic contingencies of tide and weather.

Returning home, I moved across Edinburgh to live in the old fishing village of Newhaven, with a view over red rooftops to the infinitely changeable sea: frosted, smooth, serrated, languid, sky-blue or platinum-grey, rain-pocked or dissected by an oily line of arbitrary wind. At times it can be as still as glass, sucking gently at the breakwater, the next day wild and jagged-toothed, slavering around the harbour walls. Sometimes the sun lights up Fife like the promised land across the Jordan. Sometimes the sea mist rolls silently up the estuary and there's nothing but the blank, ragged edge of the universe.

After my sea pilgrimage I resolved to allow myself a broader, more open-handed belief: less fretful about the details of doctrine, more willing to let complex realities clash, and mysteries remain. There even came a time, not long afterwards, when I thought my faith had gone for good. It was more peaceful than I expected, almost a relief – like looking down on the wet mud of an empty harbour after the tide had gone out. But then, helping a friend through a crisis – *doing*, in other words, rather than pondering - I found the inexplicable Something seeping back again, lifting the boats, lapping at the stonework. I'm learning to let go and stop trying to force myself to believe things, stop trying to understand it all. Or at least trying to stop trying.

When I find myself getting lost in my head, it is always nature which brings me back, whether that means pottering in my back garden, walking the dog, or paddling out onto the water in my canoe to rise and fall with the waves.

The Hazards Of Certainty

It's our gift and our curse to want to explain things fully. But it turns out even Cormac, the patron saint of wanderlust, had a rather more nuanced ending than his gothic legend implied. My further research reveals that the real Cormac of the Sea actually spent his last twenty years – 'the happiest period in his stormy life'[171] – ministering to the needy from his tower

---

171 Andrew L Shaw, *The History of Ballyboy, Kilcormac and Kil-loughy* (Kilcormac Historical Society 1999)

back home in Ireland. Yet if it was the place of his resurrection, it also turned out to be the place of his violent death: he was indeed savaged by wolves, probably while strolling in the woods.

Perhaps it was a fitting end for a man who loved nature in all its brutal beauty. But it's easy to sympathise with those who felt it necessary to do some posthumous embroidering of the tale: adding the prophesy, the cowering, the morphing snails to give some sort of answer to the question *why*. To bring some narrative order to a vast and sometimes terrifying universe.

I see this impulse in myself – not least in my polarised fascination with the symbols of sea and tower, my desire not to be enclosed at any cost. "I don't like the idea of living in a tower," I confessed to a wise ex-minister who gives me spiritual direction from time to time. I saw the tower as an embattled monument to religion, whose heavy blocks of doctrine I had grown tired of defending. "I'm definitely looking for a seafarer's faith… and yet sometimes I find myself wishing there was somewhere solid to come back to, just to rest…"

My spiritual director raised his eyebrows and gently stated the obvious. "Don't you think we need both? Sea *and* tower?"

Holy H2O

And he's right, of course. Nature itself is a yin/yang of permanence and flux - the reliability of seasons changing, the invitability of both birth and death - and my seafarer's spirituality ultimately demands the same balance. Every navigator knows we'd be lost without a few fundamentals: a compass of some kind, a sound hull, working mast and sails, tide tables and a chart - as well as the confidence that you'll interpret them honestly and correctly in the constant flux of a changing voyage.

And what is a lighthouse, if not a form of tower? Life, like seafaring, is about questioning our perceptions every now and then, making sure the rock is where you think it is, keeping all the information dynamic in the mix, keep the clutter off the chart table. And never forgetting the astonishing reality of tides pulled by the moon, of sudden sea mists and whirlpools.

Indeed, perhaps water itself is the best symbol for the divine mystery which sustains us. Leonardo da Vinci set out to understand water, much as the theologian tries to apprehend the Almighty. It was part scientific quest, part phobia. He had seen the River Arno burst its banks and wanted to pin down this elusive, destructive, creative substance of life. His notebooks were full of sketches of swirling eddies, apocalyptic floods and great storms, along with various devices to control or divert them: canals and lock gates, a street-washing system, plans for draining a marsh. His aim was as all-embracing as you'd expect from Leonardo: 'Describe all the forms taken by water from its greatest to its smallest wave, and their causes.'

More than five centuries later, water remains an enigma. We do, of course, know a little more than Leonardo about its iconic triptych of oxygen flanked by two hydrogen atoms. Under an electron microscope the anarchic moshing of its molecules reveals itself to be a force for transformation, coaxing and fostering reactions from other chemicals, making connections between things. Yet we can't really explain why. Scientists admit there is, as yet, no universal theory of water, or even a master equation for all its properties. Despite wave tanks and test labs and all the successors to Leonardo's whorled sketches, we still have no idea why a raindrop will sometimes slalom down a perfectly smooth car window; why whirlpools blort and eddy as erratically as they do. We don't know why our eyes leak tears when we're sad.

It's as elusive as love, as ordinary and as magical as the boiling of a kettle – that miraculous conversion of agitated molecules taking flight and becoming almost air. Water was the formless chaos from which all creation was brought forth, whether by the Holy Spirit brooding over the watery wastes or *Homo sapiens* evolving from the primeval soup. We think we know water, and yet the deepest oceans of our blue planet are scarcely more familiar to us now than in the age when maps were etched with sea monsters. We know more about the surfaces of Mars and Venus than the bottom of certain Scottish lochs.

The water of life. It protects us in our mothers' wombs, makes up 80 per cent of our bodies, mists us with the aura of its presence in every breath we take. Perhaps that's the best we can say about our quest for God, our ambivalent relationship with the untameable natural world.

In the end it's as simple and as complex as water.

Nick Thorpe is an award winning writer, journalist and speaker. His travel memoir, Adrift in Caledonia: Boat-hitching for the Unenlightened (Abacus 2007), from which this essay is adapted, was a BBC Radio 4 Book of the Week. His most recent book is Urban Worrier: Adventures in the Lost Art of Letting Go (Abacus 2012). www.nickthorpe.co.uk.

Chapter 13 – Paul Cudby

Friendships across the Divide:
A Theology of Encounter

An Experiential religion?

'Arboreal exchanges of affection may occur'.

This comment, written by Bruce Stanley to describe an aspect of 'The Grove', Forest Church's presence at the 2013 Green-belt Festival, brought many wry smiles to the faces of the participants. Those who have taken active roles in the ecology movement have long been ridiculed as being nothing more than a bunch of tree-huggers, and now those of us who are involved in forging, or at least acknowledging, a spiritual connection with the natural world are having to face the possibilities of similar ridicule with the added spice of spiritual suspicion. Christians with a more conservative theological stance have a tendency to dismiss new ideas as diluting the truth and so the role of this article is to take a deeper and more theological look at the possibilities of 'arboreal exchanges of affection' in order to understand some of what might actually be taking place. My hope is that by putting this within the context of Trinitarian theology I might be able to allay the fears of some whilst provoking debate amongst others, and because Christianity is an experiential religion, not merely a dogmatic one, narrative will take a large part in what I describe. It is also important that I add that, as within any shared experience, the conclusions that I have drawn from what has taken place are not necessarily the same as others who were present since it is wholly possible for the same experience to speak to different individuals in different ways and on different levels.

Understanding the difficulties

Ancient Arden Forest Church, led by a core group of five of us with my wife, Alison Eve, as the main liturgist, meets under the canopy of a delightful cedar tree in the vicarage garden looking across a meadow. Gradually the cedar has been taken to the hearts of the participants and is now often talked of as the 'guardian' of the space we use. But what do we mean by this? Many people name their cars and even assign personalities to them. Is that what we intend by adopting our old cedar? Is it just a friendly mascot that we have anthropomorphised into something it could never be? Or is there something taking place at a much deeper level? Some within Christianity view such a possibility as being tantamount to communing with demons but for others who have genuine experience, rather than a superficial dismissing of anything outside their narrow theology, there is a sense of connection, almost of companionship, with the natural world both within and beyond the animal kingdom. A form of Animism can often be found lurking not far beneath our logical scientific culture. Jenny (not her real name) is an elderly parishioner who I have known for some time. She has a lively and active Christian faith which is quite conservative in nature, yet she talks to her houseplants and has affirmed to me that her companionship and friendship helps them to grow. Jenny would never dream of attaching the label of Pagan to herself so this serves as a simple example of an intuitive 'feel' that many people have. If this connection is genuine rather than imagined then we need to explore two difficult questions:

1. What/who exactly are we communicating with?
2. How can we be communicating?

The answers to these questions is the subject of this article, but in order to understand just how difficult the first question is to answer we need to turn our attention to answering question two. Picture this scenario:

> *Alison, my wife, and I are sat at a dining room table with some acquaintances. The dinner topics range over a wide array of subjects. As I start to raise something of interest to me that I would like their opinion on there is a micro-second glance from my wife. No one else would have seen it, nor noticed the subtle change in tack from what I had originally intended, but that tiny glance communicated Alison's awareness that this topic might be more difficult to speak about, that it touched a raw nerve I had been unaware of, and that I should tread very carefully, and preferably in the opposite direction. Our guests remained oblivious to the unspoken words between us.*

Like a lot of couples who have been together for many years, Alison and I understand each other deeply. No one knows us like we know each other because the depths of intimacy, the time we have shared, and the sacramental bond we have nurtured means that we can non-verbally communicate more with a glance now than we could have said in an evening when we first met. Language, although not transcending words, often has little need for them. Yet it has taken us more than two decades to have reached this state of relationship; that's two decades of the day-to-day togetherness of two complementing members of the same species, bonded spiritually by the knitting of two souls in marriage. We can often know what the other is thinking, but then you would expect that to happen.

I do not pretend to have this kind of relationship with other friends, let alone acquaintances, where a glance cannot hope to communicate a sentence. Yet despite this knowledge of the difficulties of non-verbal communication within our own species, we almost blithely accept that we can somehow communicate with other members of the natural world. Indeed this is at the heart of the Pagan beliefs and experiences surrounding Animism and I find myself concerned at what seems almost like arrogance to be questioning the experiences of others. Yet there remains inherent in this a puzzle and the question we have to ask is, how can we be communicating? The answer to that question is dependent on us recognising the need to reject, or at the very least question, some of the assumptions Christians have historically made whilst at the same time challenging our notion of awareness, all of which leads us to try and deal with question one...

When Nature Stares Back...

I've described the non-verbal communication with my wife, and we are all aware of the ability of humans to transfer ideas by the written word, provided a common language is shared, but what about across the species divide? Obviously the written word is beyond us since writing is a skill possessed only by humans, but verbal and non-verbal communication can certainly take place between us and other members of the animal kingdom. Anyone who has shared their living space with a dog will know of the seemingly almost telepathic abilities that canines have to comprehend our emotions. Clearly commands can be learned but dogs seem to be able to go far beyond this to stunning levels of empathy. Romero, Konno and Hasegawa[172] have recently shown empathic yawning by

172 T. Romero, A Konno, T. Hasegawa, "Familiarity Bias and Physiological Responses in Contagious Yawning by Dogs Support Link to Empathy", PLOS ONE, August 2013, Volume 8, Issue 8, e71365

dogs in response to yawns by their human partners. Intriguingly a canine response was not demonstrated when the human yawns were faked or when yawns came from strangers in a room, regardless of whether they were real or fake. This is just one of numerous studies from a more scientific realm that show that we connect on some level with other non-human animal species. Yet when one is considering a spiritual connection with nature this is only the first step. It is necessary that we take a further, more perturbing step, to consider consciousness beyond the animal world. This takes us into areas that are usually more at home within Pagan paths which are characterised by Animism and its philosophical partner, panpsychism. Animism is far too often caricatured by those who have done insufficient research as merely a primitive religion that ascribes human-like consciousness to rocks. Animism, for the modern Pagan, is far more deeply thought out than this, as evidenced by recent books such The Wakeful World[173]. A comment which perhaps summarises the whole movement could be this from Graham Harvey[174]:

> *Animists are people who recognise that the world is full of persons, only some of whom are human, and that life is always lived in relationship with others.*

There is within this statement a deep world of mystery that is not in any way in conflict with the basic tenets of the Christian faith, simply because this is not something we have developed a theology for. I suspect that this absence is probably due to the ease with which many Christians tend to dismiss out of hand (or simply not consider) the experiential claims of those whose religions are not Abrahamic in origin. The closest we are likely to come is to lump Animism into the same box as

www.plosone.org/article/fetchObject.action?uri=info%3Adoi%2F
10.1371%2Fjournal.pone.0071365&representation=PDF
173 Restall Orr E., *The Wakeful World*, Winchester: Moon Books, 2012, 272.
174 Harvey G., *Animism*, London: Hurst and Co., 2005, xi

the kind of worship of idols so condemned in the Bible when in reality there is no connection between the two whatsoever. There is, however, the need to observe some caution. Harvey's statement does not contain nor convey any form of anthropomorphism. In other words his description of Animism does not imply that the consciousnesses in question are remotely human-like. This is instead a simple proposition, that consciousness within the natural world is not limited to humans alone, and indeed may utterly transcend the animal world. How far one wishes to take this depends on the individual and their experiences. Many modern western Christians live in a technological, anthropocentric, city-based society and are adept at assigning value to something depending on its use as a commodity. For those who function within this culture these ideas must seem like an anathema, yet if we are to move forwards in nature connection we have to take seriously the experiences of people who do feel a genuine sense of communication. For some this is little more than sitting by a sea shore being lulled to sleep by the peaceful sound of the lapping waves, but for others the connection can go much further.

So for the remainder of this article I want us to journey through three stories, taking what I have outlined above, in order to set out a theological mechanism for how the connection may take place. The three stories are all personal ones rather than borrowed from another source, and outline a progression from that which falls within recognised theology to that about which we can only speculate. Each has an arrow, a direction, which conveys something of who appears to have initiated the experience. The first is about a divine to human experience; the second is about a human to nature experience and the third *may be* a nature to human experience. I am far more speculative about this third example for reasons that will become plain, but for the sake of completion it needs to be included. This is also the chronological order in which they took place which suggests to me a divine leading that has been aimed at overcoming my own inner misgivings, coming as I do from what was once a fairly conservative theological standing. In a sense by writing this I am inviting you along to see a part of how I feel I have been led by God into recognising God's all-pervading presence within the natural world, whilst recognising that the thoughts and ideas shared here represent a snapshot of my own developing theology regarding the world of which we are a part.

Story One: the Divine-Human encounter

> Alison and I have gone on a journey into the forest. For me this was with an express purpose of experiencing the presence of God in the natural world whilst for Alison it was a part of a spiritual exercise. We begin by following one of many pathways but after a while, following Alison's intuitive lead, we leave the path and walk into the trees. We stop to scatter some seeds for those we sometimes call the 'Little Friends', those for whom this forest is their natural home. They don't need our seeds, they have plenty to forage for here, but whenever we visit the homes of our human friends we often take a gift like a bottle of wine or a box of chocolates, so it seems only friendly to do the same here. We then embark on a form of prayer walking - a way of treading slowly and carefully, listening out with all our senses, trying to become tuned to the song God is playing within creation.

> After a while we come to what simply seems like the right place. It seems right purely because we have been walking slowly and quietly and have become aware of some noise up ahead which seems to be coming in our direction, so we crouch down and wait, listening as the disturbance comes towards us. Within moments the forest is filled with the sound and vision of squirrels chasing each other. Neither of us have ever seen so many squirrels in one place at one

time. Usually they seem to be single or in pairs, and just occasionally we have seen three, but here there are many more, running after each other up and down trees, across the ground, circling and chasing excitedly. Then almost as soon as they have arrived they disappear, vanishing off into the forest, leaving us alone.

Yet this sense of being on our own lasts only momentarily. We stand up slowly then with just a hoot of warning a huge owl sweeps down in front of us, maybe no more than an arm's length from our bodies, before sweeping up into the trees, and as she sweeps past us so there comes to me a very clear sense of divine presence. I have known God's presence on many times in my life, but never like this. As I reflect now I think of Elijah's encounter when God was not in the earthquake, wind or fire, but after they passed there was the sound of stillness which was the presence of God. That is how this feels, an unmistakeably divine sense of presence and welcome. God was not in the squirrel nor the owl, they were simply heralds, trumpeting the coming One. What is so unusual for me, though, is that whilst the presence seems to me to be unmistakably God, for the first time in my life it is also very feminine. I simply cannot explain this - it must be experienced for there to be understanding on the part of another, but this, and a similar experience in another woodland just a fortnight later with exactly the same sense of presence, though encountered elsewhere, convinced me of both the genderfulness of God (that we are created in God's image, both male and female), and the presence of God throughout creation.

From an Animist perspective this kind of experience is not uncommon in ritual. Harvey[175] notes:

....
175 Ibid. 91.

> *More than once animals from the wood's edge or*
> *neighbouring fields were encountered in the depths of the*
> *woods, or acted in unusual ways seemingly indicative of*
> *welcome intentionally offered.*

And:[176]

> *...owls, herons and crows are not rare in Britain, but I have*
> *witnessed them fly in ways that have been taken to indicate*
> *participation and benediction on Pagan celebrations or*
> *activities. Merely flying past a celebrant... might seem*
> *significant only to that person or their friends. However*
> *the unusual physical proximity that sometimes occurs in*
> *encounters between particular birds and particular humans*
> *can be considered to be deliberate acts of communicative*
> *intimacy.*

For an Animist, the encounter I have described might be thought of as a show of welcome and acknowledgement from the forest to Alison and me, and that in itself may be true but seems to me to be an incomplete picture of what took place. What has led me to this belief is simply that an identical sense of welcome, as if from the same person, took place in another forest many miles from the first encounter, and with none of the unusual animal activity. The second 'welcome' took place in a simple moment of silent appreciation.

This experience changed my understanding both of the natural world and of God. I know we are created in God's image, as affirmed in Genesis 1, and that the image is contained by both male and female together. It logically follows that God must have aspects that are what we would define as feminine, yet hitherto all my encounters with God had felt powerful or gentle yet always masculine. Here though, in the forests I encountered God as 'She'. I experienced for myself what I

---

176 Ibid. 103.

had affirmed for many years. The 'head-knowledge' became 'heart-knowledge' because of God's initiation within the natural world, using some of its elements and residents to draw us nearer.

This, however, was not the end of the journey. Having convinced me that the natural world was a place of divine and animal encounter, this second story takes us deeper into a place where many Christian theologies fall short. In this second story is a sense of human - nature interaction, or as Bruce Stanley has put it to us on a couple of occasions, 'When you stare at nature - nature stares back.'

Story Two: Human-Nature Encounter

The Wyre Forest, near Kidderminster is close to our hearts and a delightful place to walk. In the winter of early 2012 Alison and I went for a wander through the Forest. Towards the end of our walk we chanced upon an unusual pairing of trees. Much of the woodland through which we had walked was oak with the occasional yew in their midst, but we found on this occasion an ancient yew tree with an oak growing up and enveloped within her boughs, their union so intimate that their trunks rested against each other. This represents such an unusual pairing because the yew is known for being very poisonous, making it difficult for anything to grow within her shadow. To us this beautiful pairing read like nature's way of affirming the possibilities of reconciliation. We left the forest that day with a real sense of wonder at having found them.

A few months later I went on a period of study leave, touring the country living in a caravan and talking to Pagans in order to learn about their beliefs in order that I could work in this interfaith space from a place of knowledge rather than speculation. As we settled back into some kind of routine on our return in the early autumn, so our thoughts returned to the oak and yew in the Wyre forest. Having not visited for more than six months we returned wondering how we could ever hope to find that unique pairing again. The leaves were full on the trees giving the whole forest a different appearance from our last visit. So we stood on the edge of the forest, on a path that we knew was not the one we had taken the first time, and we simply 'listened'. By this I mean we tried to still ourselves to heighten our awareness of our surroundings through our senses. The Wyre Forest is criss-crossed with numerous paths and so it was not long before we came to one such crossing, giving us three choices. To understand how difficult this is for me you need to consider that I have absolutely no sense of direction whatsoever, and so if the sun is not visible (such as in a thick forest) I have no hope of finding my way around. Alison had gone to look at a little brook, so I stood at the crossroad with my senses as tightly tuned as I could, 'listening' for the direction. And so it gradually seemed as if the birdsong was louder in one direction than any other, and that had a sense of rightness, almost invitation, about it. When Alison returned I tried to explain which direction we should take. She was slightly bemused, knowing how hopeless I am with directions, but agreed to go with my impression. This was how we continued, with both of us 'listening' closely at each division of paths, and throughout the journey there were little encounters with the natural world as we followed our impressions, confirming a sense of rightness to the paths we took. We passed a ring of wild mushrooms that seemed to be centred on a tree; a deer in the mist to our left; and then finally, as we came towards a bend in the path, a large black stag ambled across the track in front of us. We felt a growing sense of excitement and sure enough, as we rounded the bend, off to the left of

> *the path was the thickening of the trees consistent with a yew, but not just any yew. This was the yew embracing her oak. Starting from what we knew was a different path, and simply by 'listening' closely to the cues from the natural world around us, we had walked straight to them.*

As Christians, what are we to make of this? We explained this to two friends of ours, both on the Druid path, and took them to the same pairing. By now we now knew the way yet even then they picked up on little signs such as a bird that seemed to sit and wait for us, then fly on ahead and wait again as if to say, 'Follow me. I know what you're looking for and it's this way.' This of course is to anthropomorphise outrageously! Nevertheless our friends, who are far more adept at this than we are, were not at all surprised at what we explained had happened. They took it in their stride, but I was left with the query that, coming from a Christian metaphysic, what was I to make of what had taken place?

Story Three: The Nature-Human Encounter

Even as we affirm the possibility that we may listen to how the natural world speaks when we ask a question, so we also need to recognise the possibility that the connection may be two-way. What follows is perhaps rather more speculative purely because it challenges me more than any other encounter when I take into account both my scientific and theological training.

> *We have observed a rather unusual 'happening' around our 'Guardian' cedar. I record this incident with some trepidation because my scientific training wishes to affirm that nothing can be proven unless it is repeatable whilst my spirituality affirms that there is rarely anything repeatable in the mystical paths we seek to tread within the Christian faith. God is personal, not some experiment that must always respond in a repeatable fashion. Therefore it is*

necessary sometimes to observe apparent 'coincidences' and
allow them to ask us probing questions. Since we began
Ancient Arden Forest Church a rather curious thing has
taken place. At face-value it may mean nothing, but the
imagery is important. Out of the roots of our cedar, and
right up against its trunk, two new trees have begun to
grow; a small oak tree and a small holly tree. To the casual
observer this may be nothing more than happy coincidence
but within British folklore the oak tree and the holly
tree play a major part in the cycle of the seasons. The oak
represents the Oak King who rules from midwinter until
midsummer whilst the holly represents the Holly King who
rules from midsummer until midwinter, and whose presence
has found its way into many Christian practices of bringing
sprigs of holly into the house as decoration for Christmas.
They battle it out each year with the Oak King reaching
the height of his strength at the summer solstice before being
defeated by the Holly King who reaches the height of his
strength at the winter solstice before being defeated by the
Oak King. It is, for us, an intriguing observation that the
arrival of these two plants seems to have coincided with
the advent of Forest Church and its practice in the space
under the cedar. We are, of course, aware that in order for
a plant to grow there must be a seed that is planted, yet
having an oak and a holly growing out of the northern faces
of our cedar, on the north western and north eastern sides
respectively, at this time and in this place, has given us all
pause for thought.

These are just a very limited representation of experiences of
connecting with nature spiritually. Yet as I have said throughout, there is a genuine question of the difficulty in imagining
how this could take place. Unless we strongly anthropomorphise the natural world, assigning for example the presence of
tree-spirits, (dryads), with whom we can readily communicate,

there must be an almost insurmountable difficulty in under-standing how we can connect with consciousnesses which, if they exist, must be extraordinarily different from our own. Across these three stories are three different ways of connecting with nature. In the first we have little difficulty in incorporat-ing it within a Christian framework because it was for me so rooted in a divine-human encounter taking place within the natural world, and we have biblical examples, such as Moses and the burning bush or Elijah in the cleft of a rock, where similar encounters have taken place. However the second and the third encounters become progressively more difficult to understand, leading us to have to make a choice between four options. We can adopt a wholesale Animist approach; we can reject them as purely speculative coincidences; we can reject them as dangerous encounters with demons, or we can recognise that it is possible to describe a theology of what took place, and is taking place for many of us, which can be described using biblical ideas. Whilst I have some affinity for the first option, the way in which a sense of identical divine encounter took place in two different locations leads me to want to further investigate the theological possibilities within my own tradition.

The Panentheistic Connection

Panentheism is a compound Greek word made up of pan (eve-rything), en (in), and theos (God). It literally translates as 'all things in God' but is also often understood to mean 'God in all things'. It is quite different from a Pagan understanding of the world as pantheistic which means 'all things *are* God', suggesting that you and I, and all that can be observed and/or perceived are part of one divine whole. I suspect that most people within the Forest Church movement or who would think of themselves as Christians within the Celtic stream would affirm their belief in panentheism which describes how

God is present to us because God pervades all that we are, but at the same time God is also separate from us as One who is both immanent *and* transcendent. This has many different applications, some of which are discussed elsewhere within this book, but for the purposes of this article I am taking it to mean that God's presence can be observed within the natural world because God pervades the natural world, and indeed I would go so far as to suggest that the natural world and the whole created order exists only because it exists in God. Were God to remove God's presence it would simply cease to exist.

I choose to recognise this as another manifestation of the Holy Spirit; that the Spirit is present throughout. Now lest we over-romanticise this, as modern Celtic Christians have been wont to do, we have to accept and be challenged by the reality that if God is in the beautiful mountains and hilltops, then God is also in the volcano and the tsunami, which is a different article for a different time. However, if we affirm the presence of the Spirit of God within all things then we have a mechanism for understanding what is actually taking place within these encounters; for understanding how the connection is taking place. The answer is there for us in the words of Christ in Matthew's Gospel:

> *"Are not two sparrows sold for a penny? Yet not one of them will fall to the ground unperceived by your Father. And even the hairs of your head are all counted."*
>
> *Matthew 10:29-30*

I have queried throughout how it can be that, if the world around us possesses a consciousness other than our own, how can we possibly interact with it, yet here, for us, is the answer - we connect through the Holy Spirit, defined by John V. Taylor as 'The Go-Between God'[177]. In other words what I

---

177 Taylor John V., *The Go-Between God,* London: SCM Press, 1975.

am suggesting is that although we may feel as if we are connecting directly with the natural world, logic dictates that we cannot do this directly across the species divide because whatever consciousness exists beyond humanity must be a different (and in some cases profoundly different) kind of consciousness because it exists within a very different physical medium. Therefore we cannot be directly aware of the consciousness of an other-than-human life, but what we can be aware of is God's perception of that consciousness. Christ made it clear in the above verse from Matthew's Gospel that God is aware of everything that takes place within the world, a kind of conscious awareness that is infinitely beyond human abilities. I cannot find my way around a forest, but by listening to the Spirit of God what I can do is 'tune in' so that I can be aware of God's awareness of the life of the forest. We can thus take this further into the more speculative realm and suggest that although the cedar's awareness of the Forest Church meeting under its boughs, if such an awareness exists, must be beyond our understanding, yet in the same Holy Spirit it may become aware of the Spirit's awareness of what we are doing and be able to respond, if indeed we wish to assign an other-than-human consciousness to the 'Guardian' cedar. Panentheism opens the gateway for us to understand that in Christ, through the mediation of the Holy Spirit, all things are connected and may be aware of the Spirit's awareness of all things, thereby becoming the medium through which communication takes place. In this way Trinitarian theology has a vital role to play in nature connection.

A Theology of Encounter?

I have been very careful to refer to this with the indefinite article as 'A Theology of Encounter', and I am aware that, from an Animist perspective I have not considered the issue of animal or tree spirits here. To do so would fall beyond the confines of this chapter. What I hope I have achieved is to offer an analysis within the Christian tradition of what are for many of us a new set of experiences. I have attempted to follow the model of the Anglican Church which I serve by using scripture, reason and tradition to understand experience, although there is very little tradition here beyond a tradition of suspicion which has a tendency to limit our beliefs rather than giving us the freedom in Christ to explore. I do not expect that this will be the last theological word on these matters, and I reserve the right to change my opinion as new information and ideas become available. This therefore represents a snapshot, from early 2014, of some of what we have experienced and some of my own ideas regarding their interpretation.

Many of us within the Forest Church movement have had to cope with suspicion that we are a syncretistic group who seek to bind Christianity and Paganism into a new religion, yet what I find here is instead a deep call to prayer, to learning how to be still, how to be silent and how to listen. Far from being a subtle Paganism creeping into our Christianity I have instead been inspired by our Pagan friends and their ideas and experiences to look more closely at my own beliefs and encounters, and begin to recognise that nature connection is actually a call to prayer. Through a deep and lasting prayerfully lived life, so God's awareness of the natural world of which we are a part may become present to us, potentially leading to a joint celebration or working with willing 'other-than-human' persons. Nature connection is ultimately God connection, for it is only through the Holy Spirit who pervades all things that we can make the connection.

***Paul Cudby** used to be a scientist but is now vicar in Tanworth in Arden. In addition to working with Forest Church he has a yearning for better interfaith* *relationships with the Pagan community which he works at through being the Bishop of Birmingham's adviser for New Religious Movements. Married to Alison Eve, he plays drums and percussion for her and with Eve and the Garden, and is currently working on a book about understanding Paganism.*

Chapter 14 – Bruce Stanley

Deepening Nature Connection

New Year 2014

January 1st, the winter rhythm of nature slows. I live on the eastern edge of an upland wilderness known as the Cambrian Mountains in mid Wales, the least populated area of England and Wales. A place with big skies holding the drama of red kites and buzzards dodging mobbing crows and the night sky showing every star. The place feels wild and big, to some eyes the land looks sheep-wrecked[178] but it is beautiful nevertheless. A lively stream runs through the garden which responds quickly to any rainfall on the hills above; its babbling song turning into a white noise after heavy rain, as soothing as it is concerning when heard in the middle of the night. Half a mile from my home it joins the upper reaches of the Wye. I wonder if one day when the river is in spate I might kayak from my front garden to my mother's house in Rhayader, 10 miles away as the salmon swims. The stretch is known as the widow-maker so maybe not.

---

178 George Monbeot, *Feral: Searching for enchantment on the frontiers of rewilding* (Allen Lane, 30 May 2013).

The house we live in is named after the geographical feature it is built near, following the convention of many Welsh place names. Literally foot-of-the-escarpment[179] in our case. The land and nature of the place shape and affect its human inhabitants too. I notice this most starkly when I'm in a city. I've been changed by this place that feels more like it owns me than vice versa. We speak anthropocentrically about God calling us to particular places as if there is something in it for us or other people but I've begun to think that God may call us to the nature in a place too – that we might better connect with the unique expression of God's Divine Spirit in the location, and if we're listening, better represent its needs.

Living more in tune with the rhythms of nature was part of the point of moving here but remaining in step isn't easy. I have a deep dissonance in the depths of winter. It is easy to imagine that the season calls for stillness, silence and solitude but there is also an unquiet, restless, coiled urge to begin and do. I work on patience in the waiting, there is more winter to come. It may be getting lighter but it's going to get colder before it gets warmer; this is the thermal lag of the northern hemisphere that always tests me. I have to wait till the 19th of January,[180] roughly a month after the Winter Solstice, to celebrate the turning point. Nature too is coiled. In my corner of the world I look at the buds of the birch, the nettle tips and jack by the hedge, some of the most likely candidates to hoof-it at the B of Bang. Birds are reading nature too, wondering when to start this year's race.

This rhythm and its dancers are, for me, evidence of Divine presence. Nature is not pretty wallpaper, it is the living, complex, on-going, enveloping evidence of God's power and

179 Troed-yr-Esgair.
180 The day when the land of the northern hemisphere stops cooling and begins to warm. However February in the UK still has marginally colder air temperature on average than January.

quality[181] – and it's a dance we're invited to participate in, body and soul rather than merely visit.[182] I'm drawn, as so many are, towards this way of viscerally experiencing God, not just through quiet interior practice but rather by full immersion, every part of me engaged.

Nature is the book God writes directly. It's tricky to read, open to interpretation and communicates in surprising ways, rewarding the participant rather than the armchair onlooker. Learning the language of nature is as tricky as any language but nature is God's book so it has to be worth it.

Sensing the connection

If participation with nature is the aim of the dance, there are two steps to the practice: connect and put the time in. Connection can happen in various ways; through our senses, feelings and intuition, our imagination and intellect and our soul and spirit. Different people at different times favour different ways but I would argue connecting through the senses in the present moment is the foundation.

Much like the disproportionate benefits reaped by other simple practices (prayer and meditation for example) there is a lot to gain from just sitting and being present with the language and rhythm of nature. Each day I spend time at what is called a 'sit-spot', a place as surrounded by nature as possible, but a suburban back garden works fine, where I immerse myself in the presence of nature. Visiting the same place (within very easy access of my home otherwise I'm unlikely to do it) teaches me the basics of the tune and the subtle shifts, changes and embellishments added today, this week, this season. The first robin, the field fair flock, the spreading alarm calls as some

....

181 Romans 1:20
182 For example: Taste and see that the Lord is good. Psalm 34:8.

predator is detected by the resident passerines,[183] the sun reaching its furthest southerly rising, cirrostratus clouds heralding a new front, stronger smells indicating a drop in air pressure. I sit still and wait for the baseline to settle to my intrusion and engage my awareness. Connecting through the senses can start with the famous five, seeing, hearing etc but growing evidence and a lot of experience tells me there are more. Mainstream researchers into the subject list anywhere from 11 to 53[184] different senses[185] and they're the ones that science can measure. There are others that science hasn't nailed down yet that exist within the natural world.

For example, the way some places feel, their 'vibe' or 'energy', Celtic Christian language might describe their *anima loci* or *genius loci*, the location's soul or spirit. Some people find that through physical touch some elements in nature seem to have a detectable emotion, energy or vibration. Another fascinating area involves the sending and detecting of intention, such as the sense of being stared at, which has some convincing laboratory research supporting it as does the ability of humans and animals to detect intentions at a distance, beyond the line of sight.[186]

Have we got a problem?

None of these examples involves occult or spiritual practices identified by mainstream Christian theology as dangerous or unacceptable[187] but they can get dismissed or caught up in the same blanket condemnation. Partly because we don't have any alternative explanations for them. Take the sense of being

....

183 Territorial, resident perching birds tell us most through bird language.

184 Michael J. Cohen, *Reconnecting With Nature* (Ecopress, 2007).

185 Richard Louv, *The Nature Principle: Human Restoration and the End of Nature-Deficit Disorder* (Algonquin Books, 2011).

186 Rupert Sheldrake, *The Sense Of Being Stared At: And Other Aspects of the Extended Mind* (Arrow, 2004).

187 Deuteronomy 18:10.

stared at as an example; it's instinctively unsettling for people who think that there is nothing that is purely of us, our thoughts and senses for example, that stretch beyond our bodies. Anything that does stretch beyond our bodies is down to the work of separate spiritual powers', an example might be how we understand prayer works. There doesn't seem to be a common theology for the other possibility which is that there is something, an extended mind/sense, not of a third party spiritual force, that does stretch beyond our physical shells.

If participation with nature is to develop as an important aspect of Christian cosmology and practice, then how we connect with it is something we're going to need to investigate. If the basis for our understanding of nature connection is limited (and incorrect), so will our further thinking be. The suspicious (and sometimes superstitious) counter to that is the pervasive reaction that exploring such subtle and amorphous territory is understandable amongst first-nations or tribal people or those easily dismissed New-Agers or the less prestigious university departments – but is barmy for the modern, orthodox, rational Christian. What is the foundation for that reaction?

Our separateness from nature is an illusion and the idea that our minds and senses are contained within our skin comes from a materialist, rational understanding that is so pervasive we only consciously experience the alternatives if we're aware of our conditioning. Once we begin to recognise a wider understanding, rather than sweep them under the carpet we should bring some light to them, research them and develop a theology for them. I'm the least qualified to do the great theological task – I'm rather more in the tradition of the experiential mystics, but I trust God (no less than if I identified as a charismatic evangelical) who seems to be drawing me forward.

What I'm encouraging here is a subtle reappraisal of what it means to sense and connect with nature without the dualistic, enlightenment conditioning. If there are senses beyond the five, the implications are at the very least a rediscovery of a fuller expression of what it means to be human connected with God's creation: more vibrancy, more wonder and awe, feeling part of a richer, wider community and feeling more alive having exercised more facets of our abilities. Games are a good way to experience what I'm hinting at as play gives us permission to think differently.

Permission to explore

I play the following two games regularly in the nature connection workshops I facilitate. They originate from techniques food gathering cultures used to train their new hunters in nature connection. I think they illustrate that these super senses are very much part of nature and not in the least bit supernatural.

The first game I've facilitated a number of times asks a participant to find their way back to a tree they've previously been led to blindfolded. The conventional senses play a big part but often when participants are forced to 'feel' their way through other senses, beyond the five, they subsequently prove they're adept at using – I've yet to have a participant not find their tree. No training is required, it seems these latent abilities are just below the surface and often participants feel a profound sense of achievement and connection to their tree.

One story of the original version describes a much longer journey and the young hunter spending a day with a tree. Then they'd be led back to the start in silence via a different route. To sense and feel the way back to the tree was a sign the hunter was ready to graduate. The abilities this game was honing were vital to real life and the link between nature connection and survival. When you read the stories and techniques from American First Nations hunters you begin to understand that hunting prey (and avoiding becoming prey yourself) involved a very subtle interplay of awareness, attitude and energy sensitivity. Contemporary hunters holding guns or cameras tell supporting stories and, of those US soldiers most skilled in detecting the presence of hidden IED's or ambushes ahead of the patrol, many had either hunting or surviving the rigours of threatening urban environments in their youth[188] – sometimes the best way to avoid trouble is to sense it ahead before it senses you and make yourself invisible. Much of the wildlife we fail to see is doing that to us as we clomp along the path.[189] You'll know that both your field craft skills and your energy is improving when you begin to detect more.

The second game I want to describe is called silent stalker or fox the fox. It begins as a listening game but develops into something else. A participant stands blindfolded at the centre of a circle of all the other players. I ask the participant to choose a prey animal of some kind, she might decide to be a deer. I then ask the group to name some predators of deer and decide on a wolf. The person in the middle is blindfolded and I point silently at someone in the circle to be the predator. At first, the game works with the predator walking around the outside of the circle, back to their starting position and then into the middle to tap the prey on the shoulder. The prey has to listen and point at the predator to win. Nine times out of ten the prey detects the predator through listening and wins the game. Then we make it a bit harder, all the other participants make farmyard or jungle noises and some, but not all, prey participants work out quite quickly that to win they must draw on other senses. A further variation simply has the predator stand still and point at the prey embodying as best they can the intention of a hungry wolf. This is the most interesting stage of the game for me. Some people are so accurate and definite with a fast point straight at the predator the rest of the

188 Louv, *The Nature Principle*, Chapter 1.
189 Jon Young, *What the Robin Knows* (HMH, 2012).

group gasps in astonishment. I never explain beforehand what might be involved but questions come thick and fast after it has been played a few times. Often participants in workshops are very happy to play these games, the unease only creeps in for some once they begin to think about what is happening. Many similar games are available in two books written by Geoffrey Mcmullen.[190]

The sense of being stared at is one of the most well-researched of these phenomena along with telepathy and a number of others.[191] There is some overlap with the previous game but this time there is both the projecting and detecting of intent. There are equally surprising illustrations from combat scenarios; during the second world war, fighter pilots were told not to look directly at enemy pilots they were approaching because their gaze might be detected.

If there is a comfortable acceptance of these phenomenon within Christian theology I've yet to come across it but personal experience in my own life and through Forest Church encourages me to keep exploring albeit through uncharted territory. The Celtic tradition does have the idea that our souls extend beyond the margins of our bodies ... perhaps this is an explanation.

The next two illustrations are to do with the way some places or elements of nature feel.

Many of us are familiar with the concept of Thin Places, where the division between heaven and earth is barely there. 'Surely the Lord is in this place', we're left thinking.[192] By far the most powerful experience in my own life of such a place happened

190 Geoffrey McMullan, *Discover Nature Awareness, A collection of Nature-based games for adults and children* ... Vol 1&2 (Pathfinder UK, 2011, 2012)
191 Sheldrake, *Sense Of Being Stared At.*
192 Gen 28:16

at St Govan's in Pembrokeshire. I wasn't expecting any great revelation but visited the chapel out of curiosity.

Steep narrow steps lead straight down from the cliff edge to a semi-circular rocky bay; blocking the route down is St Govan's chapel, to get further you have to pass through the small chapel that features a cleft in the rock, roughly body shape, that was said to have opened to hide St Govan from pirates. Ok, legend over. I walked through the chapel down to explore the rocks and arches below with a growing sense that the place had something else to say but I wasn't sure what. In such circumstances it is easy for the intellect to find something to grasp – but the legend and its themes didn't seem to resonate with the now stronger, unexpected, emotional reaction that was developing in me. I glanced for a moment at Sara my wife patiently helping our 2½ year old daughter clamber over the rocks some distance away and then it came into focus. The small cove was powerfully resonating with an overwhelming sense of the enveloping, loving, caring Divine feminine side of God[193] and I found myself resting for some time in a sense of being embraced. Interestingly, when sharing this experience, others had had the same sense of a Divine feminine presence at St Govan's. Is God expressing something unique in that place or has the sense been cultivated by human interaction there? If the latter is the case, what are the ramifications?

The other story is about a tree. I was due to lead a nature connection and landscape reading workshop with a group of Celtic retreat walk leaders at a village in north east Carmarthenshire called Cilycwm. Research beforehand told me two interesting facts, firstly that the church was called St Michael's and within its grounds was one of the oldest yews in Wales, over 1500 years old. Those two features alone strongly suggest that

---

193 Which isn't to say that God's masculine side doesn't express those
things too or that the Divine feminine can be so stereotyped.

something fascinating had happened – perhaps there were still echoes detectable at the site.

Ancient churches are laid out following the cosmology (and sometimes geomancy) of the time which reveal some of the understanding the people had of the relationship between spirituality and the natural world.[194] We know that yew trees, especially groves often mark the site of pre Christian spiritual centres. Yew trees, one of three native evergreens in the UK, grow large, heavy side branches[195] which bend and reach the ground allowing them to grow into new trees, forming a circle, bestowing on the yew immortal connotations. So, this place was once a Pagan or Druid place of worship that wasn't easily quelled by the new church. How can we deduce this?

The church is unlikely to have been called St Michael's originally. The practice throughout Wales was to name the church after the local Celtic saint. When, during the reformation (or earlier), many churches were renamed, St Michael's (understood to be the saint who combats evil) was reserved for places where evil (in the eyes of the religious authorities) needed to be wiped out. Evil was understood to come from the north so cities often have a St Michael's north of the centre. Some old churches have a door in the north, opposite the south entrance, across from the font, which was opened, it was believed, to allow evil spirits to flee (north) during baptism. Anyway, this tiny village had a St Michael's. Someone at some time was trying to tell the people of Cilycwm something.[196]

All very fascinating but what about the tree. I arrived early in the village to see if the church had the door in the north and to see if there were more, older graves on the east and

....

194 Matin Palmer, *Sacred Land* (Piatkus, 2012).
195 Like holly, another understory tree, their branches seem unnecessarily strong for their height until you realize they evolved to withstand our now missing mega fauna such as mammoths and wooly rhinoceros.
196 Palmer, *Sacred Land,* 33 & 136.

south side and fewer at the north for the same cosmological reasons described before. And then I found the tree and what an impressive sight it was! Huge and obviously very old. Innocently and with no expectation I reached out and touched it and was immediately overcome with a powerful emotion of deep sadness and sorrow that seemed to be coming from the tree. Could it be that the spiritual conflict around this place was embodied in the tree? If so, does a tree have a spirit that shares some overlap with our own that enables us to connect with it in some way?

There can be more rational explanations for each of these experiences as I'm often the first to point out! Subconscious projection or giving more weight to what are really only random occurrences.[197] But there is credible research and testimony in their support.

The divisions between spirit and nature

I've chosen these two pairs of stories because they illustrate different aspects of the subject being explored, deeper connection with nature as God's creation. I'm satisfied that the first two games are using natural senses that we and other animals have, albeit ones that science can't measure yet. I call them super senses. If we were to recognise, embrace and exercise these senses, what might that mean for nature connection and participation? How might that affect our connection to and understanding of God?

I think the second two stories about St Govan's and Cilycwm are to do with spiritual elements present in a place (also undetectable to science, but more acceptable to Christians?). But instead of pursuing the detail of those two examples I want to broaden the thinking to the more general idea of the spiritual

....
197 Just as there is for prayer, healing and many other
accepted phenomena within Christian practice.

atmosphere of a place, its *genius loci,* because I think humans have a role to play in creating, developing and changing such atmospheres – which is relevant to Forest Church.

People experience certain places as feeling holy or sacred and some places as feeling dark or threatening. Often the holy places have hosted over the years countless deliberate interactions with God.[198] Ray Simpson talks about changing the spiritual dynamic of places through prayer and communion.[199] An interesting example might be the island of Iona that many would recognise as a significant thin place. Some Forest Churches that are meeting in the same location each time are beginning to sense something changing about the place where they meet, as if their actions are creating a resonance.

When comparing the stories, the clear divisions between what is explainable through natural senses and what has spiritual dynamics is often more blurred than I've described. The person detecting their way back to the tree, for example, may utilize both super senses and spiritual discernment. When Jesus knew what others were thinking,[200] was that a supernatural intervention or someone deeply in touch with a natural sense beyond the five that modern materialism champion?

In preparation for a recent landscape reading course, I located the site of a holy well, supposedly with healing properties, that gives the settlement and town of Llanidloes its foundation story. St Idloes' well is barely accessible at the back of a garage, behind unmarked wooden doors, down an unassuming side street. Without giving anything away I asked the group if the place had any sense or feeling. Some said they could feel an energy there and one girl said she felt as if there could have been a healing well close by. Whether she knew through

198 Nick Mayhew Smith, *Britain's Holiest Places* (Lifestyle Press, 2011).
199 Ray Simpson, *Healing the Land* (Kevin Mayhew Ltd, 2004), 20-26
200 Mark 2:8

spiritual means, detecting the signature spiritual identity of the place, or through other sensory vibrations I don't know. If it's the latter, maybe St Idloes detected the same vibrations before any Christian practice claimed the spot. There are, of course, some places that have never had sacraments or any human religion practiced in them, that nevertheless have a positive feel.

My own understanding is that God's Spirit is present in different ways in different places and things so that there is detectable a subtle and unique facet of God's presence just as the physical characteristics of what has been made are telling us about God.[201] God speaks through elements of nature throughout the Old Testament. Trees, hills[202] and the sky[203] above us, everything created[204] in fact is part of the conversation sometimes in personified ways. Perhaps connecting with the trees in your local park isn't such a shocking idea.

Through a monotheistic, panentheistic lens it may be healthy to re-examine and reconcile some elements of an animist view if that is possible. At an intuitive, pre-conceptual level animism or the personifying of things in nature is in our wiring. If this is how we are as unconditioned humans (tending to see nature as personified) it may be worth recognising one of the plusses that links personifying with loving. If we care about other persons, maybe deliberately seeing elements of nature as such can help us widen our compassion beyond humans and cute animals to Brothers Wind and Air and Sun, Sister Moon and Mother Earth.[205] Language is important, 'things' is such a poor way of referring to elements of nature, it doesn't

201 Romans 1:20
202 Isaiah 55:12
203 Psalm 19: 1-4
204 Psalm 148: 1-13
205 From St Frances' canticle, Brother Sun, Sister Moon.

encourage respect and care in the same way as we do when referring to persons.

Advice for explorers

Christians are understandably concerned about what is of them, of God, or of harmful spiritual influences because they don't want to get involved with the latter. So anything that seems at first glance spooky can be worrying, especially things that don't have a clean and clear bible reference or orthodox tradition in their support. We are on poorly charted territory here. Nevertheless it is worth repeating just how common these experiences are. I phoned a bishop up recently (of all people) who answered very surprised, 'I was just thinking about you'. I hadn't scheduled the call, I had an idle moment and suddenly decided to pick up the phone.[206] And if I asked a congregation of the most straight-laced Christians if any of them could describe a place that felt particularly holy to them, I'd be surprised if the majority couldn't do that. I am suggesting that we bring some superstition-free light to the subject.

For the cautious in faith this might not be the adventure for you but if this is an area you feel God is calling you to explore then wouldn't it be more healthy to do so without the nervous distraction of condemnation hanging over you? The safest way forward might fall into two parts, examine carefully the motivation and rationale for the journey and secondly put in place some acceptable parameters. I think both aspects involve love.

Why might God be calling us to a deeper connection with creation? Because we want to continue to connect with God in all ways and understand our advocacy of nature as thoroughly as possible, as participants not anthropocentrically. And because we love what God has called good and long to experience it

---

206 As many as 93% of people claim to have had a similar experience. See Sheldrake, *Sense Of Being Stared At,* 99.

more deeply which leads to greater commitment to care for it as God has asked us to.[207]

I am encouraging a gentle careful uncovering of latent nature connection abilities we've lost in our modern society. By way of support, you might talk these things through with trusted elders or spiritual directors. You can pray and ask God for guidance. You should test your call, work on your discernment and above all examine your motivation, if you make love your aim[208] then you're heading in the right direction.

Suggestions for exploration

I've used different conceptual models for nature connection or Reading the Second Book of God as I referred to it in Forest Church.[209] In that book I talked about study, awe and meaning. At other times I've talked about sense, imagination and spirit. Borrowing from Jung, a third model might be: sense, feel, intuit and think. In all of those it is clear that sense is the primary way in with feeling and intuition and imagination coming close behind. The focus of this piece is to encourage a deeper recognition of sensing, not as dualistic, materialistic, enlightenment thinking would have it but through following the subtle example of societies that still participate with nature.

The following suggestions are experiential exercises to explore and exercise your own super senses and understanding of genius loci.

1. **Visit a sit spot regularly.** Find somewhere as surrounded by nature as possible but a back garden or corner of a park works too if that is what is available. See if you can switch on your sensing and intuition as you search for this

....

207 Gen 2:15.
208 1 Cor 14: 1
209 Bruce Stanley, *Forest Church* (Mystic Christ Press, 2013).

place. Choose somewhere as close to your home as possible to make it easy to visit. Begin by getting to know the baseline of the place which will settle down after about 20 minutes of your arriving. Understand in time that as you sense, the place senses you; allow a kind of solidarity to develop. Recognise that the place will subtly reflect your inner state and will teach you much. For more about the bird language focus of sit spots, *What The Robin Knows* is a good way in.

2. **Create Thin Places.** Choose somewhere to pray and practice the sacraments and other Christian rituals. Repeat prayers to encourage God's light to come.

3. **Visit some holy places, hug some trees.** This can help heighten your own discernment of places. A good book and app to help is Nick Mayhew Smith's Britain's Holiest Places or you could look further afield with www.megalithic.co.uk.

4. **Test your sense of being stared at.** Rupert Sheldrake describes a simple test with two participants in his book The Sense of Being Stared At and online: https://www.sheldrake.org/participate/online-staring-experiment.

Bruce Stanley ran away from the circus to get involved in things even more creative. Most recently he's pioneered the Forest Church movement and works and writes to promote nature connection and participation with the hope that what we love we may care for more. These days he is to be found with his wife Sara somewhere on a beautiful hill farm in the Cambrian mountains where they're growing a permaculture forest garden.

The Sacred Circle: Elements of Ritual

The Dance

Quietly, we walk together to the circle which has been prepared with autumn leaves and fallen twigs.

We are uncertain but full of open-hearted expectancy, and a sense of rightness pervades our faltering first steps on this pathway. Singing a Trinitarian Celtic Caim, we describe a circle around ourselves, moving clockwise, and we take a long moment of silence to look and listen, to the trees that surround us, to the birds at work in the bushes close by, joining their song to ours, to the strange sense of something or someone else with us, holy, friendly, interested, supportive, amused, ordinary yet extra-ordinary.

The person standing in the North turns and addresses Mother Earth, the Womb of Creation, and clockwise we proceed around the circle to "Call The Quarters", with The Spirit of God, Breath of Life in the East, The Father of Life, passion and abundance in the South, and Christ, the Living, cleansing Water in the West. We have faced the four corners of the earth, honoured the voice of creation, and opened our eyes, ears and hearts to the immediate world of

*this gentle garden around us, and there is, in that moment,
a sense of encircling, a moving, a flowing of energy around
us in a loving and welcoming embrace.*

*I feel like we may just have started to wake up to something
important. Something that the birds and the trees already
know, but we humans just seem to have forgotten somehow:
That we are all woven into the web of life and being,
together with our little brothers and sisters the birds, the
squirrels, the trees and plants with whom we share this
garden, and with the very bones of the earth herself.*

Well over a year has passed since that Autumn twilight when
we began to explore where our hearts were leading us, and the
truth of our interwoven-ness has taken root within us. This
in-between place, out beyond the old certainties of a formative Christianity, is a strange space to find ourselves being
led to. However, "where you are when you don't know where
you are", is a precious and creative space full of possibility, a
"Gap", which sparks improvisation with an "unseen partner",
with the unknown.[210]

As we've developed in our ritual practice together in the place
of unknowing, we have indeed danced freely with new unseen
partners. We have explored this new space, which feels and
tastes ancient and primal somehow. Simply being outside,
connecting with nature seen and unseen, our many senses
opening out, we are becoming re-rooted in the changing seasons and the energies of the turning year, the currents from
which we have become disconnected in the modern world.

How can I have missed these before, I wonder as I wriggle
my fingers and toes into the damp needle-carpeted loam, and
nestle against the ancient Cedar in our garden. The Cedar

....
210 Nancy Stark Smith, 'Taking No For An Answer', Contact Quarterly,
vol.XII, no. 2, quoted in Bani Shorter, Susceptible To The Sacred: The Psychological Experience of Ritual, (Routledge, London, 1996), p. 106

has been a companion on my journey, and a guardian to the Ancient Arden Forest Church grove which meets beneath these welcoming branches, roots intertwining beneath us. In dance improvisation you have to let go and trust, particularly when working with a partner, but the joy of what you create between you is unmeasurable.

Our rituals have evolved and deepened. They have been devised by drawing upon the tools and resources of other contemporary earth-based Pagan spiritual pathways such as Druidry, and combining these with the skills gained from many years of experience with the Alternative Worship strands of contemporary Christian culture.[211] Those of us involved in leading Ancient Arden Forest Church have spent the vast majority of our lives planted deep in the spiritual ecology of the Christian Church in all its breadth and variety. It is formative, yes, and precious too, despite the differences we may have with many of our co-religionists. Christ, the Trinity, the Easter Story, these still resonate in our hearts and remain central as we explore an earth-based spiritual pathway.

As we let go and trust, finding our own new steps in this dance improvisation, it is Christ, the wild Lord of the Dance, who dances with us as we greet unknown and unseen partners. So we welcome you to our sacred circle.

The Circle

God is a circle whose centre is everywhere
and whose circumference is nowhere

211 I acknowledge that the use of Pagan resources may be contentious for many Christians (and some Pagans). We have debates within the Forest Church network too, so it is important to note that this approach is used by our branch of the many-faceted eco-system that is Forest Church. I will explore aspects of traditional, ancient and contemporary ritual and the ways in which we can incorporate these as a way of connecting in deeper and more meaningful ways to the Divine in and through nature. I hope that as this unfolds it will open up for you the possibilities, without the need for an apologetics for our approach.

A number of years ago, I found myself stepping through the portals of the Norman splendour that is Tewkesbury Abbey. Abbeys and cathedrals are always special places, but I was particularly awed on this occasion and it took a moment to realise why. For whatever reason, the chairs had been removed, and the cathedral was an open space, breathtaking, full of possibility, inviting me to dance and sing through its echoing cavernous regions, spinning in circles. I would do this to every church in the land if I could: Remove the fixed pews keeping us in line, regimented, boxed-in, knowing our place, being taught what to think by those at the front.

In much of our lives we "live and move and have our being"[212] in boxes and lines and rows, and these are shapes of separation and delineation, shapes replicated in almost every church. I imagine this God within which I live and move both as tender encircling womb, and vast cavern of possibility. But God is presented in church as linear. If we run and spin in circles in church we risk hitting the hard wooden surfaces of pews, as well as the resigned, weary defences of the folk who occupy those pews (just ask any 3 year old!).

The circle is a profound symbol for us to engage with, organic and womb-like, it reflects much of life's processes. There are the cycles of sun, moon and stars, in their ever-flowing patterns, the earth revolving, the deep slow elliptical dance of the solar system, the spinning of our galaxy around its supermassive black hole. In the study of symbolism known as sacred geometry, the circle is a potent, suggestive icon of eternity, of void, and nothingness, and has often been used to the divine source of all being, as we see in the quote attributed to De Cusa above. Pi is what mathematicians use to calculate the dimensions of a circle, but what is exciting about this is that

212 Acts 17:28

you never can get to the end of calculating it. A circle whispers to us about the infinite.

The circle is about mutuality, and many find it an inclusive, healing praxis within which to explore spirituality in community. In the circle each person is equal. Ancient Arden Forest Church, in common with many different spiritual communities, uses the circle as the primary mode of operation, and indeed, church house groups usually gather in a circle rather than replicate in miniature the chapel rows. It can be easier to communicate in a small circle as no one is excluded by being hidden behind rows of pews. But there is responsibility in a circle, which is why some prefer rows and lines. In a circle there is no back row where you can hide.

Each member of the circle has an unspoken responsibility both for the integrity of that circle, and for their own spiritual growth. Your spiritual journey is yours to make, it is your path, and in this sense Ancient Arden Forest Church is esoteric, in that each person is ultimately their own "teacher" in their inner hidden hearts. The flexibility of the small circle allows for the gentle encircling of someone in need, where we may be held by the circle in times of brokenness, and many of us have experienced the loving support and encircling that this offers. So rather than an audience model, the circle is a participative model. Theatre in the round draws the audience into the unfolding drama using the praxis of intimacy, and circle-based ritual also works with informality and intimacy.

We hold around ourselves our own intimate circle, one we often only feel when someone unexpectedly transgresses the boundary of our personal space. We are always in the centre of our own circle.

Take a moment to turn around in your space, and see if you can feel its circumference, feel yourself within your own body and within your own personal space.

Sometimes we may feel pulled away from our core, and scattered to the four winds. Much spiritual work is about integrating our circle, returning to our centre, combining the opposing forces that pull at us from the four corners of the earth. The circle helps us to understand how we can work with the Four Elements towards spiritual growth and integration. God is at the centre, and all around the circumference too - our circles are always held within the divine encircling.

Alexander Carmichael, in the 19th Century, collected many Gaelic prayers from the Hebrides and presented them in his compilation, the *Ortha Nan Gaidheal,* the Songs of the Gael, popularly known as the Carmina Gadelica. Within this compilation is found the evocative practice of the *Caim,* or protecting circle, which would be cast by turning around whilst drawing an invisible circle with an outstretched forefinger. At the same time the pray-er would call on the Trinity, on Jesus, Mary, Brighid, the angels or apostles, requesting their presence and power to create a circle offering protection from all manner of harm that could befall them.

In some Pagan rituals, the intention in casting a circle is to disconnect from the apparent world and journey to a mythical location in some other reality such as the underworld, so the energy the participants must put into casting the circle and calling the quarters, is intense and specific. This kind of circle-casting is not appropriate for Forest Church, because we are opening to the sacredness of everything around us and the shift is in us not in the space itself (this could also be said for many Pagan groups, especially Druids[213]). We may sometimes work deeply and intensely within our circle dealing with complex issues that the energy of the season is calling us to address, but the intent is never to remove ourselves from the world.

213 See *Ritual: A Guide To Life, Love And Inspiration,* Emma
Restall-Orr, (Thorsons, London, 2000,), p.86

Our intention is to connect ever more deeply to the land, to the divine spark at the heart of all being.

The circle we cast is a gentle grace and an encircling *Caim*.[214] In the name of the Sacred Three and the Christ of Peace we invite the protecting wings of the Spirit to enfold us as we meet together, holding us as we learn to open our spirits and hearts to the whole of creation around us, unfolding into the possibility of connection with all our relations, the animals and birds, the trees and the grass, the rhythm and breath of the ocean, the sun and the moon, the stars in their courses above, and the deep slow circle dance of the earth beneath our feet.

The Power of Four

> *The Lord said to Abram, … 'raise your eyes now, and look from the place where you are, northwards and southwards, and eastwards and westwards; for all the land that you see I will give to you and your offspring forever'*
>
> *Genesis 13:14*
>
> *Look around you now, and get a sense of your surroundings.*
>
> *Do you know which way is north? Are there any features to help you identify the cardinal points? Where is the sun in the sky, or the moon if it is a clear night? Do you feel the wind around you, where is it blowing from? Do you know what geological features lie in each direction, such as mountains, lakes, rivers, forests and oceans, urban conurbations, industrial centres, religious monuments?*

This sense of locating ourselves in time and space in both the local landscape and the wider cosmos hinted at by the distant horizon and the vast skies, is one of deep symbolic and practical significance to our ancestors, and many of the earthworks and wooden and stone circles which they built mark the pathways

---

214 Another meaning of the word Caim is grace.

of the celestial bodies that occupied the heavens. The number Four emerges as a powerful motif that humans employ to orientate themselves within their world. Ancient and enduring threads such as the Four Winds, the Four Elements, the Four Corners, the Four Cardinal Directions, are woven through the various archaeological and cultural remains of several different cultures.

Ancient Mesopotamian cultures used the directions of the principle winds blowing from the NW, NE, SE, NW to describe their world, and in Egypt (C.2000BCE) south was notated as 'front' – facing the Nile and the noon day sun - with north 'behind', east 'left', and west 'right'. An inscription referring to a Priestess of the Winds from ancient Mycenean Greece suggests that the cult of the Anemoi, the Four Winds, was established by the 13th Century BCE. A few centuries later, Homer names Boreas the north wind, Notos the south wind, Zephyrus the west wind, and Eurus as the east wind. The winds and the directions can also be found in the Hebrew bible which scholars suggest was written from c.600BCE, the Babylonian exile era. The *Four Winds* (*Arba ruchot* עַבְרָא תוֹחוּר) are summoned from the four corners of heaven, to scatter the Elam to all the winds.[215] Daniel sees the four winds of heaven stirring the great sea,[216] and there is Ezekiel whom we will explore below. When referring collectively to the cardinal directions, the more commonly employed phrase is: The ends of the earth, (*Qetzvot ha'aretz* צַרְאָה תוֹצְק)

> *You whom I took from the ends of the earth, and called from its farthest corners... Do not fear, for I am with you"*
>
> *Isaiah 41:8-10*

The significance of *Four* is etched deep into western culture through the work of Greek writers beginning with Empedocles,

---

215 Jeremiah 49:36
216 Daniel 7:2

in the 5th century BCE, who formulated the idea of earth, air, fire and water as the common *roots* of all things. Philolaos (c. 470-385BCE) connected these roots with the quarters of the zodiac circle, and in the 4th century BCE, Plato named them *elements*. Aristotle linked them to the paired humoral qualities developed earlier by Hippocrates, and the 3rd Century BCE Stoics gave just one quality to each of the elements.

This deep philosophical legacy alongside the biblical heritage was breathed-in by the early church, and absorbed into their world view. Mark's gospel, written around 65-75CE, quotes Jesus as saying: "Then he will send out the angels, and gather his elect from the four winds, from the ends of the earth to the ends of heaven."[217] In the book of *Revelation* also written in the latter decades of the 1st century CE, John sees the four angels standing at the four corners of the earth, holding back the four winds.[218] The 2nd century CE apologist, Athenagoras, argues in favour of resurrection based on God's ability to re-constitute the dispersed particles of a human which have been dissolved into the original elements, because God created all things by combining these elements.[219]

Irenaeus (d.202CE) uses these threads to weave his defence of the four canonical gospels: *"For, since there are four zones of the world... and four principal winds... it is fitting that [the church] should have four pillars."*[220] Irenaeus identifies Christ the Word as the one enthroned on the cherubim,[221] highlighting these angelic beings as four-faced, then proceeds to echo Ezekiel's

....

217 Mark 13:27
218 Revelation 7:1
219 "On The Resurrection Of The Dead" by Athenagoras, Edited by Alexander Roberts, Sir James, Arthur Cleveland Coxe, 1885
220 "Adversus Hereses" VIII, XI, 8. in A New Eusebius, J Stevenson, 1957/1999 SPCK, p.117
221 Psalm 80:1

vision of the '*something*' that came from the north in a stormy wind and a bright fiery cloud.[222]

> *In the middle of it was something like four living creatures... Each had four faces and.... four wings.... The four had the face of a human being, the face of a lion on the right side, the face of an ox on the left side, and the face of an eagle.*

> *Ezekiel 1:5, 6 & 10*

Paraphrasing Ezekiel, Irenaeus links the "living creature... like a lion"[223] with Mark, symbolising kingly authority, and the creature with the face of a man symbolising the incarnation of the Word, he associates with Matthew. Luke, is linked to the calf, and the sacrificial nature of Christ's ministry, and John, the eagle, symbolises the Holy Spirit hovering over the Church. These characters can be found in one of the most well-known illustrated gospels, the Book of Kells, scribed by Celtic monks in the 9th century CE.

In Old Irish, the word for cardinal point is aird, which was in use in Scotland up to at least the 19th century. In *Beannachadh Buana* (Reaping Bleassing) from the Carmina Gadelica, the farmer, before cutting the first corn, turns on his heel sun-wise

> *Bho 'n airde 'n ear gu ruig an iar, bho 'n airde tuath le gluasadh reidh, gu fior chre na h-airde deas. (From the airt of the east to the west, from the airt of the north with motion calm, to the very core of the airt of the south.)*[224]

One of the most famous Celtic Christian prayers, the Breast-plate of St Patrick, demonstrates the ancient Irish orientation, facing the east and the rising sun, the traditional direction of

222 Ezekiel 1:4-10

223 Ibid

224 Carmina Gadelica, Volume 1, by Alexander Carmicheal, [1900], at sacred-texts.com, 90. Beannachadh Buana (Reaping Blessing), pp248-9

the resurrection. Thus, in St Patrick's prayer, the word for left is the word for north, and the word for right also means south.[225]

Críst limm,	Christ with me,
Críst reum,	Christ before me
Críst im degaid	Christ behind me
Críst indium,	Christ in me,
Críst ísum,	Christ beneath me,
Críst uasum,	Christ above me,
Críst desum,	Christ on my right hand,
Críst tuathum,	Christ on my left hand,

Attributed to St Patrick c.450AD

This prayer brings us full circle, drawing together the threads of the four directions with the encircling *Caim* of our sacred circle. When weaving a circle it is traditional to walk deiseal. In the *Beannachadh Buana* above, the farmer turns "Rightways", "*Deiseil*" in the Gaelic, which is clockwise. The opposite direction is tuathal, anti-clockwise, and is used to close the ritual circle. It is also used in private meditation to create an inward pathway. Walking a labyrinth anti-clockwise is about journeying into the centre of our spiral, our souls.

These ancient, enduring threads have woven their way through the centuries, reinforcing links between the four elements, the four winds and directions. However, although strong commonalities seem to emerge which cross historical, spiritual and cultural boundaries, these are balanced by the great variety in the ways that the elements, the directions and their symbolic meanings are connected. In the Zohar, a 13th Century CE Jewish mystical text, the south is linked to the element of water, and the archangel Michael; The west is expressed through earth, and Raphael; In the north we find

....

225 Compare this with the song from the Carmina Gadelica above
and you see the same words translated as north and south.

fire, and Gabriel; Finally in the east is air, and Uriel.[226] The spiritual dance practice, Movement Medicine, follows a tradition possibly inherited from the founder's Peruvian Shamanic training: North=Air; East=Fire; South=Earth; West=Water.[227] In another Shamanic meditation east is associated with fire, south with water, west with earth, and north with air.[228] There are some traditions of Wicca that work with north=air; east=earth; south=fire; west=water.[229] A passing reference to ancient faery tradition has north=water; east=air; south=fire; west=earth. And there is no space here to consider the great diversity of spiritual meanings to be found amongst various North American native traditions.

What this means is that there are many different ways that humans have connected to the sacred in the land in which they find themselves, and there is no one *correct* series of correlations. Instead, these different systems provide us with insights into the energies that each direction offers, and resources for devising ritual. You may wish to focus on the four winds, the four oceans, the four seasons, the fours stages of a human lifespan, or the four archangels. It has even been known for ritualists to use the four houses of Hogwarts![230] It depends upon the intention behind your ritual. As previously suggested, Forest Church seeks to connect with the immanent immediacy of the Divine within the land, so one of the best ways to come up with meanings that work for your ritual community, is to spend time in the place where your ritual will take place.

....

226 Http://telshemesh.org/earth/the_four_elements_and_the_four_seasons
227 Movement Medicine: How to Awaken, Dance and Live Your Dreams, Susannah and Ya'Acov Darling Kahn, London, 2009, Hay House Publishing, Pg. 22
228 www.realmagick.com/7197/journey-to-the-four-directions/htm
229 "Calling the Quarters", by Aislynn: Http://www.rootsof-ritual.net/general/calling-the-quarters/ and "Re-Thinking The Watchtowers", Mike Nichols http://witchessabbats.com/index.php?option=com_content&view=article&id=50&Itemid=54
230 www.rootsofritual.net/general/callingthequarters, pg2 Slytherin = Water; Hufflepuff = Earth, Gryffindor = Fire; Ravenclaw = air

Ancient Arden Forest Church is UK based, and therefore we explore and interpret the ways that some British Pagan paths use the elements and the directions. The most popular set of associations we have found seems to be:

East = Air;
South = Fire;
West = Water;
North = Earth;

In Wicca, calling the quarters may involve summoning the Guardians, or the beings known as elementals, or simply the archetypal energies associated with each direction. These energies or beings aid the practitioner in the working of magic, and the efficacy of the ritual process. The calling is done with respectfully worded intention so that whatever is summoned works within safe boundaries. The ritual ends with releasing the energies or beings summoned. In Druidry, the intent is to connect with the energy and flow of life, along with a simultaneous working with the inner world of myth and archetype. Ritual practice creates an organic link between these inner and outer worlds. The quarters, often called Gateways, are opened, rather than called, allowing the energies to flow into the circle. Respectful, welcoming language is employed, and references may be made to mythical animals associated with the quarters such as bear in the north and hawk in the east.

In our Ancient Arden rituals we also use gentle welcoming language as we open up to the energies of the directions, *Hail and welcome!* and at the close *Hail and farewell!* For us this has more to do with opening ourselves to Spirit, Being, Divinity, as it is always already present around us, with us, within us, and our use of language reflects this belief in the Divine as present/presence in all things. The words are often loosely monotheistic or Trinitarian, gently expressing Christian understandings of Deity, yet remaining flexible and open enough that

Pagans who join us often feel able to meaningfully participate in the ritual.

Which direction to call first is a matter of tradition and personal preference, and at Ancient Arden we frequently change to reflect the season. As it is common to begin in the east, however, this is what we shall do now, proceeding around the circle, *deisil*, sun-wise, to the south, west and finishing with north. I invite you, wherever you are, to locate and face the east, the home of the rising sun.

East – Air

In the beginning... darkness covered the face of the deep, while a mighty wind from God, swept over the face of the waters.

Genesis 13: 14

When I was a teenager, folk from the local churches would gather at Old Redding each Easter to greet the rising sun and the Risen Lord. A local minister played his accordion, as we sang out 'Thine be the Glory', my voice hitching as the emotion of the story swept over me again. We've introduced this to the church my husband now leads, meeting in a field behind the churchyard, facing eastwards. Waiting for the sun to rise is a hushed and quiet thing, those last moments in the gloom of dawn are stretched out, and it feels like the earth is holding her breath. When that first sliver of burning red gold gleams over the horizon, you draw breath again. A new day has begun. The association of Easter, the resurrection and Christ's return with the east has led to the eastward orientation of churches, and the practice of burying people with feet facing east, so that on the day of resurrection, they will rise facing Christ as he returns.[231] When we think about awakening from sleep in the

---

231 Matthew 24:27

early morning we are reminded of the need to fully awaken from the sleep of unconscious living.

The east is about hope, new life, beginnings, the blossoming of the earth in spring after its long sojourn in the winter dark. At the start of our lives, after swimming in the waters of the womb, we emerge into the light and draw our first shocked breath. In "Breathe" one of the Nooma series of videos, Rob Bell talks about the name of God in Hebrew, the unpronounceable YHVH, as being the sound of breathing, Yod (breathe in), Hey (breathe out), Vav (in), Hey (out). We are born with God's name on our lips and death is when we can no longer breathe the name. In every waking and sleeping moment the name is on our lips, and "[i]t is the breath of God that [we] breathe – and [we] are unaware of it."[232] The dance of life is the sharing and giving of air between us and the trees, and we breathe together with all things.[233]

The opening words of Genesis could be translated as, "the *Spirit* of God swept over the waters", for the word used is חור _ *ruach*. This powerful little word means breath, wind, air, life, spirit, soul, mind, intellect, passion, direction. *Ruach* is the etymological root of the words inspiration and intuition. The hawk of dawn, the animal associated with the east in Druidry is about far-reaching vision and insight. Artistic inspiration and mindful illumination are thus located in this quarter. We catch a glimpse of an idea, the flash of inspiration comes to us, we sniff the air to gather its scent into our nostrils.[234]

Pneuma, is the New Testament word for Spirit, air, and wind: "The wind blows where it chooses", says Jesus to Nicodemus, "you hear the sound of it, but you do not know where it comes from or where it goes. So it is with everyone who is born of the

232 Theophilus of Antioch c.180CE
233 Teilhard de Chardin, The Hymn Of The Universe, New York: Harper & Row, 1965 p.
234 Another meaning of ruach, is to smell.

Spirit."[235] The air is invisible, intangible, and the unpredictability of the wind can be a powerful and destructive force, leaving us spinning in our dance with the unknown and the unseen. Hildegard of Bingen talks of being a "feather on the breath of God"[236] but this hints at a radical surrender to the elements that may not be comfortable for us. We think of St Brendan, casting his coracle out upon the seas at the mercy of winds, currents and tides. Pagans may be taught to use carefully worded intention so that they remain in control of the elements, and so that the *sylphs* or air elementals do not bring mayhem to the ritual. Instead the gospels and the mystics encourage us to release our control, surrender our agendas and in trust and acceptance lean into the wind, the breath of the Spirit.

> *Blow upon us, East Wind, the pregnant breath of the rising*
> *sun distilled with the anticipation of dawn.*
> *Breathe inspiration into our hearts,*
> *as the morning erupts with an orchestra of bird-song.*
> *We bid you hail and welcome!*
> **Hail and welcome!**
>
> *Alison Eve Cudby, Copyright © 2013, Ritualitas*[237]

South – Fire

Last summer was a rare gem of sunshine and warmth, with long days stretching on forever, and dinner parties out in the garden till dark, with open fires to take us deeper into the night. You could find me working outside with my computer or practising my harp under the shady canopy of our cedar tree. Such a delicious feeling of finally being able to uncurl, unfold and relax in the warmth. This is what the south is all

---

235 John 3:8
236 Letter To Pope Eugenius III, 1148, Hildegard of Bingen
237 From Ancient Arden's Spring Equinox ritual, 'Christ the Gardener'

about. We face the noonday sun in all its strength, we face the area of sky which never loses the sun, even in the darkest of days and the longest of nights. This quarter is associated with abundance, the earth in full bloom, the crops ripening in the fields. It is us in the strength and height of our powers. When someone is functioning at their peak we may speak of them as being on fire, or of firing on all cylinders.

Fire and light are amongst the most powerful symbols for the Divine – light of the world, burning bush, pillar of fire.[238] In the transfiguration of Christ, his countenance shines like the sun, and in John's powerful passage that we hear each Christmas, the light shines in the darkness and the dark is powerless to extinguish it.[239] There is a light in us too. Let your light shine, Jesus tells us, and do not hide it under a bushel, or a bowl.[240] The mystics talk about the divine spark in us, or the flames of love that burn in the deepest caverns of the heart, or how our dwelling place is in the "Flowing Light Of The Godhead"[241]

But there is also fear and destruction in fire, a terrifying democracy that indiscriminately transforms all it touches, reducing it to dust and air once more. The heat of the sun scorches the desert and only a few specially evolved plants and creatures can exist in this tough environment. Jesus spent 40 days in this harsh place facing down the devil, reminding us that under the scorching light of the sun, nothing can hide, and we too need to confront our demons and our shadows.[242]

. . . .

238 Exodus 3:2; Exodus 13:21; John 8:12
239 Matthew 17:2; John 1: 4-9
240 Matthew 5:14-16
241 Mechtild of Magdeburg, *The Flowing Light Of The Godhead,* Transl.
Frank Tobin (The Classics Of Western Spirituality, Paulist Press, New
York, 1998). See also St John of the cross, 'Living Flame Of Love'.
242 Matthew 4:1-10

Gathering around the fire late into the summer night, we recall that fire is at the heart of the human community. Fire is iconic of our developing civilizations, of forging weapons and firing industry, of tool making and cooking.

I will raise the hearth-fire as Mary would. The encirclement of Bride and of Mary On the fire, and on the floor, And on the household all.

We gather around the hearth fire to tell stories and share food as the long summer nights unfold in song and laughter.

Hail thou Sun, Eye of God, glorious Fire of the skies
Burning with growth and plenty.
Fire of God, call forth abundance within us this Summer Solstice
Hail and welcome! All: **Hail and welcome!**

Alison Eve Cudby, Copyright © 2013, Ritualitas[243]

West – Water

In Cornwall, by the sea at the mouth of Rocky Valley, the sea crashes up a narrow slice in the coastline, as the Trevillet river empties itself into the Atlantic. Lined with rocks, and overlooked by cliffs filled with the squeaking calls of choughs, it is a perilous and beautiful place, where the sea continues its relentless rhythm. We sit there at sunset, feeling the tidal pull that Tolkien evokes so well in the passing of the elves from the land of men to sail into the west.[244] The sea remains elusive and dark – surfers and sailors will tell you that you never really know the sea, it will always surprise, and those who dance upon its waves, do so respectfully. When you pull your boat or your board from the water, there is no sign that you were ever there. This indifference reminds us that we will surf the

----

243 From Ancient Arden's Summer Solstice ritual, 'In Full Bloom'
244 J.R.R. Tolkien, The Lord Of The Rings, (Unicorn, Unwin Paperbacks, London, 1983 Edition), see especially pages. 93 & 1066-9

tides of life for just a span, and then we will disappear into its depths without a trace.

The west is the place of the setting sun, associated with autumn, old age and wisdom. Deep pools of experience build up over the course of our lives, and are eventually emptied into the sea. There is the wisdom that comes with age, but there is also the wisdom that comes in a flash of instinctive knowing. The Salmon of wisdom, honoured at the western gateway by Druidry, lives in the pool at the source of the River Boyne, Ireland, and it is said that whoever eats the fish, instantly gains knowledge of all things. The story of Fionn MacCumhail, tells of a boy who received this wisdom accidentally, by licking his thumb when cooking the fish caught by his older companion.

Tracing the Trevillet towards the waterfall where St Nectan is said to have lived c.500CE, we encounter a beautiful glen alive with the melodic, rhythmic gurgling of the stream, dappled green branches stretching out over the sparkling waters, revelling in the refreshing flow. I often look at rivers and think of all the tears I have shed, running together in one stream to the sea. Sometimes we bottle our tears, staunch the flow of emotion, and the pressure builds up over time. They can flood towns and cities. Tears, like rain, are cleansing and releasing. They can come in a shock and a rush, taking you by surprise. These tears of emotion, contain more proteins and hormones than tears which wash away a speck of dirt, or keep the eye moist, and there is some suggestion that by eliminating these substances, the underlying feelings that gave rise to the tears are being washed away. Sometimes there is relief and letting go at the end of tears. Sometimes, there never seems to be an end - we could cry a river.

"As a deer longs for the running streams, so my soul thirsts for God" laments the Psalmist, and the exiles in Babylon sat and wept by the rivers, lamenting the loss of their home.[245] Jesus referred to a deep spiritual thirst when talking with the Samaritan woman by the well: *"The water that I will give will become in them a spring of water gushing up to eternal life."*[246] A deep well of Living Water lies within us at the core of our being, where the fountain of Life overflows into and through us. These living waters flood our hearts, the rhythm of the crash and swell relentlessly carving out new channels and shapes, just as the water which has thundered onto the rocks at St Nectan's Kieve for millennia, has slowly carved a hole and a huge basin, where the water collects before rushing onward to empty itself into the sea at Rocky Valley.

> *Christ of our hearts, the living water,*
> *By salmon and kingfisher, we welcome the welling-up*
> *within that follows the cleansing rush of nature's tides.*
> *By ebb and flow, river and rain, twilight and autumn,*
> *Christ, come to us with the blessings of the west.*
> *Hail and welcome!* **Hail and welcome!**
>
> *Alison Eve Cudby, Copyright © 2012/13, Ritualitas*[247]

North - Earth

Our Cedar Tree is a good listener. After spending sometime beneath his branches and making connection in that tenuous human to plant manner that is all guess work and instinct, I often sit with my back nestled up against his bark. I am always amazed at how there seems to be something between my shoulder-blades that connects, allowing me to feel myself as rooted too, strengthening the bond between us. All my worry and pain flows down into the dark earth. Ancient Arden

....

245 Psalm 42:1; Psalm 137:1-6
246 John 4:14
247 From Ancient Arden's Autumn Equinox ritual, 'Full Circle'

spends time in each ritual silently rooting down into the deep dark moist earth, and breathing in the energy like sap into our branches. Then, we bow close to the earth, getting our hands and noses into the grass and the soil where we often spend a long moment. The earth smells rich with life and possibility, and it is worth getting down onto your hands and knees to experience the loamy scent of active soil.

In spring and summer we saw the manifest fecundity of the earth kindled on the branches, but as we move around the wheel of the year into winter, the trees have become dormant, the energy going down into the roots rather than into the branches. Leaves have fallen and everything rests. In the dark earth the nurturing of the buried seed takes place, and this is a powerful association between North and Earth. The winter darkness, the cold winds that bring snows down from the north, the tall mountains that hold their snow well into the summer. This is about resting, hibernating, being still. The bear is considered at this gateway, now long gone from Britain but still with us mythically, and we think of her hibernating in her mountain cave through the winter.

One of the deep symbols of this direction is the tomb/womb, the deep cave in the rock, another way of contemplating the nurturing depths of the earth. That which seems dead is resting and being nourished in the darkness, it is the place both of death and re-birth, and in this way we see the earth as the womb of the Mother. We may differ from one another as to whether this is an icon of the God the Mother, or a fully incarnated expression of God the Mother, but in ritual it matters not. However, we all share this place of birth and burial, we are all formed of the dust and the clay, and will all return to it once again.

This clay from which we are formed, the shifting plates of the earth shaping the landscape as we now inhabit it, has been in formation long before life appeared, long before humans emerged in their existential separation and imagined themselves orphans from the stars. For spans of time that we can't fully imagine, the landscape existed without us, without any animal life, and from this we emerged, with the temerity to claim ownership. Long before Genesis declared human "dominion... over every creeping thing that creeps upon the earth"[248], humanity had begun to exert its influence over the landscape, pitting itself against the wilds of the planet to survive. Not even 200 years ago, landowners turfed highlanders out of their ancestral lands and homes in order to farm and clear 'their' land. Land rights and ownership has become one of the weapons that humanity has employed in the last handful of centuries to oppress other humans. "The earth is the Lord's" proclaims the Psalmist, and everything in it, including ourselves.[249] If explorations like Forest Church can play a tiny part in the radical change needed in how we view ourselves in relation to the earth, then it will have been worthwhile. Because it is the land which owns us, not the other way around. Our Mother is the earth, her blood runs through our veins, and the whole clan of humanity belongs to her, flesh of her flesh and bone of her bone.[250]

> *O Mother Earth and Sister Death,*
> *Mighty badger and Great Bear,*
> *You bring us winter with nourishing darkness,*
> *And roots that deepen there.*
> *O ancient silent sentinels*
> *Of the dark we all must face*
> *Holy Womb, come bless us with long life*

....

248 Genesis 1:26

249 Psalm 24:1

250 This may seem to contradict Psalm 24, but there is no conflict here. Our belonging to the earth in the very fabric of our being is not in opposition to our belonging to God. The early Christians felt an alienation from 'The World', but this is usually seen as the hostile human culture within which the church emerged. We are of the earth, and the earth is the Lord's.

Then enfold us in your embrace.
Hail and welcome! **All: Hail and welcome!**

Alison Eve Cudby, Copyright © 2012/13, Ritualitas[251]

The Alchemy

Nature that fram'd us of four elements,
Warring within our breast for regiment.

Conquests of Tamberlain, Christopher Marlowe (1564-93)

Empedocles imagined there were four roots of all things which began in a state of pure harmonization, a perfect sphere ruled by Love. Gradually these separated under the influence of Strife or Hate, causing opposition, a state which allowed our universe to come into being. The process will eventually reverse itself, the elements being drawn together again into pure harmony signaling the end of the universe. The continual separation and combination of elements was important in Alchemy, which flourished in the latter Middle Ages and the Renaissance, and this delicate process served to transmute the elements one into the other. "*Thou shalt separate the Earth from the Fire, the subtle from the gross, softly, and with great ingenuity*".[252] The elements all come from the One, and Alchemy is the art of returning to this oneness, the perfect union which transcends the separate elements, "*Man must know himself and recover his divine essence by reuniting with the divine mens [mind].*"[253] The end result of this *coniuncio*, is more than turning lead into gold, it is union with the Divine,

---

251 From Ancient Arden's Samhain ritual, 'Into the Dark'
252 From the Emerald Tablet, quoted in Bardic Companion, The Order of Bards, Ovates and Druids, p.24 (Private text limited to members of OBOD)
253 Smolley, Richar, 'Hermes and Alchemy:The Winged God and the Golden Word', in ', Kinney, Jay, (Ed..), The Inner West, (Tarcher/Penguin, New York, 2004)

a 'chymical marriage'[254], often illustrated as the union of masculine and feminine principles.

Alchemy has filtered into popular spiritual imagination as a metaphor for the transformation of human consciousness, and greatly influenced the psychoanalyst Carl Jung, who saw the union of opposites within the personality, the integration of the conscious with the un-conscious as one such coniunctio. Elements of the personality which exist in tension or are simply missing from the personality, are reconciled and transcended, drawing together the different aspects that lead to wholeness[255]. Jung was also intrigued with mandalas, more or less complex circular patterns which he realised was all about the journey to the centre of the Self. The process of individuation, as Jung calls it, "does not shut one out from the world, but gathers the world to one's self."[256]

We stand in our own circles, feeling the pull of each direction, the concerns and obligations, the often confusing aspects of our personality. We come into the ritual circle with a variety of needs, hurts, betrayals, and abandonments. Trauma, grief, and the simple to and fro' of living can fragment our souls, leaving us with a sense of dis-ease. Or it may be the emptiness and silence of heaven that is the pain in our souls, the spiritual thirst for Presence that we have been seeking. Many of us face hopelessness on a daily basis, but most of us, whatever language we may try to use, feel this simple desire for wholeness, a longing for integration, for the union of opposites within us.

Come from the four winds, O breath (ruach), and breathe upon these slain, that they may live again.

Ezekiel 37:9

254 Corbett, Lionel, The Religious Function Of The Psyche, (Routledge, London and New Yorl 1996), p25
255 Ibid. p25, 46-7
256 Jung, C.G., Memories, Dreams, Reflections, (Collins.Routledge & Kegan Paul, UK, 1963

Ezekiel finds himself in a desert valley filled with bones and is told that God will join bone to bone, with sinew, flesh and skin. The prophet prophesies as God has commanded and with a great rattling noise the bones come together, gathering flesh and skin. God then enjoins Ezekiel to summon the four winds to breathe the breath *(ruach)* of life into them. God explains to Ezekiel is his people see themselves as already dead and beyond hope, cut off from their land, and that his intention is to gather them from their graves, breathe his spirit into them and return them on their own soil, the land of Israel. The spiritual meaning for us is that this is a prophetic healing work. The disparate parts of ourselves are being summoned from the four winds, re-united, re-integrated into one whole, the re-membering of the soul. We are returning to ourselves. This work of integration, could be seen as coterminous with the lifelong task of attaining to the fullness of the stature of Christ.[257]

The use of symbols such as the four elements, the four quarters, the circle, help us, in our ritual, to enter into this process of integration, not just of the self and the personality, but also of the earth, and the web of relationships within which we are woven. For us, the experience of Forest Church ritual is intended to connect us with all of nature, to ground and root ourselves *as* nature. We feel the wind on our faces, we hear the communion of birds, we accept our simple, human bounds, the clay from which we are formed, beyond judgment. And ritual shows to us the possibility of growth and transformation, inscribing the sacred into our hearts, and writing its message deep in our bones.

> *We have gathered together again beneath the Cedar tree,*
> *for our Winter Solstice Forest Church ritual. It is late in*
> *December, and in the gathering dark, we light the fire, and*

---

257 Ephesians 3:19 & 4:13

*sing of the Light of the World, born in our hearts. I look
around the circle, surrounded by close friends with whom
we have been travelling this forest path for over a year, a
circle growing in strength and fellowship as the wheel of
the year turns. We always know we do not stand alone in
this circle, and I can sense stepping into older footsteps as
I step forward into the circle. Gathering my robe closer
around my shoulders against the cold, I switch into storyteller mode and begin weaving a tale from the Hebrides,
with many other voices from the circle taking up the story
as it unfolds. It is a tale of Brighid who is carried by angels
across the miles from her exile on Iona, to assist at the birth
of the Light of The World, The King of The Elements. She
is both mid-wife to Mary, and Foster-Mother to Christ,
Muime Chriosd, as they say in the Gaelic. In our telling,
Brighid nurses the baby from her own breast, singing: "Tha
mis a'cur m'ùidh an Righ nan Dùl."* [258] *I am placing my
trust in the King Of The Elements.*

*This chant as we gently sing it into the gathering gloom
of winter, encapsulates so simply what it is we seek to do
here in our strange eclectic rituals – to trust the Spirit, the
Divine, with this path we are walking together. Here, in
the centre of the circle is Christ, the King of the Elements,
drawing all things together in himself, unifying all our
contradictions, combining the elements, bringing peace. In
this fleeting moment of ritual, we are working with symbols
and icons woven deep into the collective psyche, which we
share with our ancestors. Maybe we are placing ourselves
where the alchemy of Spirit may transform our vision of the
world, and our connection to all being.*

. . . .

258 Fonn2: Sacred Chants of the Céile Dé – Words, translations,
phonetics and interpretations, (Céile Dé, Scotland: www.ceilede.
co.uk) [Pronunciation: Ha meesh a'cor moo-ee an ree nan nool]

At the close of the ritual, we bid farewell to the energies of the four gateways, and we give thanks to the Spirit for being with us in our ritual. I take my staff and walk tuathal, anti-clockwise to unwind the circle. This is the direction of the inner journey to the centre of our spiral, the Self. It is also a journey into the heart of the world and the heart of

the Divine.

O Ground of all being we give thanks to you for the nurturing depths of your heart.
For the power of darkness to reshape and remake the world.

O harsh and ruthless teacher,
midwife of light and love and possibility,
we give thanks for the courage and strength
you wrench from deep within us in the dark cycle of our lives.

For fears to be faced and monsters befriended
for the lessons of solitude and rest,
where we must come to terms with the true self
without deceit or delusion or judgment.

For bringing us safely to the deepest inner moment of the year, the centre of the spiral where we discover the Christ Light ever burning within.

Alison Eve Cudby, Copyright © 2012, Ritualitas[259]

Alison Eve *is a singer-songwriter, wedding harpist and liturgist for alternative worship. She writes much of the ritual and song used by Ancient Arden Forest Church, and has recently released an album for the yearly cycle of celebrations on her own Ritualitas label www.ritualitas.*

---

259 From Ancient Arden Forest Church's Winter Solstice Ritual, 'The Christ-Light'.

co.uk. Ali is a Bard of the Order Of Bards Ovates and Druids, and also follows the Ceile De tradition. She trained in contemporary dance, and is currently exploring free movement in the green. Along with her husband and drummer, Paul Cudby, Ali plays in the folk band Eve & The Garden, and also directs the all female voice choir, nChant. www.alisoneve.co.uk

Chapter 16 – Nick Mayhew Smith

Bathing in the Christian Tradition

Holy wells cover Britain like drops of rain on a map, testament to our damp climate and the workings of ancient beliefs. I've bathed in sacred pools abandoned for half a millennium, watery shrines lost in the margins between fields. Their rituals are long forgotten, yet they flow on regardless. My personal discovery of sacred bathing has felt at times like connecting to an older Christianity, one that seems scarcely recognisable in any of the modern churches. It is a ritual that offers a breathtaking encounter with God's creation, a primal spirituality which engages both body and soul alike.

The Reformation began by physically preventing worship at Britain's holy wells and other sacred sites. But more effective since has been the shroud of secrecy obscuring the lives and activities of our earliest saints, which continues to this day. You can find any number of books describing a modern author's personal take on Celtic Christianity, for example, but you will struggle to buy more than a handful of the actual lives of the saints themselves. Nature devotions are now seen as the preserve of the New Age and Neo-Pagan revivalists, but start to explore some of the early Christian texts and a very different picture emerges. At the conversion of Britain our earliest missionaries strove to write the Gospel not just on people's hearts but on the very landscape itself, a cosmological mission that placed people and nature on a level. We have been cut off not just from our oldest Christian traditions but from the natural environment where our ancestors once worshipped, prayed – and bathed – with joyous abandon.

Britain's oldest sacred pool

"Serve the Lord with fear, and rejoice with trembling." The words of the second psalm came to me unbidden one summer's afternoon as my bare feet stepped on to the mossy surround of an ancient sacred pool. A shiver rose from my legs, as I braced myself to enact one of Christianity's most neglected rituals. Fear before and trembling afterwards: these stone-cold waters provide plenty of both. It was this moment when I understood that worshipping with the body means more than abstinence and self-denial.

Neither fear nor trembling had played much part in my Christian life before I discovered the allure of sacred bathing. Even the sight of an austere preacher stepping into the pulpit with a sheaf of sermon notes seems positively indulgent compared to the eddying chill of a remote Northumbrian spring, a world apart from the warmth and song of the average Sunday morning service. But my immersion in the sacred waters of Britain has proved every bit as authentic and meaningful as any indoor liturgy yet devised.

I have bathed at about a dozen sites with a tradition of Christian immersion, during my travels across all of Britain's main sacred landscapes. It was easily the most unexpected form of Christian devotion that I encountered while writing my guide *Britain's Holiest Places*, published in 2011. The book was an attempt to visit and document all our country's main sacred sites in a single volume, describing not merely their history but exploring whether they could still be used today. It turns out they can, holy wells included.

The sacred function of every one of the 500 holy places I visited is still available, to a greater or lesser extent, despite half a millennium of neglect following the Reformation. It is perhaps unsurprising that the places most untouched by the reformers' anger and the passage of time are natural holy sites: islands, mountains, caves and above all pools, rivers and beaches.

The particular watery shrine where I considered my psalm lies hidden in a grove of trees near the tiny hamlet of Holystone in Northumberland. It almost certainly dates from Roman times, a natural place of religious activity that can still serve its original function, as I discovered. It is about the size of a small swimming pool but much more shallow, fed by a spring that arises through the gravel bottom. It is usually called the Lady's Well, an incomparable spiritual treasure in the guardianship of the National Trust, which allows free access at any time.

The dark leaves of encircling trees meet overhead to block out the sky, lending an oily blackness to the peat-stained water, a chapel set apart by nature as much as by human invention. I waded towards the middle of the pool, where a Celtic-style stone cross has stood since the 19th century, and knelt into this silky body of pure water for a moment of quiet devotion. Immersed up to my waist, I scooped a handful over my head three times in quick succession, drew a cross, then lost myself amidst the silence of early Christianity.

The Lady's Well might have been used for baptism at the very end of the Roman period in Britain, making it by far the oldest known natural font in the country. A tradition written down in the year 1903 states that the well was used by St Ninian, a Roman missionary who headed beyond the safety of Hadrian's Wall to convert northern Britain. He was operating at the start of the 5th century, pushing the Christian message beyond the borders of the empire just as Roman rule was beginning to implode.

The pool lies amid fields in the tranquil Northumberland National Park, a gentle uphill walk from the tiny village of Holystone. The nearest building is out of sight, a rural setting sufficiently intact to bestow a sense of timelessness to my brief devotions. Sadly a notice has recently appeared at the well asking visitors not to disturb the pool, because it is used for drinking water by the local hamlet. Health and safety rules have trumped the Reformation in putting these ancient baptismal waters out of reach. But there are plenty of other sacred sites in Britain where you can plunge without inhibition.

An enigmatic ruin

One of the most enigmatic places where I bathed is the ruin of a well chapel near Nant-y-Patrick in North Wales. Hedged between fields and woodland in a secluded valley, this atmospheric enclave is overgrown and absolutely remote. Little about the layout of this former shrine makes sense to us today, hinting at liturgies and rites unique to the sacred spring. The complex was clearly built around the holy well, which rises in a medieval stone chamber. This pool is large enough for one person to enter at a time, which I did briefly after looking back along the valley to be sure of solitude. My feet touched down on silt so soft it was hard to know where water ended and mud began. Below that I eventually came to rest on an uneven floor of fallen masonry, perhaps the first pilgrim to bathe here in decades, if not centuries.

The water from the well then flows along a channel through the interior of the ruined building, making this the only church with its own river. As you step through the entrance you have to cross this stream on a stone bridge, perhaps a symbolic reminder of the River Jordan's sacred flow. If so this place must surely have served as a baptistery, although its traditional Welsh dedication as Ffynnon Fair, St Mary's Well, hints at other miraculous legends now lost. There are many Celtic well chapels in Britain, particularly in Cornwall and elsewhere in Wales, but Ffynnon Fair was perhaps built as late as the 15th century. It stands apart in place and time.

The Jordan has done much to inspire Jewish and Christian tradition, the starting point for our religion's devotional interaction with water. In the Old Testament the Jews crossed through the Jordan to enter their Holy Land, a symbol of national renewal. John the Baptist to use the same river to symbolise a different sort of spiritual transition, as he prepared the Jewish people for the coming of Christ. The probable site where Jesus himself was baptised has been identified at Al-Maghtas, about 10km east of Jericho, and can still be visited today as large numbers of pilgrims testify. This is one of few locations where a Christian bathing ritual is still commonplace.

Baptism in the raw

Recovering the function of baptismal sites is relatively straightforward on one level, since there are Roman texts dating from the early 3rd century onwards recording the ritual in meticulous detail. What these documents describe seems a far cry from modern Christian concepts of what is traditional, devout and even decent in an act of worship – but they reflect the social and spiritual attitudes of their time. The written records also match the earliest paintings of baptism, which can be seen in the Catacombs of Rome. The oldest surviving baptismal liturgy, by St Hippolytus, dates from about 215. Chapter 21 goes into meticulous detail:

> *When they come to the water, the water shall be pure and flowing, that is, the water of a spring or a flowing body of water. Then they shall take off all their clothes. The children*

shall be baptized first. All of the children who can answer for themselves, let them answer. If there are any children who cannot answer for themselves, let their parents answer for them, or someone else from their family. After this, the men will be baptized. Finally, the women, after they have unbound their hair, and removed their jewellery. No one shall take any foreign object with themselves down into the water. (St Hippolytus, The Apostolic Tradition)[260]

So simple is the list of requirements – natural water and a naked body – this must be the only church ritual that can in theory be recreated exactly as it was first practised, identical in every regard. Out of respect for such venerable traditions and in sympathy with nature itself I bathed naked at every holy well and pool, apart from the Catholic church-run facility at Holywell in North Wales, which is next to a busy road. All this history would no doubt be an embarrassment for many modern-day Christians, particularly those who teach that the undressed body is irredeemably obscene. Indeed one American academic has gone to eye-watering lengths to argue that 'nude' means 'wearing clothes' in the context of early church baptismal liturgies. Yet even he is obliged to acknowledge that it happened on occasions, which indeed it did.

The white robes we now associate with the ritual were actually put on after the candidate had emerged from the water, to mark their entry into their new life in the church. Our modern word 'candidate' is a literal rendition of this dress code, *candida* meaning white in Latin: one who seeks to join.

Among other charges levelled against nature devotions such as ritual bathing is that they are a throwback to paganism. In truth we have almost no idea what British pagans did at their sacred springs, but overwhelming evidence that water plays a central role in early Christianity. The first element mentioned

260 Translation from www.bombaxo.com/hippolytus.html

in the Bible is water, and given Christ's own baptism it is hard to argue that water ritual is the exclusive preserve of pagan religious practice. Baptism was embraced wholeheartedly by the early church, water poured liberally over the candidates head three times as they stood in a pool, a thorough drenching from head to foot. Some churches go further still, even today, the Orthodox Church insisting on complete submersion three times beneath the surface.

In Britain today, baptism is usually a token few drops of water on a baby's head, long before they have any chance of remembering the ceremony. My own Christening, in the now redundant church of St Alban, in Teddington, certainly passed me by at the time, but I've had many baptismal reminders since, usually entering the waters and then ducking under three times, or if in doubt about the purity of the pool simply sprinkling a few drops on my head. The latter technique works in an inch or two of water, which is all some holy wells currently hold.

Baptism is clearly the archetypal sacrament from which all other immersions are derived. The baptismal reminder is a stripped down ritual, easy enough to perform on your own wherever a suitably discrete and clean body of natural water can be found. As a starting point for entering the church it harnesses much powerful symbolism of cleansing and rebirth. But for all its prominence, baptism is just one of many rituals that have developed around the use of water. And that opens up the big question: apart from the sacrament of baptism, what exactly are Christian sacred bathing rituals?

Water rituals of the early saints

Thankfully we have a multitude of early saints in this country who liked nothing more than ritual bathing, performed as a penance, for ascetic reasons, for worship, for healing, and I suspect because they rather enjoyed it. The idea that it was only practised for mortification of the flesh – numbing the body into submission – doesn't match either the historical records or my own experiences. For example, one devotional activity recorded in the lives of many British saints was to sing a psalm, an invigorating way to ward off the chill.

One such devout bather is a nun called St Ethelfleda, who lived at Romsey Abbey in Hampshire in the 10th century. She is remembered for bathing in the nude every night of the year to say her prayers and recite psalms. The queen once followed her while staying with the saint, curious to see such sincere devotion, and ended up catching a severe cold simply by watching from the bank of the River Test. The saint cured her with a blessing. Clearly made of hardier stuff than most mortals, St Ethelfleda lived to an advanced old age. If anyone were to become patron saint of sacred bathing, my vote would go to her.

The last in a long line of great British devotional bathers is a former pirate called St Godric, who hung up his cutlass in 1110 and went to live as a hermit in the forest a few miles outside Durham. Having retreated at the age of 40 he remained there for another 60 years, a life of epic proportions full of the most incongruous details imaginable. Living beside the River Wear in a hut made of twigs, he invited the local wildlife to come inside to share the warmth of his fire, and also composed England's earliest surviving hymns, following a vision of the Blessed Virgin herself. I would imagine he is the oldest British composer available on iTunes.

This wild man's penitential lifestyle was so extreme it roused even the devil into direct action, who stole the saint's clothes from a riverbank as he stood mid-torrent in penitential roar. The former pirate, who had once served as a mercenary in the First Crusade, had no doubt suffered worse.

The ruins of Finchale Priory, built in honour of St Godric shortly after his death, still stand beside the river, a simple stone cross in the grass marking the site of his former shrine. It wasn't the devil's pranks that put me off bathing when I visited, but rather a large and busy eco-campsite built alongside. A group of teenagers were returning from a bathing spot some distance downstream when I visited, hair wet and damp towels under their arms, but I didn't have time to investigate this alternative site myself.

At many other bathing places the saintly traditions have become intertwined with later superstition. St Fillan's Pool is a deep and slow-moving bend in the River Fillan, surrounded by trees but just a few metres away from the busy A82 near Crianlarich in Stirling. It is named after an 8th century missionary who presumably baptised here, but subsequently developed into a popular place for healing.

As late as the 19th century there were separate bathing areas for men and women, allowing participants to strip and dip. After emerging from the water, they would walk three times round a cairn, drop nine stones in the pool and then leave behind an item of clothing most closely associated with their ailing body part. Visit a holy well today and you will often see a nearby tree festooned with similar rag strips, which are known as clouties. I was feeling relatively healthy when I slipped into the chilly water so contented myself with one of the bathing rituals practised by the early saints of Britain, standing on a boulder mid stream and gasping out a quick prayer.

Bathing in the wild

Probably the most famous devotional bather in Britain is St Cuthbert, the 7th century abbot of Lindisfarne. He was observed early one morning entering the sea near the monastery at Coldingham, a few miles over the modern Scottish border from Berwick upon Tweed. This was no mere bath: St Cuthbert waded into the sea in order to pray, the sanctity of his act underlined by the fact that two sea otters rushed over to him after he emerged and attempted to dry his legs with their fur. The otters might be an embellishment too far for some, but St Cuthbert was unarguably a man of the sea, seeking out the lonely shore and remote islands for his devotions.

I visited the beach at Coldingham below the site of the long-abandoned monastery, hoping to bathe myself. But the waves were crashing against the rocky bay, unsuitable conditions for sea otters let alone humans, so I marvelled at St Cuthbert's devotion from the safety of dry land. But on Lindisfarne a few weeks later I visited the little crag of rock just offshore from the parish church, known as St Cuthbert's Isle, where the saint used to retreat from his monastic duties. Wading over as the tide went out, I had this little scrap of grass and rock to myself. The land shelves into the sea on the far side, so I quickly undressed in the cool morning fog and waded into the green water, losing myself for a moment out of time. A seal surfaced shortly after I emerged, but merely watched from afar as I dried myself with a towel.

Into healing water

One function of holy water has clearly been surpassed by modern technology, and that is its role in healing. Leaving aside the question of miraculous cures, the supply of pure fresh water alone would prove beneficial for a wide range of complaints, particularly eye infections and skin diseases. Given the short supply of medical alternatives in the middle ages it is hardly any wonder that healing pools earned their place in the public's affection. The NHS has long since taken over the role of the church in ministering to the sick and crippled, and yet our affection for ancient springs has somehow survived. Bottled mineral water is proving a lucrative market for modern purveyors of health-giving waters.

Perhaps our collective memory runs deep: the word 'holy' and the word 'healthy' derive from the same source, the Anglo-Saxon term 'haelig' covering both. It is also the root of the word wholesome. Water is one of the best ways to reconnect with the natural world, to become reconciled to God's creation, at one with the elements.

Its link to symbolic and actual rebirth is nowhere better demonstrated than at the medieval pool complex in Holywell, North Wales. Older than Lourdes by more than a thousand years, this amazing little site even managed to escape the Reformation relatively intact. The fact that Henry VIII's grandmother had built the chapel and pool complex that still stands today probably helped to stay the king's hand. Holywell still has bathing times set aside each day, and a row of changing huts beside the pool so you can put on a swimming costume before entering St Winefride's Well. The current devotional practice is to wade around the perimeter of the pool three times reciting prayers.

The saint who was reborn – indeed physically resurrected – here was a young woman who fled to her uncle's chapel on this site to escape the unwanted attentions of a local prince. The wicked Caradog cut off her head with his sword, and where it fell the miraculous spring began to flow. The uncle, St Beuno, emerged from his chapel and miraculously reattached St Winefride's head. She lived in the 7th century, her story similar to other Celtic well traditions which involve a beheading and a miraculous cure.

The Bible refers to one sacred healing pool, at Bethesda, where Jesus heals a cripple according to John's Gospel (chapter 5). It certainly feels like being reborn each time I emerge bright pink and dripping from the water's embrace. It is invigorating of course, but almost feels like an act of humility, a show of innocence even. Healing and the rebirth ritual of baptism are never far apart.

Birth of a tradition

As far as I can tell – and I continue to research this topic – the earliest reference to Christian sacred bathing comes in a remarkable book written by a woman from Gaul in the early 380s. Clearly an intrepid soul, the lady Egeria took herself on a tour of the Holy Land and wrote an early form of travelogue about her adventures. She captures so much rare detail about life in the late Roman church it is a wonder her book is not more widely known. Added to that is the fact that she is probably the first female author in the whole of Western Europe.

Egeria is a cultural marvel, and she also writes about a holy well at Aenon near Salem, thought to be another baptismal site once used by John the Baptist (it is mentioned in John 3:23). Egeria records not only baptismal use but also some sort of sacred bathing tradition at this pool:

> *Then the holy priest said to us: "...Many brethren, holy monks, direct their steps hither from various places that they may wash there." So at the spring, as in every place, prayer was made, the proper lection was read and an appropriate psalm was said, and everything that it was customary for us to do whenever we came to the holy places, we did there also. The holy priest also told us that to this day, at Easter, all they who are to be baptized in the village... are always baptized in this spring.*

Rather frustratingly, this is the only detail that Egeria provides about the ritual activity. "Everything that was customary for us to do" begs several questions, but at least her description of monks visiting the site to wash confirms a Roman-era sacred bathing tradition, in particular one that has been laid on the firm foundation of baptismal precedent.

Holy well rituals steadily developed in the church. By the 8th century in Syria there are liturgies for the Great Blessing of the Waters, an annual festival held on 6 January each year to celebrate Christ's baptism in the Jordan. A second holy water rite, the Lesser Blessing of the Waters, can be performed at any other time of the year, and is still used by the Orthodox churches. The date of Christ's baptism overlaps with epiphany, which tends to steal the limelight in the Anglican Church's calendar. In the northern hemisphere this date happens to be in the dead of winter – something that doesn't stop the Russians from their annual holy immersion in natural water today. They usually need a chainsaw to cut a cross-shaped hole through the ice for the devout to line up and immerse themselves three times.

Cold all over

The coldest water I encountered on my aquatic pilgrimage across Britain was in the Forest of Dean, though even this needed no chainsaw to enter. An enchanting little medieval stone pool lies secluded among trees, dedicated to St Anthony and once tended by the monks of Flaxley Abbey, which was a couple of miles to the east. This stone bath is filled by a powerful spring, which emerges from the hillside and then pours into the chamber at one end before draining at the other end into a stream. When I visited a family were cheerfully throwing sticks in the water for their Labrador to retrieve. I waited until they were out of sight and tried to convince myself that the dog's bathwater had been circulated away before stripping and entering.

Spring water hardly changes in temperature whatever the time of year, since it emerges from deep underground. St Anthony's

Well is deep, and by the time I had walked down the slippery stone steps to the bottom my legs had lost all sensation. I emerged quickly and tried again a minute later, this time managing to recite all of the Lord's Prayer. I left my clothes a few steps away, to avoid muddy paw prints, and took a towel to the pool edge in case the dog walkers returned unexpectedly.

I have to admit that getting undressed outdoors to bathe in natural water is easier for me than most. The first guidebook I wrote was on nude beaches around the world, an interest that started when I was on a gap year trip to New Zealand and discovered the joys of skinny-dipping at the age of 18. Apart from one Scottish saint who kept his clothes on, all the other early saints I encountered stripped off completely to bathe. The Venerable Bede recounts that St Drycthelm at Melrose Abbey would stand in a river up to his neck and then refused to change out of his soaking wet clothes afterwards, not out of reasons of modesty but in order to prolong the chill.

I don't think the human body can be inherently indecent in Christian terms – not least because Jesus had one. I think of the human body as an entirely natural creation, with the same inherent decency as a tree or a rock. All three can be used for good or ill, as the Bible so often illustrates. Nakedness crops up from time to time in the Bible, but has different meanings to the one that is in vogue today. To Jesus it can be a mark of poverty, for example.

Ripples in the water

Christianity may have abandoned sacred bathing, but its psychological appeal still ripples through the mind. People are still drawn strongly to water as a symbol of renewal, as the detox regime of any modern spa amply demonstrates. I once started a sermon by asking the congregation to remember their favourite holiday, and a few moments later asked which of them had been by the sea or a lake. All hands went up except for my vicar's wife, who it turned out had spent a blissful week beside a swimming pool. As a place for refreshment water has no equal, the sea being the greatest visitor attraction on earth to a degree even Disney couldn't calculate.

The recent revival of wild swimming is another example of this deep-running need for immersion, a communal yearning that was once served so well by the church. Sacred bathing is of a different order to wild swimming, though I have often stayed after my moments of ritual in order simply to swim. Either way, wild swimming and sacred bathing absolutely require outdoor natural water. It would take a mind more devout that mine to use the local public swimming pool as a place to reconnect with the rhythms of our ancestors' worship.

By the same token you don't need somewhere that is a dedicated holy pool, although I find it helps. Holy places are those given over to prayer or contemplation, favoured perhaps by creation, a setting of trees, hills and meadows conducive to a peaceful mind. A truly holy place needs no interpretation, its function as plain as a box of matches beside a row of votive candles. Shrines invite you to kneel and to touch, and holy wells draw you to immerse yourself with wordless clarity. The endless expanse of the sea is perhaps the most eloquent of all spiritual encounters with water, but rivers and lakes are just as suitable.

My most recent act of devotional bathing managed to combine a wild swim with a visit to a local ruined monastery, a site that seems out of reach when viewed from the land. Newark Priory lies on an island in private water-meadows, a couple of miles from the M25/A3 interchange. Other than the distant hum of traffic this setting could not be more untouched, literally so since it is impossible to visit the ruins. After gazing at them across the fields and on a map, I eventually worked out that a meandering tributary of the River Wey runs right past their northern end.

I returned to this riverbank one evening in late July, the whir of insects drowning out any intrusion from the 21st century. A blue sky overhead and a mirror-flat river dotted with yellow water lilies beckoned. I chose a spot on the bank opposite the tributary, affording a long view up and down the empty towpath, and hurriedly stripped and entered the water in absolute solitude. Carrying my shorts, shirt, shoes and car key in a waterproof bag, I slipped across the river and hid them in the hollow of a tree. Bereft of all worldly possessions, and desperately hoping no squirrel would turf my bag into the stream, I set off against the current.

After 20 minutes I eventually drew alongside this haunting ruin of a building and pulled myself up on the opposite bank, safe from the herd of bulls. Sitting in the golden sunshine surrounded by wildflowers and the sounds of nature preparing for nightfall, I was rooted to this blessed spot for a moment out of time. The last monk had left this building some 500 years ago, yet still the river flowed on.

We have been cut off from nature devotions, but holy places and their rituals are as much a feature of the landscape as they have ever been. My visit to Newark Priory was final proof that holy places need not be alien or other: they are not sites to visit as a pilgrim but local haunts, created, cared for and revived in every instance by the people who dwell around them. The near universal response to the phrase 'holy places', even among committed Christians, is an assumption that I am talking about pilgrimage, about travel to somewhere other than home. It is a sign of how disconnected we are to the silt beneath our feet.

Nick Mayhew-Smith is a writer and Anglican lay minister, author of the best-selling guidebook Britain's Holiest Places, a guide to 500 sites of sacred heritage. His book was made into a six-part BBC Four television series in 2013, 'Pagans & Pilgrims: Britain's Holiest Places'. He is currently researching a PhD on nature devotions in the early British church, at Roehampton University.

MYSTIC CHRIST PRESS

Also from Mystic Christ Press...

Forest Church

A Field Guide To Nature Connection
For Groups And Individuals

Brimming with insights and packed with information,
this book draws you out, quite literally, into nature
to experience a new, well thought through pattern
of spiritual practice. Bruce Stanley gives you all the
resources you'll need, both practical and theoretical,
to get going with a group or on your own.

By **Bruce Stanley**

Wheel Of The Year

An eight-fold calendar of fire festivals and solar seasons with
Celtic and Christian festivals – exercises, meditations and
reflections on the seasons. Suitable for any year.

By **Bruce Stanley, Steve Hollinghurst,**
with illustrations by **Stu McLellan**

Available from: www.mysticchrist.co.uk/press